The Sky Behind Me

The Sky Behind Me

- 2nd Edition -

Extended Downwind

Byron H. Edgington

Dedication

To my dear wife who happens to be my best editor, too. How lucky am I? And to the following who tried to make me a better writer, especially to those very few who succeeded: Terry Jacobs from H.S. English class, Lee Martin, Connie Shelton, (Hawaii was fantastic advice), the critiques were even better. Randy Mains, full rpm brother, and keep 'em coming. Maura Heaphy for her efforts to get me on the map, and to my fellow Buckeyes, especially the class of 2012. O-H! And to my wonderful readers who find ways to keep me writing. The heart of a man can want no more than this.

BE
Columbus Ohio
June 2015

Published in the United States of America in 2015 by
The SkyWriter Press. www.theskywriterpress.com
5854 Aqua Bay Drive
Columbus Ohio 43235

©2015 The SkyWriter Press

Paperback Acquisition of this title:

ISBN-10: 0996447105
ISBN-13: 978-0-9964471-0-2

Cataloging-in-Publication data is available from the Library of Congress.

Printed and bound in The United States of America

Available at Amazon.com & through Smashwords.com for E-readers.

For a complete list of The SkyWriter Press publications contact the
editor: www.theskywriterpress.com, www.byronedgington.com.
614-634-3774

Cover design: Pixel Droid Design Studio:
pixeldroiddesign@gmail.com

Cover and back images: iStock Photo

The Sky Behind Me

1

The Island of Kauai: 12/14/2005

I step out of the cockpit, and the cold, hard ground comes up to meet me. You've been there, felt this, the realization in your bones that something is finished, something so important, so fundamental to who you are that you can't allow yourself to think about it yet, though you know it's true. You get through the next minute, hang up a phone, watch a train pull away, a face at a window—or close a cockpit door and walk away, and you just know. As much as you ache for it not to be true, it's done, and you know it. Something in your life is finished forever.

I land, shut off the engine of the helicopter. The rotor blades spin down, slower, slower still. The trade wind catches them. Each blade dances and bends, like a hand waving goodbye. I yank the rotor brake and they creak to a stop overhead. In the cabin with me six passengers peel off headsets, their helicopter tour of Kauai over. With laughter, and even some tears, they chat about the flight, voting on favorite parts.

I listen to their bubbly conversation: *"NaPali Coast, stunning, the volcano, unbelievable, Hanalei Valley, waterfalls, gorgeous, how'd you like that double rainbow? Love to go again."*

Typical comments. After flying 2,500 tours of the island I can predict them. I remove my headset, and click open the seatbelt lock. I was forty-five minutes into the tour when the spell washed over me, a sudden dizziness, narrowing vision, creeping loss of consciousness. It scared me to my bones. If I'd passed out...I'm listening for something else in their voices now, wondering if, during the spell, whatever the hell it was, a customer noticed me trying to stay conscious? I parse their comments, cringing when a woman says *'turbulence.'* Was that when I shifted in my seat? When I squeezed my gut, and gulped in air to fight it off? When I did that, did I jerk the stick around and she saw it, felt it?

No, she hadn't. *"...wonder if it's always that bumpy on the NaPali Coast?"* she says, and I breathe again. The bumps during my near syncopal episode happened just as I shook my head and sucked in slugs of air trying to stay awake. Coincidence. Air pockets on the NaPali are a common occurrence. The spell was out of the blue, immediate, frightening in its intensity. I tune in to comments again, but none of them refer to my efforts to avoid passing out in the cockpit. None of my customers know how close I'd been.

Nor do I. A shiver of shame washes over me; why had I not landed? Another spell may have started, and been worse. I'd continued flying, assuming that whatever the hell it was, it had run its course.

But I knew something was forever changed. I knew my position, my status as a tour pilot on the island of Kauai, the ultimate job in my forty-year career was over. I saw myself asking the boss for time off. Envisioned entering the doctor's office, the same place I went every year for my up slip, the FAA medical clearance without which I couldn't fly. I heard myself tell the doctor about the spell, describing how close I'd come to passing out with six people in the cabin with me. I hear my urgent questions: why had it happened, what can I do and will it happen again? I see the whole thing, hear the conversation. And I watch myself absorbing his verdict.

The Sky Behind Me

~*~

I step out of the cockpit, and the hard ground comes up to meet me. I latch the door. Despite the anxiety squeezing my chest, I manage a smile, shake hands, accept tips. People thank me for a *'wonderful tour.'* They sneer, and slap my back, saying *'what a tough job you have.'* They produce wallets, peel off tens, twentys, the occasional fifty, fold the bills, sneak them into my hand. I thank them for flying with me, watch them walk to the shuttle. The bus pulls away under swaying palm trees, and the helipad falls silent. Behind me a colleague hovers in, lands, and his engine winds down. At that moment it hits me. I'm done. My flying career is over.

When I was ten years old I snuck out of the house to play baseball with the neighbor kids. I had to sneak out because mom forbade me to play that day. It was Good Friday, and in my Irish Catholic house it was unthinkable that I'd ignore the sacred day of Christ's crucifixion to engage in something as crass as a ball game.

Despite the admonition, I grabbed my mitt and the lumber and headed out the back door. Before you could say bless me father I was on the diamond with the lads, in the bright spring sun, with swish of bat, loft of ball, smack of leather, the thrill of the grass.

I remember swinging hard, connecting, the satisfying thunk, and the silly sizzle in my chest at the pleasure of a solid hit. I see white ball arc into blue sky over pitcher Bill Peckham's head. It continues climbing. I'm sure beyond doubt that what's his name, the new kid on the block, the kid wearing a flannel shirt on such a warm day, the kid no one has seen play yet, that he'll for sure miss it. And he does. The ball tips flannel shirt's upraised mitt, skips upward, slows a bit, but heads for the outfield. Sure as I am that, on that very day Christ died for my sins, I've got second base made standing up. No way the new kid'll field that ball. No way. I punch first with my right foot, dredge dirt with my left, put my head down and dig for second.

Second sack is 90 feet away, seventy, fifty, ten... Then a blur, a swatch of flannel, and a terrible whump. I see stars, but this is a day game, isn't it? My head throbs. Stars twinkle out. Why are guys standing over me in a circle, staring, a blue hole of sky between them? Blood? What are they talking about, blood? I'm sweaty, and my head aches like I've been hammered. I can't focus my left eye because of...the blood.

I reach the emergency room for stitches ten minutes before the flannel shirt kid. I met him, finally, at second base, when we collided, skull against skull, opening a penitential gash in my forehead, like one of Christ's wounds. Only mine is well deserved. I've had my fun; it's time for payment. In the car, bloodstained towel at my throbbing head, Mom scolds. "No Good Friday baseball," she says. "You see what happens?"

Eight stitches later I'm released to the loving, forgiving fold of my family. Easter comes and goes that year and many others. But I never forget the lesson. The lesson Catholic school taught me above all others. Balance. For every good there's a bad. For every bad, a good. I never played baseball on Good Friday again.

Why that long ago incident came to me as I walked away from the helicopter I don't know. It wasn't Good Friday; it was December 14th 2005. I'd not been enjoying myself too much; I'd been working. Or had I? This wasn't some kind of balancing act, was it? My mind raced with possible reasons I was being punished. Divorce and remarriage? That describes half the world these days. Moving so far from family? Leaving Iowa when I told them I'd stay? It was a no brainer for my wife and me. Another winter in Iowa City, or a move to a mid-Pacific Paradise? Was it work? People threw money at me, a lot of it, for flying them around the island while music played and I entertained them with anecdotes, local color and what I knew about Hawaii. Was it just too rewarding, and I loved it too much?

If so I shared the emotions of my passengers. With laughter, and even some tears, I walked away from the flight line for the last time.

Byron H. Edgington

2

Balance

Maybe I was booted out of Eden, just like in the Baltimore Catechism. Maybe I'd lived in Paradise too long, and it was time to leave. Could that be? If so it made no sense. I'd long ago given up those fairy tales, virgin birth, water to wine, bodily ascension into heaven. Useful narratives for a sixth grader, but not for adults, as Orwell said about the incompatibility of faith with maturity. If there was an Eden, I'd come to believe we hadn't been kicked out of it; we got bored and left.

If it was about balance, what about all those frigid nights flying in wintertime Iowa? The phone rings at midnight, ten below zero, wind chill minus forty. I dress like an Aleut to fly a hundred miles for a drunk who curses me and my nursing crew for forty minutes, then he vomits on us. Was that work? What about the flights in Indiana with those crude businessmen, listening to their sexist jokes about women their daughters' age in the Playboy magazines they slobber over, as I fly them to job sites? Where's the balance there? Never thought I'd be relieved to lose a job, but I was. What about scrapping for my first commercial flying job, those postings at the end of the road nobody else wanted just to scribble hours in my logbook? Where was the payback for that?

What of the dues I've paid, the harassment of my first flight instructor in Texas, the Darwinian demands of flight school, an endurance test all the way to graduation? What about the war? That was work just staying alive most days, work a lot of friends failed at. I'd thought living on Kauai was my reward for forty years of paying attention to the flying god, keeping my safety record intact, taking no chances. The After the Fall scenario made no sense. I'd spent forty years as a pilot; my job description was simple: it was to not fall.

I go to the office, tell the boss I need time off. I call my wife, say I'll be home early but don't tell her why. I can't say it to myself yet. The appointment with the flight doc won't be easy, but I have to make it, and I have to keep it.

I sit in the car a long time scanning the flight line. A colleague climbs into his cockpit, and straps in. The door closes, engine whines, blades turn, faster, faster, disappearing in a blur. A strange feeling comes, achy, tenuous. It makes me feel, what? Invisible. When my colleague takes off I know I'm watching my past.

I see myself board a tiny, two-seat helicopter in Texas almost forty years ago. Wayne, my first instructor, starts the engine, engages the blades and we lift into the searing Texas sky. How easy for him it seems. How hard it is for me in the next few weeks to learn to fly. How frustrating failing over and over. How satisfying, finally, when I do what Wayne says, "...just think about moving the controls, Edgington, and it'll do what you want."

I see my first solo flight, feel the rush of success knowing I've flown, by myself, that I've done it. Then advanced training at Hunter Field in Savannah, instrument flight, tactics, navigation, first flight in a Huey. Flight school graduation, then on to Vietnam in February 1970. The company, and missions, and fear, and fire and friends. Some die. Twelve months pass, and I come home.

My colleague takes off low overhead, and the car wobbles. In his rotor wake palm leaves frolic, then settle down. The aroma of burned jet fuel washes over me like incense, and my eyes fill with tears. The helicopter heads for the interior of Kauai. Part of me is on board. And always will be.

The places I've flown: Southeast Asia, Alaska, South America... The missions I've done: spotting tuna, herding bears, dousing fires, rescuing emergency patients. Winter night, 100 miles to Iowa City, 3 in the morning. The dim cast of the instruments, altimeter, rpm, torque, compass glow red like backlit rubies. My hand grips the cyclic, steady, the touch of experience. The ship surges through the frigid night, blades whipping overhead while Iowa sleeps a thousand feet below.

Another night, newly dark, ominous. I see gauges sag, needles droop, warnings flash like fireworks as my engine fails and the Huey plummets. I take charge, adjusting, maneuvering. Ground rushing up, I flare the Huey and slide it on smooth and safe, like a thousand practice runs before.

I see my whole career in that one takeoff. And in one landing.

I grab my seat belt and snap it shut. The other tour ship becomes a speck and then disappears. The island shimmers through a mist: all the tours I've flown; satisfied customers; the camaraderie of peers and fitting in with an elite group of pilots. I see Wendy, a woman completing her bucket list with her pungent leis and brave smile. I remember the letter about her weeks later. I see the envelope from my Chinese passenger, a five and two ones inside, smallest tip ever, and the best. I hear the questions: *"how long you been doing this?" "Ever crash?" "What's the worst that ever happened..?"*

I know that answer. The worst incident ever was stepping from the cockpit minutes ago.

I start the car, and put it in gear. On the phone, my wife wonders what's wrong? I never leave early; I always stay late on the flight line. She's used to it. Today something's different. I'm looking for balance, and not finding it. But I will, one way or another.

I leave the airport, and head down the hill.

3

August 1970: Vietnam

Headwinds, the storm, rain in buckets and the restriction to visibility on an August afternoon in Vietnam in 1970 made me a pilot, and showed me the balance I'd be seeking my entire career, though I wasn't aware of it then.

I was assigned that day to fly for a detachment called U.S. Army Vietnam, USARV, (You-Sar-Vee) a liaison between the U.S. and South Vietnamese military. I made several routine air transfers that day, of equipment, mail, documents, beans and bullets. The flying was easy, until it wasn't. I logged five flight hours in my Huey, refueling twice. During a previous leg, Sergeant McKay in company operations had radioed with orders from the 101st Airborne's commanding General. McKay told me to be on the ground by five p.m. A major storm was forming in the South China Sea, moving in from the east, and the General didn't want his aviation assets damaged. I called Sarge McKay back. "Roger...on the ground by seventeen-hundred. No problem."

I carried more materiel, ammo, hot chow, the stuff an army needs to do its job. The day slipped by with more of the same, an easy mission. But, as I'd often joked with colleagues, an easy mission can turn nasty in a heartbeat. At four o'clock I finished my last sortie, I thought. At four-fifteen USARV released me, and I headed to home base at Camp Eagle. Looking forward to a shower, dinner, and a cold beer at the club, I aimed the helicopter that direction with plenty of time to gas up and lash things down by five o'clock.

Sometimes insights are so brief, so obscure, that we're unable to understand even their outline much less its meaning in our lives. Like the shards of lightning that zippered the Asian sky that August day, illuminating my cockpit like flashbulbs in a dark room, the insights were so brief that I was unaware of their defining purpose in my life. Short and subtle as they were, they showed me who I was, and the balance I was yet to see. They also showed me the pilot I would become. Sometimes it takes years to tease out the truth of those insights. That doesn't make them any less true, or real, or valuable. Indeed, their brevity can make them sacred. As Anne Morrow Lindbergh wrote in *North To The Orient*, "*...at the time of the incident, one was not conscious of such a feeling, and only became so in the retelling.*"

That August day I was a 21-year-old Army helicopter pilot. The war was going badly for me. I'd been under fire numerous times. I'd lost good friends. I was tired, hassled by military bullshit, fearful of the unknown, the random violence that came in an instant. I felt weary beyond my age, wary from being off balance. My ambivalence about the war, and the reason I found myself there, had turned me cynical and angry.

Growing up I was a happy, carefree kid, hopeful for my future, confident that the world was a good place, and that what I did mattered. Second pup in an Irish Catholic litter I was, by tradition and temperament, the one tagged to become the family priest. That selection was reinforced, my resolve strengthened, when I was in seventh grade at St. Andrew school.

A priest from a missionary order came calling. He showed a movie to boys who entertained thoughts of the priesthood.

~*~

The forty-minute film was titled *"The Heart of a Man."* It featured the life of a mission priest in Burma, a real cleric named Father Colombo.

The priest arrived in a jungle clearing in a small plane. He said Mass, heard confessions, gave communion. He ministered to the simple people of his village, cared for them, kept them safe from local thieves. One scene showed Colombo trudging through the dim village late at night with a hypodermic to comfort someone in pain. The film ended with the narrator's simple yet magnetic message: *"The heart of a man can want no more than this."* I was hypnotized. Watching that priest gather his flock around him, smiling, eyes lifted to heaven, a look of pure joy in his face, I wanted to be him. The narrator was right; I could want no more than that.

That insight, too, was brief. Like a flash in the night it gave little by way of explanation. Even so, that day, as the film's ragged end slipped through the projector and whap-whapped against the takeup reel, the light may have blinded me but I saw what I wanted. I would become a priest. In September 1962, at age thirteen, I entered the seminary.

My dream was not to be. When I was fourteen, a priest took advantage of me for his own sexual gratification. His perverted actions, and the dismissal of them by church authorities were the biggest crisis of my young life. Making it worse, instead of punishing him, church authorities subsequently dismissed me from the seminary. My dream of the priesthood died. Lost, confused, feeling out of all balance I questioned heaven for some explanation but found none.

The echoes of that supreme betrayal followed me for a long time. It broke my heart because I loved the Catholic faith, its comforting rituals, the solemnity of its liturgy. Church music exalted me, filled me with joy. As a choirboy I led the procession every Sunday during High Mass. I warbled liturgical melodies while candle smoke tickled my nose, my whole being lifted, almost a weightless, glorious feeling that only near rapture can provide. Participation in the liturgy gave me a feeling of clarity, exhilaration. I knew I was valued by the Church, that I was among the select. The Church entrusted me with a secret, powerful message: my beliefs were the truth. Everyone else labored in a dark jungle of ignorance awaiting the light I would offer them. The knowledge was intoxicating. I immersed myself in the rites: Baptism, Confirmation, Holy Communion. I dreamed of Holy Orders, the priesthood. I yearned to administer those sacraments, perform those rites, to be that jungle priest. It was my childhood dream to soar, my first aspiration toward flight. And it was my first experience with the heartbreak of a crash as well.

One of my most vivid childhood memories is watching a helicopter land, almost in my back yard. It must have been about 1958 when I was ten, and likely after my stitches had healed. Home was on the near northwest side of Columbus Ohio, near the Olentangy River Road. The house was literally across the fence from the local NBC affiliate, Channel 4 TV. One summer afternoon I heard the percussive wopping of rotor blades, and ran to the back yard. The old Bell model 47, with its bubble canopy like the helicopter on M*A*S*H, kicked up a swirl of grass and dirt as it clattered to the ground. The pilot idled the engine, slowed the blades. Then his passenger unbuckled and stepped out. As she and I watched, my mother informed me that the passenger was Van Johnson, a popular actor at the time. But the star of that scene, for me, was the helicopter and its exotic landing and takeoff.

I first flew in a seaplane with my dad and brother when I was seven. The plane's engine roared, and lake spray spattered the windscreen as we took off. Vibrations in the fuselage made my gut giddy as the pontoons lifted, dripping water. The sparkling lake fell away as the plane's nose grappled skyward. People really were like ants. Cabins and trees and cars looked like the ones on my train board. The engine thrummed, sunlight flickered through the prop, the salt-sour stench of av-gas and burnt oil tingled in my nose. The only bad part of aviation, near as I could tell, was landing. The experience was over much too quickly.

Considering my romantic, carefree nature, flying was the best career match in the world for me, the perfect fit. It was much better than the priesthood as it turned out. According to my mother, and several nuns I managed to annoy in Catholic school, I spent most of my childhood with my head in the clouds. I was the kid who, as the Peter, Paul & Mary song has it *"...always looked out the window, failing tests in geography."*

Aviation was a natural extension of my predilection for dreaming, for overlooking the real and mundane in favor of the insubstantial and ethereal. I'm a loner, mostly, perfectly happy by myself curled up with a book, or solving a crossword, while a soothing symphony sounds in my headset. As a priest, I knew I'd have a life of quiet contemplation surrounded by books, solving people's crises, reveling in music and ritual. But I was turned away from that dream, and fell into aviation as a replacement.

The replacement was a perfect fit. As a pilot, I was almost always alone, ensconced in the cockpit, poring over charts, solving aviation challenges while the lyrics of flying lingo hummed in my headset. I was at home in the sky, never lost, never afraid of what the air, or clouds, or wind or weather might bring. The sky was my element; returning to the ground was the alien part. Like that seaplane ride when I was seven, it was always over too quickly.

I grew up in Ohio, so flying was in my background courtesy of the Wright brothers, Neil Armstrong, John Glenn, Jim Lovell, Jerry Mock and numerous other aviation pioneers. My mother's brother worked for North American Aviation. Three or four times a year 'rich uncle' Dick took my brother and me to a local hobby shop where we could pick any plastic model we wanted. My bedroom ceiling was littered with models: A P-40, MIG, P-51, a Japanese Zero, an F-4U Corsair, and several century-series jets, F-100, 101, 102, 104. The ceiling tiles disappeared behind plastic Revell or Monogram model planes dogfighting with each other on strings. Orange and black painted cotton streaming from a fuselage meant an enemy aircraft.

As the Pauline letters read, "...as a child, I spoke as a child." Once I'd been dismissed from my earlier fantasy and put childish things aside, the adult world provided a richer, more satisfying way for me to pursue my dream. It was aviation, not religion that gave me the chance to help others. Especially in my hospital flying, I used skills that made a difference at a critical time in people's lives. In my corporate and other flying I put people's fears to rest, allowing them to relax and do their job. While flying in Hawaii I gave more than 15,000 tourists a vision of paradise they'd remember forever, including many newlyweds who received a memento of their honeymoon they'd cherish. The heart of a man can want no more than that.

Aviation gave me a unique perspective on human behavior, especially that part of my career in Air Medical aviation. Flying for a hospital for twenty years matched my skill with the needs of people in crisis. It was a gratifying convergence. The ability to use our skills at a critical time in another's life, and to possibly save that life, is a privilege few people ever have. I held that privilege in my hands for twenty years. It was like balancing two kinds of gravity at once, the physical principles of flight, and the grave crises of medical emergency, or traumatic injury. And I was damned good at it.

Tour flying on Kauai seemed like a reward for my twenty years of jump through your ass, oh-dark-thirty take off in ten-below zero snow-shrouded Iowa flying. Maybe it was. If so, the balance makes me smile. Aircraft must be in balance, or they simply won't fly. Flight surfaces, airfoils, control rigging, all must be tuned, balanced, or the machine will not leave the ground.

That necessity goes for us, too. Our attitude and outlook must be balanced, or we'll miss a critical part of the flight. I learned pretty early that the ripples we create go in all directions, and they spread in a balanced, equal way.

If dismissal from the seminary was my first crisis, getting drafted out of college was the second. Losing a dream isn't easy, and finding a replacement for it isn't either. Aimless, and uncertain how to proceed, at the height of the Vietnam conflict my grades went south and I lost my 2-S deferment to stay in school. Days later I received a letter from Selective Service changing my draft status to 1-A. It was the only 'A' I'd received in a long time, and it made me eligible for immediate induction.

In a remarkable display of government efficiency, within two weeks my draft notice arrived in the mailbox, and my future was chosen for me. I was removed from campus, given a uniform, a military skill, and shipped to Vietnam to participate in a cause that seemed marginal at best, hopeless at worst. The irony was too rich. In choosing the missionary priesthood I'd dreamed of anointment to an elite group, then traveling to an exotic land, finding people in need, showing them the light of my religious truth, while helping them at critical times in their lives. Instead, I was anointed a Warrant Officer in the U.S. Army, shipped to an exotic land to locate people in need of conversion to our beliefs, and to assist in killing them.

The similarities with the seventh-grade movie were eerily similar: I arrived in jungle clearings in a small aircraft; the Vietnamese looked like the people in the film; we called our flying assignments 'missions'; the American 'mission' was an effort to 'win hearts and minds.' I tried not to become cynical.

I'm afraid I failed.

The happy, carefree kid was gone. My psychic terrain was littered with shoals, ruts, dark valleys. The war changed me, defeating the last vestige of my boyhood optimism. It made me someone I didn't recognize: I joked about human suffering; I shared negative outcomes with fellow pilots; I developed a morbid sense of humor that even then I knew I'd need to change if I survived. All that had happened made me doubt the human capacity to love, the compassion that, as a choirboy at midnight Mass I'd assumed was present in everyone, and especially in me.

I no longer recognized the man I saw when I was shaving, and I didn't like the fellow very much. There was no balance between what I saw, and what I knew in my heart to be true. I was "East of the sun, West of the moon" in my inner exploration, cast into that foreign land where no one goes willingly. I might have been flying in Vietnam, but in reality I was crossing the landscape of my own soul.

Then, on that August day in 1970, based on decisions I made, and my actions following them, I was given an insight, a glimpse of the terrain ahead, the rise and fall of it. It would take years to cross. But after that day I knew I was headed the right direction, back to myself. The curious thing is, that unlike my day to day flying where I studied the sky in front of me for its clues, its traps, its benevolent breezes that ushered me along, unlike that necessary vigilance for what lay ahead I could only know the truth about myself by studying the sky behind me. And that clue, the first generous spark of wisdom was given the August afternoon when fate showed me the pilot I would become.

The unit released me from my mission, so I turned the Huey toward Camp Eagle. Then the aircraft radio sputtered. It was the USARV fellow calling. He had another mission, a Medevac flight down the coast to a village called Vinh Mỹ. A young Vietnamese woman was in labor, he explained. The baby was breech. "If she doesn't get to a hospital soon..."

I checked the time: four-twenty. The fuel gauge showed enough for about forty minutes of flying. I did the math. A flight down the coast, back to the hospital in Huế, off-load time, back to base, then time to gas up... I'd never make the General's five o'clock curfew. Fuel was iffy as well. I scanned the blackness, like a shroud across the ocean, and a chill crawled up my back: the storm was close, and marching closer. I had to decline the mission. My finger hovered near the transmit button to send my regrets. Then something stopped me. *"...the heart of a man..."*

I simmered in irritation. Why didn't those people in Vinh Mỹ call sooner? They'd known the girl's condition all day. Am I responsible for their poor planning? She's been pregnant for nine months! The cynical me pressed forward. I touched the transmit button again, almost squeezed, released it, waited. *"...no more than this."*

The USARV fellow called again. In that moment, after listening to his calm, even voice on the radio all day, and then hearing a different tone, I sensed the urgency in his request. That urgency raised the tension between the new cynical me and my old compassionate self. Imagining the girl in trouble I saw my earlier dream, a foreign land, people in crisis, a small plane landing. I saw Father Colombo moving through the dark to provide comfort.

With my finger on the button, I tried to strike a balance. I have orders to be on the ground, orders from the General himself. The girl needs help. I've done the damn mission all day, and done it well. Her baby is breech, and may die. I'm tired; my crew needs food and rest; fuel is low; the war is wrong. The storm's closing in. But a young woman and her unborn child need my help...

I looked at my crew for support. My crewchief nodded. The

gunner's thumb went up. My right seater looked outside at the glowering sky and he hesitated. Slowly, he nodded yes.

I mashed the transmit button. "Comanchero 2-3, off to Vinh Mỹ."

4

Air Craft

I learned to fly way back in the twentieth century, when sex was safe and flying was dangerous. Since then, I've flown all over the world at the controls of more then twenty kinds of helicopters. In addition to flying combat in Vietnam, I flew 3,200 medical patients to a hospital in Iowa, counted several thousand utility poles across the Midwest, delivered executive Kahunas to their appointed busy-ness in a corporate posting that made the pole count job fascinating by comparison. I flew 15,000 camera-snappy tourists around a fuzzy little rock in the middle of the Pacific Ocean, the island of Kauai. Over a 40-year flying career I logged 12,500 hours of flight time, flew almost a million miles—at a top speed of 120 knots, which is why it took 40 years. I carried more than 100,000 people, some happy to be aboard my helicopter, some not so much. I landed aboard ships at sea, flew across Lake Superior once carrying an open dumpster of toxic waste slung beneath my aircraft. I lifted a lighthouse and laid it on its side. Flying a Huey landed me overnight in prison once. I played airborne shepherd in Alaska, with bears. I took Hollywood's *Golddiggers* for a ride, flew a U.S. Senator, a fragrant Miss America runner up, hundreds of not so fragrant GIs, and too many dead bodies. Once, a live grenade rolled into my cabin. Once was enough. Once I scared myself spitless when I landed downwind on an LZ with a half ton of troops on board, a full bag of gas, out of luck, lift, and ideas. That landing was a ten—on the Richter scale. One of aviation's solid aphorisms is this: Gravity's not just a good idea; it's the law. I proved it that day, as if it needed proof. One afternoon, 3,000 feet over Laos, I was almost hit by antiaircraft fire. The bad guys missed, or this memoir would be a lot shorter.

Indeed, I seemed to avoid all the common traps that trip up a lot of pilots. I left Vietnam without taking a single hit. Throughout my career, in the National Guard, and commercially, I had many close calls in the air, but I sidestepped every one. After many years of avoiding perils and pitfalls in the sky, I began to believe I had some purpose waiting for me on the ground.

As my career progressed I gathered not only flight hours, I gained wisdom, and insight. I believe the world is a beautiful place. I've flown over a whole lot of it, and seen it from an angle not many have. I believe we humans are mucking it up. I'm a firm believer in climate change, because I've seen evidence of it. I believe flying is the safest way to travel between point A and B, and back again. After flying for forty years I believe that what I heard once as a rookie isn't true. The fellow said, "You can't fly forever without getting killed." I don't believe that. You can live forever without flying. That part *is* true. But why would you want to?

In Vietnam I saw the depths of depravity, man's inhumanity to man. After the war I saw the depths of human misery and wanton suffering among medical patients, and the ravages of modern sources of comfort—cigarettes, alcohol, neglected seat belts, as I flew patients to a hospital. In twenty years of Air Medical flying I also witnessed the better angels, the altruistic side of us. Flight nurses and Air Med crews are dedicated to making others feel better, live longer, or at least die with a modicum of dignity.

I saw the savaging of the earth from a perspective few have. If more people were exposed to the trashed and poisoned slurry pits of coal country, the tree-stripped landscapes of the Western U.S., oil-fouled rivers, sheeny pollution, and acres of refuse in Alaska, the Sierra Club's membership would skyrocket.

I flew over beauty too rich for words—The NaPali coast of Kauai, frigid nights under a February full moon in snow-covered Iowa, shimmering drapery of the Aurora Borealis in northern Michigan. I saw flight nurses comfort casualties of highway trauma, birth emergencies, and medical anomalies, a different kind of beauty.

Flying wasn't like work. If not for utility bills, car payments, groceries and the like, I'd have flown for free. Flying was forty years of living a childhood dream.

Some say 100% of all accidents are caused by flying. Some say that if you fly helicopters long enough, you'll sooner or later ball one up. I never bought that. It sounds too much like predestination, or some Calvinistic hocus-pocus that denies personal ability. A kind of helplessness or inevitability that dismisses competence and a good preflight inspection. I do believe that some of my colleagues put themselves in harm's way. A colleague of mine once took off for a sixty-minute flight with twenty minutes of fuel in the tank. I was never good at math; it's one reason I elected to fly for a living. But even I knew that equation had an unhappy solution. I've read too many reports of pilots entering clouds, then diving toward the ground to regain visibility, only to find the unsentimental side of a mountain awaiting them.

An old aviation adage says if you don't believe you're the best in the game, you're in the wrong game. I was the best helicopter pilot in the game. I maintained a lot of respect for the aircraft, never got complacent, always flew the machine till I was done flying it, "...till it's in the fucking hangar," as Wayne said.

Wayne Alexander was a profane, no-nonsense fellow from East Texas, and my first flight instructor. Wayne taught me to fly. It could not have been easy.

It all started at Fort Wolters Texas way back in 1969.

5

Army Primary Helicopter School, Fort Wolters Texas
Summer 1969

At Wolters I remember heat, mostly. Both kinds of heat: the searing Texas summer sun, and the scathing torment of black-helmeted Tac Officers. Those individuals were the flight-school equivalent of the Gestapo, men assigned to harass us into quitting. At the stage fields, instructor pilots, IPs, had orders to push us through, teach us to fly one way or another, and get us on to Vietnam where more pilots were needed by the day. None of the Tacs or IPs at Wolters gave passes, because the war didn't. I'd either sink or swim on the merits of my ability. Helicopters fly only by constant attention, arcane scientific formulae, and the grace of the flying god, who, thank goodness, gave me a pass from time to time.

I left Fort Polk, Louisiana, on a March afternoon surrounded by fellow Warrant Officer Flight Trainees. We WOFTs pulled into Wolters around five p.m. The bus crossed under a gate with a wrought iron arch. The arch wore a plaque with a simple phrase: 'Above the Best.'

Before we stopped, a cabal of black-helmeted Tac Officers descended. They banged their swagger sticks against the sides of the bus, screaming like besotted soccer fans. "Off the fucking bus, ladies! Welcome to flight school, girls!" Bang-Bang-Bang, the bus rocked and swayed till I was nauseous. It was my first encounter with turbulence in aviation.

The reception at Wolters was designed to be terrifying, and it was. Hiding under the seat of the bus not being an option, I filed off, not quite sure that a trip back to basic wouldn't be better. Once off the bus I cowered with my colleagues in formation. A Tac charged at me, took my duffel bag, and dumped it on the ground. He kicked its contents around, my cherished letters from home, military documents and other papers scattering to the Texas wind. I'd heard once from a fellow who'd washed out of flight school that the saving trick was to never take the harassment personally, or it would be all over but the shoutin.' At the first sign of a tremble, a shiver, or God forbid a tear in the eye, he said, the Tacs would exploit the weakness, and soon the broken individual would quit, opting for the infantry, or cook school instead. It happened to him, he said. I was determined not to let it happen to me.

It was tough to *not* take it personally. The Tac tossed my duffel aside. Atop the pile of my recently dumped belongings was a photograph of the owner of my heart. The girl I'd left behind back home in Ohio, Patti G was a comely 18-year-old virgin, whose fetching countenance, electric smile, and raven tresses would rivet the attention of any red-blooded American male.

And so they did that day. The Tac picked up Patti's photograph, and he made a lewd remark about those very same exquisite female attributes. Inches from my face, he uttered a salacious query concerning my carnal affiliation with Patti, a question that he'd likely not have asked in church. The scapegrace then studied me, anticipating my reaction, hoping I'd bite the lurid lure. He loomed close enough to my face that his breath, I'm able to report with some authority, was like the bottom of a disposal. I held back, sensing the game that was afoot. He wanted me to react, to lash out. I refused to engage him.

Discretion being the better part of valor, and naive enough that, still a virgin myself, I truly didn't grasp the physiological implications of the Tac's question, I said nothing. I must have passed flight school's first hurdle, because he flipped Patti's picture aside, and moved on to the next terrified WOFT.

For the first month at Wolters I was called a Snowbird. Old people in Arizona who drive golf carts to afternoon shuffleboard are called Snowbirds. They flock south to escape chilly northern weather. When I was called a Snowbird at age twenty I wasn't quite sure what it meant.

What it meant was, that even though I'd escaped the chilly northern weather, and come to Texas to learn to fly, I wouldn't shuffle off in a helicopter for the first month of flight school. It was 30 days of constant harassment, continuous physical demands—even more so than basic training—and ongoing psychological gamesmanship. The harassment was designed to discern which of us would crack under the stress, and opt out of flight school. More than a few did, those men ceding under harsh taunts, the din of derision and latent threats to their physical well being. Of 250 men entering my flight school class, fewer than 120 graduated with me.

One of the harassment practices at Wolters was called bracing the wall. Crossing through a corridor, if I encountered a Tac officer I had to snap backward against the concrete blocks with enough speed that my head bounced. Sadistic as it was I did it anyway. It was tradition, and part of my re-socialization, a requisite ticket punch. Why I didn't have a concussion is a mystery. Maybe I did. I had few brain cells to spare anyway, so I was careful to avoid corridors at certain times of the day.

In the mess hall I ate 'square meals.' This had nothing to do with the nutritional content of the food. Considering the manipulation required to eat, the taste and quality of the food were a non-issue. The square meal required me to move my fork straight up from my plate, then bring it ninety degrees toward my mouth, then return it using the same square routing. Across the chow hall my colleagues and I looked like so many robots, forks hovering straight up, a sharp turn, ingestion, back out, sharp turn, and back down to where the food was. It was part of a plan, of course. The more I thought for myself, the less room the Army had to squeeze in its helping of rote discipline.

Speaking of discipline, just like at Boy Scout Camp, there were demerits. I was slapped with them for deficiencies on the flight line, in class, in formation, in the billet. It was all rather junior-high, but I put up with it. If I didn't make my bed just right, got out of step in formation, or dozed off in class I got demerits. Considering how few privileges I had to lose anyway the system was ludicrous. But, with sufficient demerits amassed, I'd return from a hot day on the flight line, or from a classroom period, to find my room plundered, bedding on the floor, closet trashed, toiletries in the hall and festive shave-cream greetings decorating the walls.

I had to display my personal gear just so. I was given a diagram with each item's placement depicted—toothbrush, paste, shoe polish, brush, etc.—like a kid's stencil. I had to display all my stuff using that outline: belt three inches from socks; toothbrush four inches from toothpaste; razor two inches from comb. The Tacs took a tape measure to every item. If my comb was half an inch off-kilter, toothpaste tube perilously close to hair brush, or any other egregious error, the Tacs tossed my room. Then I had ten minutes to put it back together.

My boot heels were notched. I had to have two pairs of boots, one with a single notch in the heel for use on odd-number days, the other pair with two notches for even-number days. The Tacs checked our boots during formation. If on the 4th of June I wore the one-notch boots I'd get demerits. The purpose of the even/odd boot exercise was to ensure that I actually wore the boots, instead of using one shiny pair for display only. Some guys tried wearing one of each, and were quickly discovered. Demerits ensued.

One item of discipline was the infamous 'Pillow.' A standard-size pillow, complete with cover, kept us awake in class in the somnolent summer heat. A man carried it. Anyone who dozed off in the un-air-conditioned classroom was fair game. Always looking to rid himself of the hated 'pillow,' the carrier scanned the room. If a man's eyes closed longer than it takes to say goose-feathers, the pillow sailed across the room and plumped him awake, branding the blinker as the new carrier of 'The Pillow.' Years later, when I saw the Monty Python sketch with its punishment by 'The Comfy Chair,' I knew where it came from. At Wolters I often wondered, with a war on, who had time to think of such tomfoolery?

It convinced some men to quit. I understood why they grew tired of the harassment, the adolescent taunting and the grade-school-mentality punishment. It was re-socialization, the Army's method of weeding out those men who would question bizarre behavior and make their own decisions. Considering what I saw in Vietnam, checking the number of notches in a man's boot heels was the definition of sanity.

I understood the desire to quit under a barrage of tedious demands, demerits, and duress. The tossed beds, bounced heads, flying pillows and square meals. The only mystery to me was that some of my classmates quit with the end of our 30-day Snowbird status in sight. First day, first week I could understand. We were reduced to cowering zombies at times. But quitting on day twenty-eight? Later on I understood that part of the psychological game plan was to discern our level of judgment and maturity. And part of it was this: those who opted for infantry, or truck driver school, harbored some ambivalence about flying, and they took the honorable way out when it was offered. The hazing and head bouncing were designed to see which of us under the strain of innocuous demands would crack. Better at Fort Wolters Texas after a silly square meal than in the heat of combat when men's lives depended on our (reasonably) calm, even temperament. We had to be able to square the circle of insanity called war.

6

First Takeoff: The Mattel Messerschmitt

Once my Snowbird month was over it was time to head to the flight line where I met my instructor. Wayne Alexander was a burly East Texan who could have been a linebacker, except he may have been too big. Six-two, 220, with a Fu Manchu mustache and a paunch coming at age 23, Wayne liked his suds. He looked like he'd be more at home ham-handing an eighteen wheeler down the double-nickel, grinding gears, CB in hand, yakking about Smokey-Bear *'takin' pitchers.'* But looks were deceiving; Wayne's delicate touch on the controls, and his smooth, professional transmissions on the radio exuded a quiet confidence.

But he was a big man. Wayne didn't board the helicopter. He more or less strapped it on his back like Santa's toy bag.

My first day in the cockpit with Wayne was an orientation ride. He did everything; I sat mesmerized, watching his hands fly through the start procedure. He flipped switches, twisted knobs, tuned radios, adjusted gauges and prepared the machine to fly.

The helicopter was a Hughes model 269, the Army's aircraft of choice for initial flight training. With two seats, a four-cylinder 180 horsepower piston engine, and a twenty-five-gallon fuel tank, the Hughes was purely a training helicopter for the military, thus its designation TH-55. With a bulging plexiglass canopy divided by a center strip, it looked like a big orange fly that was more than a little pissed. When the four-banger Lycoming chattered to a start it even sounded like one. Over the years more than 6,000 Army pilots learned to fly in what we called, with some affection, the Mattel Messerschmitt.

Wayne mashed the start button, and the engine roared to life. Then he flicked the clutch switch, moving eight drive belts forward to engage the rotors. Three blades whipped overhead, and the helicopter was ready to fly. Wayne called for takeoff clearance.

I studied his hands and feet. He mostly didn't move the controls, just pressured them. Wayne told me time and again not to, "wipe out the cockpit," as he said. "You barely move the controls; just *think* about moving them, and you'll go the right direction."

He made it look so easy that I couldn't imagine *not* being able to do likewise. Wayne was right; I barely saw his hands and feet move. He made it look so easy, so simple. When he lifted the collective the helicopter rose smooth as wet glass. Wayne pressed the aircraft's nose forward and we took off. Simple. He banked this way and that, zipping around with what seemed little or no effort. I watched him, a giddy warmth rising in my chest. I can do this, I thought. Heck, just relax, take it easy and let the machine do all the work. How tough can it be?

Wayne took us to altitude. He showed me basic maneuvers like straight and level flight, standard turns, climbs, descents and basic navigation. "Let's turn to the North," he said. We were then headed East. He banked left, stopped, leveled off. The compass bobbled and bounced on the panel, then a big 'N' settled in the glass as if painted on. Easy, nothing to it.

Wayne talked about what he called air sense. "Never let the aircraft go where your brain hasn't been thirty seconds before," he said. Air sense is another phrase for situational awareness while airborne, but that takes too long to say. Wayne was a man of few words, and many of them were crude. But his vulgarity was surpassed only by his aviation knowledge. "Treat the aircraft like a woman," he said. "Don't manhandle her; let her think she's in charge. Be gentle, but show her who's boss." After every dab of flying wisdom Wayne cackled like a madman. "Let me tell 'ya, Edgington," he'd say. "Flyin' ain't dangerous; crashing is. So try not to crash! Ha-ha-haaa!" I can hear him cackling even now.

This is as good a time as any for a short primer on how helicopters fly, the aerodynamics of rotary-wing flight. The main blades provide the lift, of course. But they also provide the steering mechanism for all intended directions. In the cockpit, the main stick the pilot holds in his or her right hand is called the cyclic. The cyclic is for horizontal flight. Ease the cyclic to the right, the aircraft goes right. Ease it left, and left you go. Forward, backward, sideways, all maneuvers in the horizontal plane come from moving the cyclic.

To the pilot's left, on the floor of the aircraft, is another stick called the collective pitch, or collective for short. It's for vertical flight. Pull the collective up, you go up. Push it down, down you go. The important thing about the collective is that, as it changes, the pitch in all main blades changes 'collectively' and equally. Moving the collective up and down also changes the amount of torque produced by the blades spinning around upstairs.

This is where the two pedals on the floor come in. Those two controls put pitch in and out of the tail rotor, which acts against all the torque mentioned above. The technical name for the tail rotor is the anti-torque rotor. The easiest way to explain what it does is to remove it from the aircraft, and show what would happen. Without the tail rotor, when we pull the collective up, the aircraft would come up, as it's supposed to. But the entire airframe would also spin around in the opposite direction of the main rotor. The upshot of this is, that when changing collective settings, up or down, the correct amount of pedal must be used to add or remove pitch in the tail rotor as well. It's simple; it's complicated.

A safety feature of any helicopter is its built-in ability to autorotate, and to land without engine power. If the engine fails,(in a single-engine helicopter), the pilot lowers the collective all the way, removing all pitch from the main blades. This action, going to 'flat pitch,' puts the machine 'in autorotation.' In that state, wind swirling upward through the rotors keeps them turning. This allows the pilot to safely land. The first day we flew together Wayne showed me an autorotation.

We shot up to 3,000 feet, where the air chilled the sweat on my arms. Wayne looked around for other traffic, both sides, and below. Then he snapped the throttle back to idle, lowered the collective, and adjusted the pedals. The bottom fell out of everything I owned. Sucked down by gravity, the little Hughes screamed toward the center of Texas. In autorotation we dove almost straight down, the vertical speed gauge pegged on 2,500 feet per minute. My stomach was still at three grand when, at five hundred feet, Wayne cackled like a circus clown. He twisted the throttle, raised the rpm and stopped our hellcat dive. Leveling off, he skimmed fifty feet across the tar trees and sagebrush. Then he cackled again. "Hardest thing about learnin' to fly is the ground, Edgington! Ha-Ha-haaaa!"

But he made it look so easy, that's the thing. After my orientation flight I was filled with confidence, eager for the next day, and my first attempt to fly. That night in the billet my colleagues and I chattered about the following day's session. It would be our first opportunity to show that we were indeed god's gift to aviation. I couldn't wait to grab the stick the first time, to pull the collective up, to ease in just a touch of pedal, correct with a tad of rpm, ease the nose forward. What's so hard? I was quite certain mine would be the perfect takeoff. Wayne made it look so simple. On day two I discovered just how good a pilot, and how good an actor Wayne Alexander really was.

7

Day Two

It's 1 p.m. at a stage field outside Mineral Wells Texas, and hotter than jackrabbit sex. Wayne straps on the helicopter. I board, snap into my seat belt, helmet up. This time Wayne walks *me* through the start-up procedure. I prime the engine with just enough fuel, check battery power and move switches into position.

"Always yell clear before you hit the starter," Wayne says. "You never know when some ya-hoo will walk into your fuckin' tail rotor."

I nod, look outside for stray ya-hoos and yell, "clear!" Then I turn the key. Soon the engine purrs, the blades whip overhead and the aircraft is ready to fly. I watch Wayne's big hands again. The size of skillets, they stay millimeters away from the controls, just in case. My confidence is such that I almost tell Wayne to relax, sit back and enjoy the ride. I don't do this. It's good that I don't.

About to try my first liftoff to a hover in a helicopter, ever, I squeeze the cyclic and collective for all I'm worth in the world. In more ways than one it will be the first high point of my aviation career, which is then two days old.

Wayne cackles at me. "If you can hover the bastard you can fly it! Ha-Ha-haaaa!"

Hovering is indeed the most difficult part of flying a

helicopter. Move one control, and you must move all others correspondingly. I'd heard this fundamental truth in the classroom, then from Wayne. I'd discussed it among my fellow students. I even read it in the Army's book on how to fly good. Still, I'd watched Wayne the day before, his subtle control pressure, his utter lack of jerkiness or force, and it really didn't look that hard. "Treat it like a woman," he'd said. (Bear in mind that in June 1969 I was still a virgin.)

I take the controls. Wayne hovers near them, his hands ready to override any overcontrol or misplaced input his virginal student might make. I suck in a breath of Texas humidity, lift the collective and feel a wave of ticklish emotion in my gut as the machine 'gets light.' Rotor rpm dips, so I inch the throttle up a tad to compensate for it. So far so good. I pull a teensy touch more collective. The skid gear skitters on the concrete, and the aircraft fishtails in a fancy dance. I push pedal to correct the yaw, and Lordy Magordy, it stops. Great! See; what's so hard?

Already I'm sweating. Globs of salty water sting my eyes. Rivulets course from my pits, and tickle my sides. I decide to be a bit more aggressive, show her who's boss as Wayne said with his signature cackle. I pull a bit more power to see what happens, jerk the collective and... She rears up like a swatted wasp, nose high, nose low, yaw right, yaw left, a Texas cowpuncher's got nothin' on me!

I hear the crudest cackle ever from Wayne. "Holy screwin' Jesus here I come, 'cause I'm gonna die today! Ha-Ha-Haaaa!"

The helicopter leaps off the ground, to a ten, or six, or twelve-foot unstable hover. "Yee-Hahh!" The nose swings right, then left, then right, through about 80 degrees. "Yoooowwweee!" The damnable little machine pitches ten degrees up, then twenty down. "Ride 'em cowboy!" Engine rpm staggers between 2,500 the low point, and 3,200, screaming above the red line. "Ha-Haaaa! I've got it!"

Wayne's hands touch the controls and the machine stops like a roped calf. Frozen at a hover, rpm steady as a rock. "Okay, try again, and remember, just *think* about moving the controls, don't actually move them."

Exhaling with conviction, my heart doing whifferdills, I take back the controls. With the same result. Like a scalded alligator the aircraft bucks and bolts, up, down, sideways, backward. It seems to resent my attempts to master it. "Yee-Haaaa!" Like a bronc refusing to be ridden it bucks and kicks, tail up, nose down, rpm all over the gauge, screaming, then sagging. Wayne's cackle fills my helmet. "Yowwww—eee! I got it!" Once again the machine freezes in place. The word bastard floats through my head. Not Wayne...necessarily. I think I hear the aviation god chuckle, but that may have been Wayne, too. I hunker down, shrug off my humiliation, wipe away a half-gallon of sweat and try again.

The rest of the period was more of the same. I arrived at a semblance of stable flight only by passing through it to another extreme. My hour-long session finally over, I unsnapped my seat belt, unplugged my helmet and cowered away from the helicopter like a throwed cowpoke. Thoughts of the infantry came unbidden; or truck driver—I was sure I could drive a truck; or cook school, if they'd have me. It was obvious I could flip pancakes, and scramble eggs with some authority.

On the way back to base the crew bus was silent. Heads sagged. I wasn't the only overwhelmed, overmatched trainee. The Mattel Messerschmitt looked harmless enough. But the little bastard had taken my earlier confidence and smashed it like a bully with a sandbox toy. Instead of looking forward to the third day's session, I was dreading it.

I'd love to report that day three, four, five were different, but alas they were not. I did my best to destroy every TH-55 I got my hands on. Wayne cackled his way through every session, his patience wearing thin only about day six when he hinted, in his signature subtle fashion, that perhaps I needed to 'settle down and learn to fucking fly.'

The yawing, swaying, out-of-control near-mayhem that passed for flight training lasted another two weeks, give or take. Little by little I managed to find the key to controlling the aircraft, gaining the touch that Wayne talked about. Day after day I learned better to *not* move the controls, to just let the helicopter fly. When I screwed up, which was still often, Wayne shouted, screamed, cursed. "Stop wipin' out the cockpit!" he yelled, his subtle way to tell me I was moving the controls a bit too much. "Quit poppin' the collective. You're losin' all your lift! Do that in Vietnam and you'll crash and burn."

When he referred to Vietnam my arms chilled. I knew that was my destination; I didn't need to be reminded of it. It was perverse. When Wayne mentioned the war his unspoken message seemed to be that I was doing okay, or at least no worse than my colleagues.

The crew bus had a few more open seats each day. One by one men decided that driving a truck, scrambling eggs or collating Army documents might not be so bad after all. (The Army did have a lot of documents.) I could have quit. I considered it many times. I knew my folks would have preferred it. But looking at all those disillusioned, disheartened men, my colleagues, the shared bewilderment told me I was okay. Like the first day, when the Tac tried to make me lash out at him over Patti's picture, I sensed that quitting was what they wanted me to do. If all of us were doing badly, none of us were. I sucked it up and went on.

My parents were nervous, and every phone call home reinforced that. Mom always mentioned alternatives, "...if it doesn't work out." Dad talked about his work, and my siblings. His only mention of the war was about my older brother's return home from

Vietnam, which was imminent. Both of them were afraid for me, afraid I'd be killed, a reasonable fear, I suppose.

It may sound odd, but never once did I consider the danger. In the five months I was at Wolters there were two fatal accidents. One of those was a mid-air collision between two solo students with two fatalities. The other involved a student and instructor. Both men were killed in that crash, too. It's not a bad record considering the low level of experience, and the high number of aircraft hours flown, likely 60,000 per month. The danger didn't phase me. Compared to the danger I knew was coming a few months hence, the flying at Wolters was tame.

So I put up with the hassles, the heat and the constant pressure to settle down, do it over, do it right. The cursing and swearing and sweating. It wasn't hard to understand. I wanted to fly. I would, by God, learn to fly. The heart of man had always yearned for that ability, too.

Something else pushed me. After two failures, the seminary and college, I needed success for its own sake. Two years before I'd been expelled from the seminary, my dream of the priesthood shattered. Then I'd been drafted out of Ohio State. If I couldn't be a sky pilot, or soar in academia, I'd be a helicopter pilot and no one would deny me that. Looking back, the high school expulsion may have been the best outcome of my life. It crushed me at the time. Losing a dream will do that. But the dismissal activated an inner fire, an anger that took me years to tame. The determination pushed itself into my head and would not let go. No, I would, goddamit to hell, learn to fly.

8

Silver Wings

I soloed on June 27th 1969. That afternoon, in an aviation tradition whose origin escapes me I was tossed by my peers, fully clothed in my flight suit, into the water. The crew bus pulled up to the Holiday Inn in Mineral Wells, and I was advised to take off my boots. As I left the bus my colleagues carried me aloft, and threw me in the deep end of the motel pool. I don't know which was more refreshing, the chill of the water in the June heat, or the release of tension from my solo success. Yes I do; the water was refreshing, but....

Graduation from Wolters in September was a bit anticlimactic. I'd moved into phase two of basic flying by then. I learned about landing in tight spots, so called red tire areas. These were small clearings in the Texas hills that approximated the LZs I'd find in Vietnam eight months hence. I learned about night flying, map reading, emergency procedures and more aerodynamics. At Wolters I learned the fundamental skills that would see me not only through Vietnam, but into my commercial career as well. The most important thing I learned at Wolters was confidence. I'd made it through a grueling selection process. Half my colleagues washed out. As little aviation experience as I had leaving Wolters I knew I could fly. The rest would come in time. In aviation they say the test comes first, then the lesson.

~*~

I say I learned to fly at Fort Wolters, but what I mostly learned there was how to stay alive between takeoff and landing. I became an aviator in Vietnam, where staying alive was more than watching gauges and rotor rpm while Wayne vented at me about "airspeed!" or "RPM!" or "x%#! Altitude" over cackles and broken pencils in a steamy Texas traffic pattern. Vietnam was a crucible that didn't know what a pass a pencil or a cackle was, and didn't care.

At Wolters, and then at Hunter Army Airfield in Savannah I absorbed tons of aeronautical info about helicopters—mechanical stuff, instrumentation, loading, armament, servicing, aerodynamics, pieces and parts, and a myriad of aviation data too boring to include in a memoir.

Wayne supplied the basics: any landing you walk away from is a good one; if you can still get the doors open it's great; if you can use the aircraft again the landing was excellent. Thus, I learned another aviation truth. Flying is filled with conflicting messages: number one, it's deadly serious; number two, joke around to get through it. Hours of boredom interrupted by moments of terror.

I learned a lot from Wayne. Rest his soul, Wayne was a good flight instructor. He gave no passes, broke a lot of pencils, cursed like a Cleveland cabbie. But he taught me to fly. Wayne Alexander died a few years ago, not in a helicopter crash, but of a heart attack. He was forty-six.

For the rest of flight school I polished skills needed to earn the silver wings of an Army Aviator. At Hunter I learned instrument flight, military tactics, formation flying, and a smattering of officer and gentleman protocols I'd need to mix with Real Live Officers, the RLOs, and not get more demerits.

Something else I learned at Hunter prior to graduation was that, regardless of my rank, despite all my technical skill and the year-long school I'd endured to collect those skills, the Army still considered me an infantryman, albeit one who could hover a Huey. The United States Army is little more than a vast collection of infantry troopers with different skill sets. Generals, Colonels, Captains of the engineer corps, MPs, Majors in the artillery, cooks, clerks, quartermasters, everyone's job description starts with humping a weapon. This glorified grunt status was reinforced by the final exercise in flight school. It was a mile-long trek to finish the escape and evasion route—on foot. Meant to simulate a real escape and evasion if we had the unhappy event of being shot down in Vietnam, the E&E course involved groups of OPFOR, opposition forces, planted here and there along the way only too happy to capture us. For a lot of reasons, chief among them that I was never cut out for the infantry, the high point of the all-night exercise was the end. Along with three comrades, I hauled into camp at daybreak, exhausted, but still among the uncaptured. A veteran Army chef welcomed the successful escapers and evaders into the safety of the compound with a hearty breakfast, standard Army fare of scrambled eggs and grits, this was Savannah Georgia after all. But no bacon. That portion of the menu was satisfied by chunks of white meat from a ten-foot long rattlesnake the good sergeant field stripped in front of us, then cooked up in a tasty broth. Yes, it tasted like chicken.

My parents came to Savannah for my graduation from flight school. Mom pinned silver wings to my chest, while Dad beamed. My father also envied me to some extent. My accomplishment in learning to fly was a vicarious success for him. His dream, during WW-2, had been to fly. His brother, my uncle Don, was a Navy pilot in the Pacific during the war, and dad had yearned to follow in his older brother's footsteps. The war ended too soon, and dad's dream to fly died, just as mine of the priesthood had. His pride in me, his pilot son the day of my graduation, was mixed with a bit of envy. With ten kids, and little income, any dream my father may have had to fly was much too expensive to pursue.

Looking back, it seems my decision to pursue the priesthood caused my folks the same ambivalence as flight school had. As determined as I'd been, they didn't want me leaving home at thirteen, believing I was too immature to handle the demands of the seminary. Watching me, at twenty years old, leaving for Vietnam must have given them similar concerns.

I never discussed what happened to me in the seminary with either of them. As devout as they were in their Catholic faith it would have broken their hearts. As they sent me off to war they must have wondered what my fate would be. Little did they know that I'd already faced a danger more insidious, perhaps more threatening to my well being, than war.

Flight school finished, I returned to Ohio for thirty days. The next thing I knew I was in Vietnam.

9

Fire Base Kathryn: RVN April 1970

I'll never forget my first girl. I'll never forget Kathryn, either. Kathryn—the name of a firebase in northern I-Corps in the Republic of Vietnam. The mission was to put troops on Kathryn's mountaintop crag.

April 10th 1970. Chief Warrant Officer Ray Woods was company flight lead that day. I was a new guy, "still pissing stateside water" as John Lipski, my left seater said. Our string of Hueys laced across the sky in a circle, like charms on a bracelet. We were waiting for the artillery prep to end so we could land on the LZ, dump our grunts and go home.

In the twenty-four-ship formation, I tried to ignore my place in the lineup. I was right seater in bird number thirteen. John and I followed the twelve Hueys in front of us like so many sheep in a line. Careful to avoid the artillery trajectory, Woody kept his flight a mile north of Kathryn.

Round after heavy artillery round pummeled the firebase. Its cratered surface, mangled tree stumps and arid ground resembled a brown blister festering atop the mountain. Artillery had pounded the firebase all night. It was nine a.m., and still we circled, twenty-four Hueys cutting holes in the sky over northern I-Corps.

We were waiting for Willie Pete, two final rounds of White Phosphorus. When the twin marking rounds of WP popped above the firebase, their presence marked the end of the artillery prep. Only then could we land.

Minutes dragged on. We circled. Radio silence. Watching shell after shell explode atop that ridge I couldn't imagine anything alive up there. I almost felt sorry for the bad guys, the ones the intel people told us were there waiting for us to land. Surely, I thought, they'd all be killed, or run off. Nobody could survive that massive bombardment. I was a rookie about to learn an important lesson. I was about to see how resilient the enemy was.

At nine-ten a.m., only a few minutes late, two ghostly clouds appeared a hundred feet above the LZ like twin thought balloons. Willie Pete; the arty prep was done. John slid his visor down and locked his shoulder harness. "Okay, guys," he said. "Let's go to work."

In the rear of the cabin the crewchief and door gunner sat up alert. Crewchief on the left, door gunner right, they cinched their monkey straps tight and swiveled the business end of their .30 cals up. "Ready in the rear, sir," they said in unison. As the gunners' weapons came up, and their charging rods clattered, the grunts stirred. Five GIs flicked cigarettes out. Their M-16s banged against the floor of the Huey as they adjusted their backpacks. Time for them to go to work, too.

Woody's ship angled off, aiming toward Kathryn, and lined up for landing. Two Cobra gunships slid into position near the lead Huey, one left, one right. The Cobras would escort Woody as he neared the LZ, then they'd break off. Together, the three aircraft flew toward Kathryn's ragged, shell-shot surface.

Woody called his approach. "Thirty seconds out," he said.

I watched from my aircraft, a mile behind, twelve UH-1s ahead.

"Short final," Woody said, the rattle and pop of Cobra suppressive fire in his radio call.

Woody's Huey touched down on Kathryn, and men streamed onto the firebase. Then a radio call that chilled my arms. Woody screamed into the ether. "Taking fire," he yelled. "On the firebase. My gunner's hit. He may be dead."

John looked across the cockpit, and shook his head. "Son of a bitch."

After an all-night bombardment, a pummeling no one could possibly have survived, an enemy soldier leapt into the open on Kathryn and shot Woody's door gunner. It's gonna be a long year, I thought.

Our turn. John steered the Huey toward Kathryn's landing spot. I watched gauges, called out readings. "Torque's good; rpm's good." I focused inside the cockpit, from fright or denial I'm not sure. I'll never forget my first girl. But I don't remember landing on Kathryn. Before I knew it the Huey was empty and John had lifted off. We took no fire, no hits. Still, what I'd seen gave me a lot of respect for the enemy. That respect helped keep me alive in Vietnam, that and a simple rule: never underestimate the North Vietnamese.

I arrived in Vietnam on March 17th 1970. The first two weeks of my year-long tour I was at Camp Evans, up the road from Huế, attending a required in-country orientation. Evans was a dusty, nondescript base of about 100 acres on Highway 1, halfway between Huế and Quảng Tri. I bunked in a wooden shack with three other pilots, new-in-country 'Wobbly-1s.'

Charm school, so called, was designed to teach GIs about Vietnamese culture, habits, cuisine, politics, religion, you name it. The fact that the Army tried to cover a couple thousand years of a rather intricate culture in a couple of weeks told me something about our efforts to win the hearts and minds of the Vietnamese. I tried to give the military the benefit of the doubt; they did have the two-week school after all, but still it seemed a bit inadequate.

At Evans I learned about the war and our place in it, from the

U.S. perspective of course, along with dibs and dabs about the Vietnamese people and their preferences. I watched a demo of how easily an enemy combatant could slither under the wire, devious movements hidden by their signature black pajamas. I stood guard duty one night on the Evans perimeter, convinced that every sound I heard was Victor Charles sliding under every three yards of the wire. When the wind changed direction I heard the stealthy fellow crawling forward, undetected, gamboling in every bunker, slitting American throats with abandon. It was a long night.

At Evans I tried to stay awake during classes on Vietnamese culture and religion taught by a young spec 4 who, it was clear even to me, misunderstood the difference between a Buddhist and Muslim. I was embarrassed for him. But I was glad the infamous pillow tradition hadn't made its way across the Pacific. I would surely have inherited the thing more than once while dozing off in military tactics, or enemy-resupply-capability class. As for Vietnamese food, I ate Nướcmắm only once, learning afterward that the delicacy was half-rotten fish. I managed to keep it down, but never had it again. I learned to distinguish between incoming and outgoing rounds, a valuable skill. And I learned to sleep through the outgoing stuff, which may have been more valuable.

Another embarrassing gibe made me ashamed for my colleagues, something I never expected. One of the immutable realities of war is the way it relaxes sexual restraint among otherwise upright, responsible men. Specifically, war seems to grant those men easy access to women who are caught up in the conflict. More than once I saw my colleagues takes liberties with Vietnamese women, and it bothered me. It should not have, I suppose. I tend to be a prude about such things, perhaps a bit self-righteous. It wasn't rape, since money did change hands, still... The sergeant's answer to this age-old convergence of war and sexual license consisted of just seven words. "Watch what you stick your dick in." Charming.

In light of that admonition, *charm* school ended on a rather curious note, I thought. I was told that we GIs were confined to our bases. We were not to mix with the Vietnamese people except on official business. It seemed a curious way to spread our brand. On April 1st 1970 I left Camp Evans and Jeeped down to Camp Eagle, home for the next twelve months.

Eagle was a sprawling, mile-long military complex, home to the 101st Airborne Division. Several aviation companies called Camp Eagle home, including Chinooks, Cobra gunships, an ARA company, a Cavalry outfit and two lift companies. I was assigned to one of those lift units, so called because, with twenty Hueys, what a lift unit did was, well, lift stuff. My unit was 'A' Company, 101st Assault Helicopter Battalion. At Alpha company our radio call sign was the Comancheros.

When I checked into the company the monsoon season was just ending. Like all else in SouthEast Asia the war had a cyclical, seasonal pattern. During the dry season—April through October—mountain firebases became a hive of activity, as artillery crews kept the big guns firing to protect troop movements, and to prevent the enemy from gaining the upper hand. But those bases had to be resupplied by air. Roads were few, rugged, often mired in mines and mud and unsafe. Because of the weather, during the rainy season firebase resupply by air was impossible. So toward the end of October the firebases were evacuated. Then, like clockwork, when the monsoon eased in the spring those bases were remanned, until the rains came again. It was all very mystical and eastern, which pattern was lost on us crude westerners.

Speaking of cyclical things, veteran pilots rotated out of the company as new ones arrived, each tour one year in duration. New faces appeared all the time, new pilots, and new crews as well. Veteran pilots left, freeing up positions for newer pilots looking to improve their situation, the chance to be in command of our own helicopter. We were all new guys once, but we didn't wish to stay where new guys were assigned, in the right seat of the aircraft. As a new pilot I did the preflight inspection, prepped the aircraft for flight, held down the right seat, kept the maps and checklist from flying out the window and tuned radios. After one or two early missions I knew the right seat was not the place for me.

10

The right seat is the wrong seat
...and other stories.

When I signed into the Comancheros on April 1st 1970 flight activity was ramping up with a vengeance. The company was flying six, eight, ten hours per day, per aircraft. All that flying allowed me to learn as much as possible in a short time, and to pick up tips from the veteran pilots. Aircraft Commanders, ACs, were those pilots who'd earned their stripes in combat, logged a set number of combat flight hours, and been assigned their own aircraft. New guys were posted in the right seat, and were called Peter Pilots. The life of a Peter Pilot was not glamorous. As a PP I secured the right seat of a Huey all day, like so much ballast. I dialed frequencies, made radio calls, monitored instruments. I reminded the AC when it was time to gas up. On rare occasions I was allowed to fly, like when the left-seater wished to light a cigarette, or when he left the cockpit at the fuel site to take a leak. Right seat duty was a grind. I couldn't wait to move across the cockpit.

The day after my check flight with the company instructor, a fellow named Tom Kearsley, I flew my first combat assault mission. It was a simple troop insertion to a small landing zone (LZ) five miles from base. The LZ was reported cold, with no enemy detected there, so no big deal as far as missions went. The big deal for me, however, was that, after I held down the right seat all morning, performing an outstanding job as a Peter Pilot, my left seater, a veteran named Tom Handy gave me the controls, and let me fly.

"Pay attention to your crew," Tom said. "They can see outside the aircraft a lot better than you can, so do what they say." He ceded the controls to me on final approach to the landing zone. "And don't ever take off till they tell you to." I aimed for my first ever LZ, and did as Tom said, although I wondered about his last injunction. As the pilot, I'd assumed I'd take off when I felt it was right, when I sensed the need to do so. But Tom told me otherwise, to wait for my crewchief and gunner to okay the liftoff, and to defer to them.

I lined up with the LZ, angled just right to avoid trees, and kept the power in so I didn't undershoot the landing, a common error with a ton of troops on board. The crewchief and gunner began their alternating talk-down, first the left side of the aircraft, then the right. "Looking good sir, keep coming forward. Good on the right, fifty feet. Left side's good, trees thirty feet, don't slide left. Clear on the right, got a little slope down on this side."

My crew chattered on like that till the skids touched the ground. Then the grunts jumped out, and the back of the Huey was empty. Instead of taking off, I waited. Tom stared across the cockpit at me. I waited longer. Three seconds. Five. The ship behind us radioed in. "Chalk three, short final." Then the crewchief piped up. "Clear up left," he said. "Clear right," the gunner echoed. I lifted the collective, and the Huey grappled into the sky.

After the mission I shut the aircraft down. Tom and I checked it for bullet holes, nicks and scrapes. We helped the crew clean things up, put covers on, closed cowls and put the machine to bed. As we walked around the helicopter Tom dissected my performance, my first day of combat flying.

"Not bad," he said, a man of few words. "Most new guys can't wait to get out of an LZ, so they ignore their crew. Not bad." The true test, I suspected, would come when waiting meant staying in an LZ under fire, when any sane person wants to get the hell out of there. It wouldn't be long before I got that test.

My first day of combat flying was over. I logged four hours, thanked the crew for their help, and checked with operations for the next day's assignments. Then I went to the club and enjoyed a beer. Or perhaps three.

There were a number of times in Vietnam that I looked at the chaos and disruption inside and outside the cockpit and wondered how in God's name I got there. Sometimes I'd indulge in a laugh or two. Such a reaction wasn't conducive to survival under the best of circumstances, so I did it rarely. Mostly how I stayed alive in Vietnam was paying attention to signs, listening to veteran pilots and taking no chances. In other words I flew like I was half, or sometimes wholly scared to death. But those sublime times when everything unfolded like a GI Joe cartoon strip, those times were almost, dare I say it, fun? Guess you had to be there.

The incident was like the rest of the war in Vietnam, a combination of terror and hilarity. I angle toward the landing zone, a ragged patch of cratered dirt blasted out of the jungle. On the floor of my Huey, five well-fed American grunts huddle, waiting for me to land so they can go kill something. August air wafts through the cockpit, oven-like, sultry as steam, and thick with the sweet stink of cordite. And other things. There is grunt-sweat, and the astringent military equipment smell we associate with government handouts. There's the green-rotten stench of bombed vegetation. War may not be hell, but it sure as hell smells like it.

Thirty seconds out. I'm number two bird. Sliding my visor down, I shake myself to calm the nerves, swallow more dry cotton. The intel brief last night didn't mention enemy activity. But I've been in Vietnam seven months, long enough to know that Army Intelligence is an oxymoron. I've acquired my own metric for when things are safe, and when not. For one thing, if there's a pending dustup with the enemy, jungle critters sense it. Like farm animals clearing fields, or house pets whimpering for no apparent reason before a storm breaks, they know, and I watched for it. I drop lower and lower toward the LZ, and my gut clenches. Last time I'd landed there I'd seen monkeys scampering around. This time, not a monkey in sight, so I lock my harness, and drop my visor. Twenty seconds out.

Ahead, a plume of dust blooms upward as number one aircraft lifts off the LZ. "One-eight's out."

"Two-three, short final," I bark into the open mike.

Just as I release the mike button, number one screams into the radio, a call I don't need to hear. "Taking fire, taking fire," he yells. "...right side of the LZ, fifty meters!"

I forget the smells and the dirt. The monkeys were right; tracers thread past the lead ship, red arcs targeting him. Gil, my crewchief, yells at our huddled customers, "LZ's hot!" It's something the grunts no doubt already know. On the left side my gunner, a fellow named John, rams his load rod home. Men shuffle; bodies shift. The Huey sways with the nervous movement of men wanting to be on solid ground, while wishing to fly home. I hear groans, the metallic clack of weapons being readied. Cigarettes arc outboard. Then a new smell. It is fear.

Tracers whip past *my* cockpit, red arcs creasing the sky, trails of lead ratcheting closer. I ask for and get permission to suppress.

Gil's voice: "Clear to fire, sir?"

"Got the friendlies?"

"Roger."

"Go for it."

Behind me, two .30 caliber machine guns erupt like a twin shit-storm. The clattering blast stings my ears as rounds snap outbound, and zing into the jungle. Ten seconds out. The chaos of thundering ammunition delivered at 500 rounds per minute. An odd comfort, the deafening din soothes me: no enemy troops would dare move under those commanding guns, that deafening chorus of hot lead. I continue forward, the LZ seconds away. Then, in an instant, exactly half the deadly noise stops.

On the right side of the aircraft the silence is louder than gunfire. John's 60 is jammed. Barely audible above the rasp of Gil's outgoing rounds I hear—a whistle. I think I'm imagining the sound, like waking from a dream. But I'm not dreaming. I'm hearing...shreet, shreeeeet....a whistle, like a cop directing traffic...shreeeet...a referee at a suburban Friday night football game. What the hell..?

The ground rushes up, the LZ seconds away. Shreeeeet... I half turn to look for the source. John jerks the gun's load rod, bangs its separator. He blows...a whistle!

Shreet! shreet! shreet!

"John, what the fuck're you doing?" It's Gil.

I guide the Huey below the treeline, onto the LZ. The skids furrow the dirt. Grunts leap off and dive for cover.

John's whistle stops, drops on its lanyard, dangles in the breeze as he wrestles with the silent gun. "Jammed," he yells. "...I'm callin' time out!"

What I remember about Vietnam comes roughly in this order: smells first, of human fear and exhaustion, and decay. It seemed like decay was the reality, not effulgence, but decay in a place characterized by wild and incessant growth.

I remember weather. More than just air and wind and water, weather was enemy and friend, peril and protector. Weather was more than seasons; it was structure, and schedule.

I remember change. From wide-eyed youths into wizened soldiers, clear-eyed true believers into squinting, snarling cynics. Change was everywhere, and nowhere, as weeks flew by while days dragged on. Hours lasted forever. Seconds an eternity.

Mostly what I remember of Vietnam is the facade we hid

behind to maintain regard among our peers, to not be shunned as fearful, or hesitant, or God forbid cowardly. I remember fire. A lot of fire, and the uses of it. Fire, too, was enemy and friend, marker and mark, symbol and scar, offense and defense. Nothing happened in Vietnam without fire. Even our waste was addressed with fire. Vietnamese civilians were put to work. Job description: shit burner.

I wondered how I came to be there, what fiery initiation I'd somehow failed. It seemed as if there was always more of it to come.

By the time I entered Vietnam I'd been in the Army a bit longer than one year. I knew about the chain of command, rank structure, the various courtesies and protocols the Army demanded, like enlisted men saluting officers and the like. When I received my W-1 bar, a rather homely brown rectangular spot in a field of gold, I became a member of the Army's Warrant Officer Corps, a curious middle ground. The rank of a Wobbly-1 suited me just fine. Neither fish nor foul, Warrants are indeed part of the officer corps. But they're kinda, sorta enlisted troops as well. I relished the status; it gave me access to both levels of rank at once. The true officer corps, what Warrants derisively refer to as RLOs, or Real Live Officers, consists of Lieutenants, Captains, Majors and the like. RLOs derisively refer to Warrants as Corporals with a club card. At its root it's a class thing, with the usual overtones of privilege and status.

The distinction played out in various subtle and not so subtle ways. I did indeed use the Officer's club, spending many evenings there in various stages of sobriety after long, tedious missions. The enlisted troops saluted me, though I was always a bit chary of that habit, allowing it only because the Army demanded that it be so. But RLOs had a way of asserting their dominance over us Warrants. This arms-length relationship marked the introduction to my company commander, an RLO named Snider. The first time

I met Major Snider he tricked me with what may have been the oldest commander's ploy there is to show who's boss. He informed me that to fit in with his company I had to shave my mustache.

Late morning of April 1st 1970 I schlepped into Major Snider's office to report in with the Comancheros. As I scanned the compound I noticed that every aircraft revetment was empty. Every Huey and crew was gone, out fighting the war. The place was quiet as a church.

I entered the CO's office. Snider welcomed me to the company with these exact words: "Mister Edgington, welcome to the Comancheros. I don't allow my men to wear a mustache, you'll have to shave it off."

Distressed at the flavor of the greeting as much as the demand to shave my long-time 'stache,' I nodded, allowed as to how I was glad to be in the company, though somewhat less glad at that point, and Major Snider and I parted. I had no idea his ordering me to shave was to approximate the biblical story of Samson, insofar as it was his way of showing me who held the reins, or the shears if you will. Dutiful if hirsute subject that I was, I retreated to the latrine, took a razor to my fluffy growth, and returned to my hooch, cool air oddly chilling my upper lip.

Astute reader, you already know where this story ends. At five p.m. local time the war ended for the day, and the compound buzzed alive with the clatter and shake and thrum of twenty Hueys returning to roost. The walls of my hooch shook. Kicked up debris misted the air. The slap and wop of rotor blades and engines and pummeling wind blasted the company compound. I wandered to the flight line to watch my colleagues land. Hueys glided into their assigned revetments, a graceful dance choreographed and precise. Soon every helicopter was aground, engine noise tapered off, and rotor blades coasted down.

Then pilots streamed from cockpits, crewchiefs and gunners

appeared, helmets slipped off. Imagine my chagrin when rugged faces revealed themselves, every damned pilot and crewchief and gunner sporting a full, fluffy, raggedy-ass mustache. I'd been had. Exposed. Marked and branded as the shorn new guy. And I'd done the shearing to myself.

I suspect the Major was at that very moment somewhere watching, his evil grin and feeling of satisfaction almost too much to bear. He likely laughed at me. I had to as well.

A postscript to this story was even more humorous. I grew my mustache back right away, of course. Then I was promoted by the enlisted crews—to Major!

When I joined the company I was issued flight gear, including two shirts and two pair of pants made of Nomex fire retardant material. It was my job to get the appropriate labels and insignia sewn on the uniforms. I took the pants and shirts to the PX sewing center, where Vietnamese women did the work for me. Instead of the standard black, subdued Warrant Officer insignia and rank, I chose bold, gold items. My bright yellow Warrant Officer insignia and W-1 rank stood out at fifty paces. The Warrant insignia is a stylized bird of some kind, a rather flamboyant looking creature with its arms outstretched, feathers aflutter, as if it's squirming in pain. We referred to this symbol as a squashed bug.

My squashed bug was gold. And even up close it looked very much like a Major's oak leaf. It wasn't long before one of the crewchiefs spied my brazen yellow tag and branded me with the nickname I would carry my entire tour. The first time the fellow saw me crossing the compound, gold Warrant insignia on my lapel, he saluted me, and screamed, "Major Edge!"

I didn't correct him. Of course he knew I was a Warrant Officer. It didn't matter. I'd been tagged. From that day forward, to the enlisted crews and most of my colleagues, I was Major Edge. They liked my mustache, too.

~*~

To be designated an aircraft commander, an AC, and take command of my very own Huey became a cherished and urgent goal. I wanted to chart my own course, to be in command of my own aircraft. I flew with most of the company pilots in my time as a FNG, or Fucking New Guy. The men I flew with were, for the most part, reasonably competent. But holding down the right seat of a Huey while another pilot flew it gave me no control over my destiny. That sense was heightened within a week of my arrival in the company when a left-seater, a guy named Bill, tried to kill me entirely dead.

I was holding down the right seat, and doing an admirable job of it. Bill was on the controls in the left seat. Behind the two of us five sweaty, well-nourished American type GIs rested with their firearms and camping out gear. The LZ was a brown spot atop a ridge. I forget what number I was in the formation, but my number almost came up during the final descent. Bill dropped power, angled in on a pretty steep approach, I thought, one where I could almost look through the chin bubble and see the landing spot. It was not the best view, considering how heavy the helicopter was, and how fast the airspeed. Even as a raw rookie in the right I sensed that Bill was doing it mostly wrong.

Bill approached the LZ much too fast for anything but a crash landing. As we screamed toward the ground I was helpless to intervene. It was an unpardonable sin to grab the flight controls away from a veteran pilot. As the ground rushed up, my life flashed in front of me so fast I needed a rerun. Several emotions passed through my stupid brain: disbelief, fear, exhilaration of the Coney Island kind, matched with a certainty of death. I was pissed that my tour was ending so damn soon without a chance to see Sydney or Hong Kong on R&R like I'd planned. I'd heard about the great deals available on Panasonic stereos, and Seiko watches, and I wanted to buy some of that swag. I was pissed that I'd put up with Wayne and all his hyperbolics back at Wolters so I could spend a lousy three weeks in Vietnam. Mostly I was paralyzed by my lack of ability to intervene.

At the last second Bill realized he was much too fast to land, and he broke off the approach. The ridge zipped by underneath. We skimmed overhead at about eighty knots, branches and leaves shuddering in our wake. If Bill hadn't veered off there'd still be parts on that hillside stamped with Bell stock numbers, my folks would have a nice folded flag on their mantel and there'd be an etching on a wall in DC they could go visit and run their fingers over. A few other incidents like the one with Bill convinced me to get my AC orders ASAP, so I could move into the left seat, call my own shots and stay the hell away from marble etchings, at least for a time.

The plan sounded well and good—and relatively easy if I kept my nose clean, and did what the veteran pilots told me. But as it turned out, company check pilot Tom Kearsley stood in my way. Other ACs gave me high marks. Some ceded the controls, and let me fly for several minutes at a time. For whatever reason Kearsley didn't like me. My in-country orientation flight with him had gone well enough. He did most of the flying, which I considered a bit odd, but that was just his way. Something he said when we landed, though, told me that Kearsley had his BVDs in a bunch about me for some reason. I never did figure it out, and never will. As Kearsley filled out the logbook that day, my orientation ride in Vietnam complete, I mentioned that I couldn't wait till I was no longer a 'fucking new guy.' He stopped scribbling, and glared at me. "You'll always be a fucking new guy," he said. Nice.

Kearsley seemed to seek me out for criticism. He picked at everything I did, commented on perceived mistakes—even when I flew with other guys—and generally made my life miserable. I heard from other pilots that Kearsley thought he was God's gift to the flying game, and those comments gave me a bit of comfort.

Maybe it wasn't just me? But he *was* the company check pilot. My advancement to aircraft commander went through Tom Kearsley. Sensing his disdain, and the need for his endorsement moving forward to a left seat assignment, I imagined being stuck as a Peter Pilot forever. Then, overnight the situation changed.

May 4th 1970. I'd been a Comanchero for just over a month. I'd flown all day—in the right seat once again. At five p.m. I was tired, hot and hungry. My logbook showed 140 hours of combat time. I needed 300 hours to qualify for Aircraft Commander orders. After putting the helicopter to bed I checked the mission board for the next day's activity. Then I went to my hooch, tossed my helmet and chicken plate on the bed, and slipped into the club where there was a lot of buzz about four dead college kids back in Ohio.

At seven o'clock I wandered to my hooch, lit a few candles—the generator was out again—and picked up a paperback. At eight-thirty, and just fully dark, a Huey cranked up on the flight line. The helicopter soon blasted into the moonless night. "Kearsley," I said. "Flareship mission. Glad it's not my night for flares. It's dark as perdition's back yard in those mountains." At nine o'clock I closed my book, blew out the candles and dropped onto my cot. I don't remember hitting the pillow.

At ten o'clock I woke to muffled shouts and scuffling feet in the company compound. They weren't the usual voices and grunts of inebriated pilots staggering to their bunks, laughing, playing grab ass, throwing up; these were sober, incredulous voices. Something was wrong.

It was Tom Kearsley. He was dead. Two weeks to the day before his return home to Utah he'd been killed, along with six other crewmen, in a midair collision with a Cobra gunship. The investigation was inconclusive. Troops on the ground saw two aircraft pass overhead, then a bone-chilling whump. Flaming aircraft parts rained from the sky, then two fires lit up the jungle, then silence.

The loss of Kearsley's crew marked the first company fatalities during my tour in Vietnam. That accident was a chilling reminder to me that the enemy was not the only peril. Indeed, the enemy was a minor factor in the number of casualties. While I was with the Comancheros the company lost more troops from friendly fire, aircraft accidents, mission errors and pure stupidity than from enemy activity. A man was crushed in our hangar one night when a helicopter he was working under slid off its jack; another man broke his neck diving into shallow water and died; a captain on a night perimeter patrol was shot by his own troops. Kearsley's midair killed seven men. If I had any doubt about the vagaries of war before that night, I didn't the next morning. But I learned how war turns things around as well.

One outcome of Kearsley's death was the creation of two AC slots in the company roster. And Tom Kearsley was no longer there to reject my orders. By the end of May 1970 I'd logged 180 hours in combat. Due to the pressing need for pilots at that time, and because I was earning high marks from the veterans, I was issued Aircraft Commander orders. The company CO, the very same Major Snider, assigned me—despite my fresh mustache—to UH-1H Huey tail number 69-16252. In June of 1970 I flew 252 a total of 180 hours, spending six hours a day on average in the cockpit. There were even a few ten and twelve hour days in the saddle. I didn't shut down the engine. There was a war on. I'd land at the refuel point, keep the blades turning and fuel hot. June 1970 was a very long month.

An addendum to the Kearsley midair story. We were young males, so we didn't do a lot of introspection. To discern the emotional or psychological state of our fellows would have been much too airy-fairy, especially in a war zone. Men give little heed to such touchy-feely stuff anyway; in a war zone even less. Long after Kearsley and his crew were shipped home for burial something occurred to me that may have been a factor in their accident that night.

The day before Kearsley's ill-fated mission I'd flown with his right seater, a fellow named Larry Mattingly from Indiana. May 3rd was the first time I'd flown with Larry, but I could tell he was distracted, that his mind was on something besides aviation. Halfway through the day's missions we approached a hilltop LZ to deliver C-rations to GIs there. The LZ was cold; there were no enemy troops nearby. So what happened on approach wasn't due to anxiety or fear, but something else. Mattingly steered the Huey toward the wide-open LZ. Then, despite repeated warnings from his crew, he drifted left toward the only tree within 100 yards, a dead snag about thirty feet tall. He seemed to be aiming directly for it.

I was about to open my intercom to warn him, when the crewchief did it for me. "Got that tree, sir?" The man's voice cracked.

As if he hadn't heard, Mattingly continued toward the tree. I watched in disbelief as he flew right into the snag. The main blades hit dry branches, and wood chips exploded like a sneeze. Shattered limbs clattered against the windscreen. Out of instinct, I ducked. The helicopter jerked and then righted itself. The next instant a hiss and whistle sounded, the peculiar noise caused by rips in the damaged blades. I cringed, hoping all that exploding wood missed the tail rotor, and it apparently did.

We landed on the LZ and shut the engine down. As the blades wheezed to a stop we looked up at them. Daylight glared through holes in both of those rotor blades. Larry didn't say a word. He shook his head, and slumped into the cockpit. The crew looked at me in silence, then with some reluctance they boarded, too. Larry cranked the engine and flew back to home base, blades whistling. I was glad to be done for the day. Then came the insight that may explain Larry's midair the following night.

I left the ops center, headed for my hooch. The fellow who'd tried to warn Mattingly about the tree saw me, and he wandered over. "Can you believe he just ran into that tree?" I said.

"Lot on his mind," the crewchief said. "He got a dear John yesterday from his wife."

The man walked away. I watched him go, knowing that my instinct had been correct: Larry Mattingly's head wasn't in the cockpit that day; when he plowed into the tree he was back home in Indianapolis trying to save his marriage. He probably should have been grounded, or grounded himself. The next night he was killed, with Tom Kearsley and his crew. Much later I wondered if I should have said something to him that day, asked more questions, let him vent? But we were too young and too male for that kind of thing. He would have thought I was weird asking about his personal life, even if it might have saved his real life.

It's a damn shame what happened to Tom Kearsley. After his accident that night he'll always be a new guy, too.

11

FNG meets Lady Hooker

As much tension, tragedy and mayhem as the war provided it gave a group of crude, vulgar young pilots a fair amount of fun, too. The officer's club was the hub of our hormonally driven behavior. It was where we drank ourselves silly to release the tension and bravado endemic to twenty-year old males, in or out of a war zone. The club was our sanctuary, watering hole and mailroom. It was our hello and goodbye spot where, as the saying goes, everybody knew my name. But before I could fully partake of the blandishments of the club I had to pass in front of my fellow pilots. I had to get the secret handshake, to undergo the inevitable ritual without which Kearsley would have been right: I'd always be a new guy. The protocol involved an encounter with a lady named Hooker. (It's not what you think.)

As young men, we had an affinity for fire. Our affection for flaming things may have been second only to our affinity for alcohol. My initiation rite involved a combination of the two. The concoction was labeled a Flaming Hooker. Lady Hooker was rum in a shot glass, ignited. She sounds innocuous; she wasn't. But, to be welcomed among the veterans, I had first to commune with the intoxicating, overheated lady. There were pilots who refused the opportunity. After doing so they were shunned, and never quite fit in. Peer pressure was more intense than fire, and more damaging it seemed. Zorba the Greek was right: the only real sin is if a woman invites a man into her bed and he will not go.

I stepped forward like a sacrificial lamb to offer myself up to the old guys for their blessing. Madam Hooker waited in the wings. With its requisite monastic vesting, flickering flames, and imbibed offertory, the ritual took on a religious aura. Veteran pilots set the altar and prepared the nave by dimming lights, and lighting candles. The raucous music of Led Zeppelin ceased, and blessed silence flowed through the club.

I was shriven of my new-guy top. A veteran pilot stripped off my fire-retardant shirt, which made no sense considering what was about to happen. I was cleansed. Like a priest performing ablutions, another veteran doused my chest and arms with beer. The door squeaked and slammed, men filing in for the ritual of initiation. Men chanted, and spirits filled crude chalices so all could partake.

The offertory commenced. From the shadows a shot glass appeared, and a disembodied hand tipped it full of holy rum. Another hand proffered a Zippo lighter. With a click and a scritch, an ardent light leapt from the lighter's wick. When the flame blessed the surface of the rum a blue fire burst upward. It danced atop the glass, glowing with an eerie sheen. This was Lady Hooker in her evening finery. Druidic and solemn, men intoned the company hymn.

The climax of the sacrifice arrived. Men stepped away.

I took the flaming glass, and caressed Ms Hooker's warm figure. I held her at eye level, at arm's length, the slow dance beginning as a growing warmth tingled my fingers. Despite my efforts, Ms Hooker led this dance, her feathery tendrils of fire, blue, yellow and red licking upward, riveting my attention. I brought her close to my face, and the broad's alluring heat tickled my nose. To complete the rite, and to atone for my new-guy sins, I had to down the liquid, then set Ms Hooker on the altar with flame still alive in her bowl. No man tempts fate by putting out a lady's fire.

Time stands still. The next few seconds will tell the veteran pilots who I am, and if I'm welcome among them, a fraternity of men who fly fragile machines at war, men who want no pilot among them who can't stand the heat. Despite its femme fatale overtones, the rite is my baptism of fire among these men.

Like the square meals of flight school, I bring the glass straight to my mouth, close enough that it sears my face.

Now or never. Without thinking I tip it into my mouth, and jerk my head back. Fierce heat gags me. I swallow. Searing fire singes my lips, and gibbets of flame dribble onto my beer-soaked chest. The acrid scent of burnt hair assaults my nose. I'm glad my mustache is gone; it would be now in any case. The taste of thick, viscous rum stains my tongue. My throat constricts. I almost eject the foul mix, but manage to hold back. Then slowly, deliberately, my hands shaking, eyes streaming tears I ease the glass onto the bar. A taper of flame burbles, dances. It almost goes out, but no... A fragment of fire rims the edge, and then snuffs out. Lady Hooker is happy. I've made her so.

Men erupt in cheers and drunken shouts. They slap my back so hard I forget about the scorch of my flaming throat. A hand comes forward holding a beer. I grab it, down it in record time, letting half of it spill onto my blackened chest hair. My new-guy sins forgiven, the club welcomes me with cheers.

Then veteran pilots transition as smooth as burning rum into a raucous rendition of the company battle hymn. It is *Camptown Races*, with our very own morbid lyrics. *"You're goin' home in a body bag, doo-dah, doo-dah, you're goin' home in a body bag, all the doo-dah day!"*

My flight shirt sails at me out of the darkness. Another beer lands in my hand. Open palms come out of nowhere to slap me on the back, shake my hand and welcome me to the unit. I suck down the beer, relief flooding my body. Then another sensation takes over as the world swims, weaves, my vision shimmers in a kind of vertigo. My mouth fills with hot liquid, and my stomach clenches. I cover my lips, barge outside, and puke like a veteran.

I'd received the blessings of Lady Hooker, and was accepted among the veteran pilots even if I *was* still technically a FNG. There were men who refused to romance Lady Hooker. One of them, a fellow named Jon who arrived in the company with me. Jon never did fit in. His estrangement started with his refusal to dance with Ms Hooker. The rite itself and its branding had a lot to do with our affinity for fire.

We loved fire. Everything about fire attracted us. One of my first nights in the company I wandered to the flight line under a moonless sky. No place on earth is as dark as Vietnam at night. There's no ambient light to speak of, especially in the mountains. So the cascade of fire in the mountains that night was riveting, hypnotizing.

It was a Cobra gunship doing its deadly job. I stood in the company compound, enveloped in darkness, watching the Cobra make pass after pass, its minigun blazing at an enemy position miles away. When the Cobra wheeled around at the top of its arc, trimmed up into its gun run and nosed toward the target, the fireworks began. The gatling-gun weapon spewed 4,000 .30 caliber rounds per minute. That's 65 rounds every second. Every fifth round was a tracer. Like a crimson river of fire dancing, weaving, a ribbon of light lasered from that gun. Sparkles of fire zinged upward, ricochet rounds off rocks on the ground spitting into the black sky like Roman candles. I didn't think about the poor shits on the receiving end of that torrent of lead; I was mesmerized by the technology, the firepower of it all. It was a use of fire Prometheus could not have anticipated. And it was awe inspiring.

Later in my tour that capability would have a different effect on me. Once I'd flown several missions, been under fire numerous times and seen the persistence of the North Vietnamese, I sensed the futility of our efforts in Vietnam. With all the technological advantages, and the sheer weaponry at our disposal, the enemy was not repulsed. Wearing simple sandals from discarded tires and cardboard helmets, toting old AK-47s, riding bicycles instead of helicopters to get to the war the NVA continued their efforts undaunted. Week after week, month after month, they pedaled down the Ho Chi Minh trail resupplying themselves. No amount of firepower, no additional or more sophisticated weaponry deterred them.

We were young, foolish men with a case of testosterone poisoning, often bored to distraction. So we used fire in other ways as well. We used it to amuse ourselves.

I returned from my missions one afternoon to hear two colleagues arguing. Frank and Jim didn't get along anyway, so it wasn't unusual to hear them yelling at each other. But this argument seemed different somehow, almost important. Then the shooting started.

Jim hated snakes. It was common knowledge in the company that he was terrified a snake would somehow slither its way into his hooch. There were indeed cobras in the compound. We left them alone because they kept down the rat population.

Frank was a great judge of character. Whatever his sour relationship with Jim, the reason and the origin of their antipathy, no one knew. But we knew they hated each other. And we knew that someday, somehow, Frank would find a way to have the last word with Jim.

So when I heard shots coming from Jim's room my arms chilled. Surely, I thought, those two haven't actually taken to gunfire? We all had a .38 revolver to carry with us on missions. Those tiny guns would have been almost useless against the enemy. One of the guys, whether being serious or not, proposed using his pistol on himself if he was captured. He kept two rounds chambered. One for him, he said, one for anyone else who wanted it. I used my pistol as protection for the family jewels. It fit very well in my crotch, holster and all, a dandy piece of armor if I ever wanted sex and kids and all that peripheral stuff.

The bottom line is that Frank had a .38; Jim had a .38. Surely, I thought, as four shots clapped out in the dusky afternoon, surely Frank hasn't shot..?

I raced into Jim's hooch, where Frank stood over a dead snake. Adjacent to the carcass, four bullet holes had ruptured the floor around the unscathed serpent. Then Frank's ploy played out perfectly, as Jim burst into his room, saw the dead snake and lurched back in terror.

Frank waved his empty pistol. "I shot it for you, Jimbo! Killed a snake, right here in your goddam room!"

Jim stared at Frank. At the snake. Back at Frank. "You son of a..."

"Jeez, you ought'a thank me, Jimbo. You could'a been bit. A snake, man. There might be more of 'em!" Frank grinned like Satan slithering up the apple tree, and left.

It took Jim perhaps eight seconds to sort it out. He saw the .38-size holes in his floor. Saw the snake's limp, undamaged body and a black rage bloomed on his face. He snorted, left his room, went to Frank's. Frank was still enjoying his serpentine coup over his hated rival when Jim entered. Jimbo slipped his .38 from its holster, cocked the pistol and fired four rounds through Frank's floor. Bam-Bam-Bam-Bam!

Frank curled up in a corner. When the echo of gunfire died away, Jim did that 'whiff the smoke from the barrel' thing you see in western movies after the bad guy drops. Then Jim holstered his pistol, swiveled, and left. He and Frank were even again for a while.

Vietnam was a boring war. Especially during the rainy season, we'd often go days and weeks without turning a blade. To pass the time we filled the hours with anything we could think of. As might be imagined, some of those activities involved fire. We'd set three Sterno cans up in a makeshift barbecue grill. Then we'd take a pot stolen from the mess hall, and make 'Comanchero Stew.' The concoction had a very simple recipe: we took the contents of an entire case of C-rations, and dumped all twelve main courses together. Beans and weenies, chicken and rice, spaghetti and meatballs, beef stew, ham loaf, pork loaf, scrambled eggs, every meal went into the pot. Then we'd fire up the Sterno cans, and boil the mess together. Just because we'd survived Lady Hooker didn't mean we'd live through Comanchero Stew. But when the rain came in buckets, and flying was on hold, we'd be stuck in our hootches. A walk to the mess hall was out of the question, thus the birth of Comanchero Stew.

The mess hall itself was the scene of a fascinating proof of our attraction to fire. I'd been in the unit for two months when the building burned to the ground. Our cooks were under strict orders to not use jet fuel in their cookstoves. Jet fuel was too volatile, and inappropriate for those devices. But the supply system broke down, the cooks had no standard fuel for those stoves, and the troops were hungry for lunch. What to do? The stoves were filled with jet fuel, and voila,' fire and mayhem. And laughter.

I was in my hootch at eleven o'clock that June morning when I heard shouts in the compound, and running feet. Then I smelled smoke. I ran out of the little cabin I called home hoping it wasn't on fire. It wasn't. In the center of the compound, the mess hall was almost fully involved. Flames had already burst through crevices in the corrugated roof, the tin was charring black and curling up as I watched.

The episode was one of the funniest memories of my tour, for a lot of reasons. First because of the Camp Eagle fire department's response to it, second because of my own, and that of my colleagues.

I heard the whine of a siren. Soon a fire truck roared into the compound and stopped by the erupting mess hall. The Vietnamese were hired on base to do various chores for us. We had civilians in the compound to burn the contents of our outhouses, the so called shit-burners. Local people clerked in the PX, they did laundry for the brass, ran the Camp Eagle sewing store, post office and class six store where we bought booze.

And they manned the base fire trucks. Three Vietnamese firefighters leapt off their truck and began dragging hoses toward the mess hall fire. One of them swiveled a fitting onto the truck's pressure port. At a signal, he cranked open the pump, sending high pressure water surging through the hose like a gopher through a snake. Two of the tiny men reached the fire. As a bolus of water pushed toward the end of their hose they aimed toward the flames, and waited.

The pressurized water snaked through the hose, reached the outlet, then gushed like a Las Vegas fountain, slamming the two men backward to the ground.

The two miniature firefighters clabbered backward on their asses. Like they'd roped a bucking bronc they skittered around on the ground, refusing to let the writhing hose go, hugging each other and that evil, swaying hose for dear life. Water gushed everywhere. Across the compound like a geyser, back, forth, across the flight line, into the CO's hooch, everywhere but on the mess hall fire. The two tiny men wrestled that full-size hose for all they were worth. Like Laocoon and his sons, the hose whipped them around, knocked them over. The fellow at the pump was laughing as hard as we were. Finally he turned off the pressure. Soaked and battered, the two hose men lay exhausted, while the last timber of the mess hall crackled and fell in a gush of sparks.

We laughed. Lordy, we couldn't stop. I thought I'd wet myself. Men held their stomachs, tears streaming in laughter, slapping each other at the comic relief of seeing that building collapse, and at the firefighting circus sideshow along with it. We didn't consider the injuries, the potential fatalities there may have been. Didn't think of the days and weeks of Comanchero Stew we'd be forced to eat. We saw fire, and we laughed.

When we weren't playing with fire, or flying, which activities were often the same, we drank. And, like boys the world over, we had a dog. Unlike most boys, we got ours drunk, almost every night. Smokey was a Vietnamese version of the Heinz 57 dog, several varieties, none of them dominant. Smokey the alcoholic pup was part beagle, part terrier, shnauzer, pit-bull, on and on. He was a little black dog with white-ish feet, and ears that stuck straight up, except when he'd been imbibing. I'm not sure where Smokey came from. He likely wandered on base looking for scraps of food. Ever the cynical GIs in an Oriental setting, we joked that the pup came in fear of his life, to escape a Mamasan's wok. Regardless of where he came from, Smokey settled right into the company. We adopted him, and made him official pet of the Comancheros. And fit right in he did; Smokey loved his beer.

Of an evening, after the flying was done and the war closed down for the day, we'd retire to the 'O' club. Soon the sound of snapping beer tabs filled the dim room, and suds flowed like water. Georgia Peach, Tony Lowe seemed to be in charge of Smokey's entertainment, and vicariously of ours. Tony spilled PBR directly onto the bar, and the little pooch lapped it up. Little did I know at that age that dogs have the same affinity for booze as their best friends. Smokey drank, and lapped, and drank some more, with predictable results. It wasn't long before Smokey's ears sagged, and his beady little eyes crossed. Soon the little dog's already too short legs would no longer reach the top of the bar, and he had to stoop to find it. So, his canine manners somewhat better than ours, he took one last slurp, his furry little knees buckled, and Smokey went nighty night, sweet dreams little pooch. Cheap drunk. Hair of the dog, one might say.

We waited for the intoxicant to work its magic on 'ol Smokey. When it did, and his little peepers yawed out of trim and then shut down, we'd roar with laughter at the animal's almost too perfect imitation of the likes of us. Despite his drinking problem Smokey was a great little dog. Tony had ideas of taking him back to Georgia when he, Tony, left Vietnam. Alas, it was not to be. Rest his beer-soaked soul, Smokey succumbed, (from cirrhosis of the liver?) at the tender age of three, which is twenty-one in dog years. Oblivious men that we were, the chilling similarity never occurred to any of us that Smokey was, in fact, our age. We buried Smokey on the flight line where, with every takeoff, we tipped our helmets to a real, hard-drinking pal.

Any officer worth a nickel knows that enlisted men run the military. The EMs allow officers to think they're in charge. Knowing this, I sought to get on the good side of the company enlisted men as soon as possible. It was particularly important for Warrant Officer pilots, since we Warrants relied on our crews to keep us safe, and to tend to the maintenance of the aircraft. In late June I showed my enlisted crew where I put them in the pecking order. I pissed off a Captain in the process, but it was worth it. I didn't fly with Captains. When the incident happened I was still new to the war. But I knew one of the most important things, that I didn't know very much. So I sought the counsel of the veteran enlisted guys. There's no room for inflated egos in a war zone. Also, I didn't make a habit of pissing off maintenance people. Life as a helicopter pilot in Vietnam was short enough as it was, I didn't need to irritate the guys who fixed the things I broke. But the fellow in charge of our unit maintenance, a Captain who shall remain nameless to protect his blinding arrogance, took exception when I questioned his opinion. I didn't have a lot of experience with the mechanics of a Huey. It's the pilot's job to break the helicopter, not fix it.

I was halfway through an inspection of my Huey when I noticed something amiss, an odd bluish, blackish mark on the turbine's burner can. It wasn't a big blemish, just not something I'd seen before. I showed the mark to my new crewchief, a Spec 4 from El Paso. Gil grabbed his chin, frowned and marched to the maintenance hangar for an expert opinion.

Five minutes later Gil returned with our chief of maintenance, the aforementioned Captain. Captain Bluster—not his real name— took one look at the blemish on my engine. He scowled, sneered and acted offended. "You called me all the way up here for that?"

"Yes, sir." I allowed that I had. I wasn't going to argue, but I did believe something was wrong with that engine, and my enlisted crew sensed my unease. Go with my gut? Or believe the haughty Captain and go fly? I chose to go with my gut. This involved going over the maintenance fellow's head. Captain B might fall off his bar stool; Gil and I on the other hand...

I asked the Captain if he was sure of his diagnosis? His response was not something he'd say in front of Aunt Alice, and he stomped away. I walked to the commander's office, where the Major and I shared thoughts. The day I'd reported into his company, right after he ordered me to shave my mustache, Major Snider listed his priorities: he said that his door was always open to his pilots; that it may be a war zone, but safety comes first; and to take care of his enlisted men. Expanding on that topic, Snider had been quite clear: "Edgington...if you hurt one of my EMs you'll be extracting my boot from your ass," he'd said, and then added... "...then I'll get mad." I sensed that the EM were important to *him* as well, thus my desire to define my maintenance dilemma straightaway. The Major and I were on the same page.

Snider phoned Captain B's big boss. Soon the ranking Captain was eyeballing *my* engine, while Captain Bluster gave *me* the stink eye.

Snider asked the big Kahuna about the mark on the engine. "Will it fly tomorrow or not?"

"Yeah, it'll fly," the fellow said.

Vindicated, Captain Bluster smiled like a boy with a new cordless drill.

Then the big guy continued. "...about five minutes," he said. "...then the turbine will blow up, and things will get real quiet."

It was my turn to smile. I felt like a million bucks, tax free. The mark was fixed, the engine fired up, tested, checked out and the helicopter flew again—three days later. Tales of a pilot's competence, or lack thereof, swept through the crew ranks like shit through large migratory birds. I had a lot of respect for the guys behind me in the cabin, my crewchief and gunner. They had no access to the controls. They were along for the ride, smooth or bumpy, either way. I imagined being in the well of the Huey, as they were, with no control over my destiny. It was the same way I'd felt about the right seat the day Bill tried to get us both a posthumous medal. So I always flew with the crew's safety uppermost. It paid dividends during my tour in Vietnam; men never hesitated to fly with me. I retained that attitude toward safe flying long after the war as well.

The down side of the incident was that Captain Bluster didn't speak to me for a very long time. I was worried sick about that.

12

In war, men die—or not...

War is filled with opportunities to get yourself killed. Sometimes these opportunities arise in seconds, unanticipated, their outcomes something not even Hollywood could manufacture. I suppose if I'd died on this mission I never would have felt a thing. It would have been a classic case of one second alive, chuffing one breath out, another in, then zap... I suppose that's the way it always is. It seemed like a routine mission, an easy LZ in a place as serene and green as the bucolic fields of my Ohio childhood. I suppose if I'd been killed that day it would have been as good a place as any to fulfill life's ultimate function.

The mission was to insert a special operations team onto an LZ in Laos ten kilometers west of Khe Sanh. I was flying lead ship that day. The escort plane marked the LZ for me, and three other Hueys to follow, and then the Air Force 'covey bird' zipped away. The marked spot was a half-acre field covered in elephant grass six feet deep. Gil was behind me in the well of the aircraft, John of whistle fame was once again on the right side. I briefed them for landing, slid my visor down and entered final approach. Down I went, the LZ a hundred yards ahead. Soon I was over it, and ready to land.

As I hovered above the deep grass the Huey's rotorwash blasted it flat. And there he was. Forty feet away, a lone North

Vietnamese soldier, gray-green fatigues, jungle hat, as surprised to see me as I him. His AK swiveled up, aimed directly at me. The next three seconds were a blur to me then, and they are now. I turned my head slightly left at the anomalous item in my peripheral view and wondered what it was? It was the enemy soldier, of course. Then a shriek of M-16 fire exploded directly behind me, and I jerked so hard I locked my inertia reel. Hot rounds snapped out, a burst of six, or perhaps twenty, I cannot say. The enemy soldier crumpled like a burst balloon, his lifeless body a heap of gray-green camo. His hat flew off. His weapon clattered away. The man was dead. One instant a breath chuffing in, then out, and then...

But I wasn't dead. Somehow I'd escaped. Not my time? Coincidence? I don't know. Yet another dodged bullet, this one literal. The GI who fired had anticipated the scene. Because of his training, or instinct, or a sixth sense he knew that NVA soldier would be there, and before the enemy could pull the trigger he caught a hail of hot ammo. The guy who saved my life leapt off the aircraft and never looked back. I had no chance to say thanks, or how did you, or holy crap.

I lifted the collective, took off, and ceded the controls to my rookie right seater. My knees shook like a dog passing busted glass. I remember this part so well that years later I'm still ashamed of myself: I had to fight an urge to laugh. Terror and hilarity. It wasn't the only time in Vietnam that I saw the ugly truth of what the hell we were doing there, the unvarnished part of war that Hollywood won't touch. Friendly and enemy alike we were just a bunch of kids playing with fire, trying to kill each other while joking around to get through it. Or trying to stay alive. Or wondering who decides? That day I was twenty-one years old. The other fellow was as old as he was going to get.

My year in Vietnam was marked by a dozen such incidents, times that other men anticipated danger and dispatched it for all the others. Soldiers look out for each other. Call it bravado, or the invulnerability of youth, or a collective survival instinct, we did it without a second thought, even with the possibility of getting dusted ourselves. It wasn't long before I had a chance to return the favor. August 12th 1970. I was number three in a four-ship lift to rescue a squad of men from the top of the so-called Rockpile near the Demilitarized Zone (DMZ). The landing zone was the only clear spot atop the ridge, a flat spot the size of a backyard patio. Men were pinned down on the LZ, their backs to the ridge with nowhere to go. The mission had popped up suddenly when those troops found themselves surrounded, and called us to get them the hell out of there. We launched without gun cover, something we hated doing, but did anyway, since the nearest gunships were thirty minutes away.

Our four Hueys took off from Quang Tri, and headed west. The Rockpile was a mountain that looked like a giant dump truck dropped it there in one load. It sat at the southern boundary of the DMZ. As we circled overhead we saw that the embattled team was hanging by their toenails. Their radio calls became increasingly frantic. The enemy troops saw the precarious position of those men, and they knew the helicopters would soon arrive.

And so we had. Flight lead and number two both took fire going in and coming out of the LZ. There was only one way in and one way out, no room to get fancy or deviate. The North Vietnamese were plenty smart. They sensed consistencies in our flight patterns, and they reacted to them right away. I briefed my crew, circled just out of range waiting for number two ship to take off, and headed in.

Chalk two was on the LZ about six seconds. Then he lifted, and zipped off to the south. It was my turn. I raced toward the LZ, zig-zagging on the way in. I'd flare hard, then plant the skids on the ridgetop. In seconds, I hoped, the troops would scramble aboard, then I'd blast off.

I raced at 100 knots toward the ridge. At the last second I lowered the pitch, and flared. The Huey shuddered, rotor rpm building. I'd soon need the extra rpm so I let it climb. As I arrived over the LZ I jerked the collective up, and stopped my forward momentum. Coming out, I yanked the collective again, inched forward, and fell off the ridge. Banking hard right, I kept power high as the helicopter gathered speed in the sticky air.

Number four ship landed, and the last five GIs scrabbled into his Huey. I looked behind at four weary men I'd rescued. Nothing but teeth. For that rescue, all of us were awarded the Distinguished Flying Cross. I still have the medal in a box somewhere. When the commander gave it to me I wondered why? Would I have left those men atop that ridge? No, I would not. None of us would have hesitated to do what we did. That attitude was the biggest, possibly the only morale booster we had in Vietnam. Regardless of the danger, we knew we weren't alone.

The closest I came to getting waxed in Vietnam wasn't out in the boonies, landing in a hot LZ, or flying missions into Laos. My closest brush with mortality happened in one of the safest places in Vietnam, the traffic pattern at Camp Eagle.

I'd finished the day's missions and was heading home. I called Eagle control tower for clearance, entered the traffic pattern and angled toward our company compound. It was dusk, and in early July, the dry season was marked by a continual haze. The setting sun illuminated the haze, rendering a soft pastel to the scene. It also blinded any pilot approaching from the east, because they'd be flying into the opaque sunlight. Which is likely what happened with the aircraft that almost hit mine.

I cruised along on a base leg at five hundred feet feeling fat, dumb and happy when Gil screamed. "Traffic two o'clock! A &%$#@ Loach!"

My arms chilled, my drowsy eyeballs went to high alert, and my head shot to the right. A scout helicopter loomed in my blind spot in the windscreen. It was converging—quickly. I could tell by the other pilot's straight-line flight, his casual progress directly at me that he didn't see my Huey. This story takes a lot longer to scribble than it took to happen, but here's the gist of it. Out of instinct I jerked the controls, sending the ship hard up and right. The Huey shuddered in wild response, rpm sagging under the strain. My right seater yelped, since he'd not seen the midair developing either. I'd like to report that my heart raced, sweat dripped, focus narrowed, all that autonomic stuff bodies do to get themselves into the next six seconds still alive, but there wasn't time for that. It was a hand on hot stove response. I sensed the danger, my head, or my hands, or some part of my gristle or grit reacted, lucky for the rest of me.

The helicopters missed each other by thirty feet, about the length of a rotor blade. Mouth dry as dust, heart hammering, I leveled off and reentered the traffic pattern. I shared thoughts with the tower operator, who sent his apologies. I don't think the other pilot ever realized how close he'd come to a posthumous purple heart. At some point I got mad. Mad because I realized how stupid it would be to get killed that way. I projected ahead to all the hero talk back home, all the 'he died for his country' baloney when I'd screwed up, killed a bunch of guys, and gave two serviceable helicopters back to the taxpayers. All in all it would have been a lousy career move. Like a lot of my experiences in Vietnam the near midair taught me something: I could never pay too much attention.

I praised Gil for his good eyesight, and promised I'd be more alert. Except for the need to change underwear, my landing and postflight were near normal. I had a number of beers that night. One in each hand.

~*~

Another incident happened exactly when the old man said it would. The grey-head Korea vet, one of my early instructors, told me that a pilot is safest when he has enough hours to solo because he's scared shitless, and most dangerous with around 500 logged hours, because by then he thinks he's God's gift to aviation. Counting flight school and Vietnam, by mid July 1970 I'd inked 500 hours in my logbook. I didn't consider myself anyone's chosen aviator, much less a deity's. But as I swaggered into the club after the war shut down for the day I felt pretty darned slick about myself and my ability to commit aviation. Slick doesn't mean competent. You can look it up. My cocky attitude came with a lesson I never forgot. And it scared me enough that I was grateful for it afterward.

The LZ was close to base, about ten minutes flying time. There's a reason I mention that. I was number six in line to land. Weather was stifling, and helicopters don't like stifling. Engine and blade performance suffer when the weather is stifling. Helicopters like a bit of headwind on landing, especially if they're heavy, which our Hueys almost always were. A headwind creates extra lift, and lift is a very good thing. Helicopters don't like landing with tailwinds, for a number of reasons. Like any other aircraft, helicopters weren't designed to fly backward, and that's essentially what tailwinds feel like.

So there I was, on a stifling day, heavy helicopter, descending onto an LZ. A fickle wind swirled around the top of the landing zone, a scarred hilltop in the middle of a valley, like a berry in a bowl. None of us knew what direction the wind would be blowing when it was our turn to land. Flight lead said wind was from the West; chalk two said East; chalk three and four West again. Five said North for Pete's sake. When I lowered the collective and started down, the wind was all over the map. The LZ was close to home plate, so I hadn't burned off much fuel. The Huey weighed close to 9,000 pounds. As I approached the LZ, with a full bag of gas and a thousand pounds of truly healthy Americans and all their gear on the floor behind me, the wind shifted onto my tail. I knew this because, when I glanced at the airspeed indicator, though I was still moving forward smartly, the needle was pasted on zero. This was not good.

Fifty feet off the ground, with five tons of helicopter strapped to my back I was directly downwind, and descending a lot faster than I wanted or needed to be.

I brought the collective up to arrest my descent. It was too little, and a bit too late. I should have abandoned the approach. But I'd logged the magic 500 hours; I was an aviation phenom, I reasoned. Indestructible. Well, indestructible or not, I slammed onto the LZ like a bag of Buick lug nuts. Sticks and dust flew everywhere, and the ship did a crazy rocking motion. I'd rate the landing about a nine—on the richter scale.

It got worse. When the grunts dove off—and who can blame them?—their departure changed the aircraft's weight equation. The Huey rocked backward like it might flip end-over- end. With my heart in my throat I jammed the cyclic forward to stop it. That settled the machine a bit, and I regained a modicum of control. Lifting the collective, heart muscle flexing for all it was worth, I stabilized things and took off. Why I didn't ball up one perfectly good UH-1 that day is a mystery even now. The upshot was a clear warning, and I took it as such.

The flying god wagged a gnarled finger, and I felt his chilly breath. "You're not such a hot-shot after all," he said. "Pay attention, rookie." And I did. That near accident was the best thing that ever happened to me in aviation. I'd avoided yet another bullet. My reputation grew from there. But it wasn't time to relax just yet.

Whatever my febrile brain cooked up for potential mishaps, the insanity of war would always do me one better.

I landed in the pickup zone, and six south Vietnamese troops hustled onto my Huey. As always, the ARVN packed along their chickens and ducks, either for food or pets I never knew. And rice! After an ARVN (Army of the Republic of Vietnam) mission we always swept enough rice out of the Huey to hold a wedding.

The ARVN were tiny. Set on a scale, the combined weight of six South Viet troops was perhaps 500 pounds, give or take a sack of rice. They looked like GIs that were put in the dryer. The standard troop load for a Huey was common knowledge: Five U.S. type GIs, and as many ARVNs as we could cram on board. The ARVN piled on, chattering their squeaky chirps back and forth at each other, ducks flapping, chickens cackling, the aroma of fresh vegetables, squash and beets and corn. And the tangy scent of Nu'ớc mắm, otherwise known as rotten fish soup. I could never decide whether Nu'ớc mắm tasted worse than it smelled or otherwise. Vietnamese soldiers never left home without it. When I flew ARVNs into battle I felt more like a farmer headed to market than a pilot off to war.

But the ARVN were a wiry bunch, energetic and vocal. They sounded like chipmunks on speed. What the ARVN lacked in fighting spirit, they made up for in entertainment value.

The South Viets treated their military equipment in fairly cavalier fashion, for instance the M-79 grenade launcher. The M-79 was a launching tube for a 40-millimeter grenade. The weapon came in handy against everything from North Vietnamese troops to enemy elephants. The weapon had a trigger guard designed to prevent the inadvertent launch of a grenade. Some troopers filed the guard off because it got in the way, and slowed them down when enemy elephants hove into view. A missing trigger guard almost slowed me down to zero.

On the floor of my Huey sat the six ARVN troops chattering away. Duck feathers floated across the cockpit. Rice sifted around the flight controls. On the floor behind me, one of the ARVNs carried an M-79 with its trigger guard removed. I took off, fell into line behind my leader, descended onto the LZ and touched down. The aircraft shifted as the ARVN troops scurried off, chittering away, ducks and chickens quacking and cackling, rice spilling onto the ground. I waited for the requisite call from my crew clearing me to take off. But, instead of the usual call, Gil opened the intercom and cleared his throat. Gil wasn't easily shaken. This time his voice quivered. "Sir,...you're uh, clear up left."

I wasn't used to hearing hesitation from Gil; something was amiss. But there was another Huey on my tail about to land, so I took off. I soon learned what caused Gil's trepidation, because the dilemma was now mine as well. As I climbed higher, the intercom crackled again. Gil spoke with the same hesitation. "Sir," he said. "...a guy shot off his M-79 back here and the round hit me in the foot."

Tunnel vision is a real thing. It comes on in a trice, ofttimes regardless of our efforts to allay it. My ears processed what Gil said; my brain took a bit longer. As I climbed through three hundred feet I managed a confident, professional response: "He what!"

"When he jumped off, his '79 caught on something and it fired," Gil said. Then he continued. "The round hit me in the foot...and it's rolling around back here."

"Holy crap!" I yelled, then I added to the already surreal atmosphere when I said, "Don't touch it Gil," as if I had to mention that. My right seater scoured the back of the aircraft. Then he unlatched his seat belt. His plan was to be the Hollywood hero throwing himself on the live round. I stopped him. "We may as well *all* dive on it," I said. I knew if the grenade went off we'd hit the ground at the same time anyway, unless Galileo had it wrong.

With my wits assembling in some kind of orderly fashion I remembered an important feature of the M-79 round: to prevent premature detonation leaving the barrel, the projectile had to rotate fourteen revolutions to arm itself. That may have been the only piece of data I remembered from ordnance class, but I knew that to be true. For one silly second I considered asking Gil how many times it had rolled? Then I thought better of it, and slowed the aircraft.

Excellent crewchief that he was, and by that point able to read my mind, which can't have been easy just then, Gil was already in the cabin. He took a healthy drop-kick-me-Jesus boot slice at the errant M-79 round, punting the sucker into the jungle where it exploded with a harmless whump.

Gil had a bruised foot for a few days. I thought about putting him in for a purple heel award, but he wouldn't discuss it. It took my nerves a while to settle down. The incident gave me something I never expected to acquire in Vietnam, and it bothered me. I began wondering if there was anything I could do to make it out of there alive? Or was my fate in the hands of some capricious entity that I had no way to control, or even gauge? I'd been in country six months. I'd worked hard to acquire my own aircraft. I'd not taken any chances that might jeopardize my crew or myself. All that caution could have been blown to bits that afternoon, because some trigger-happy chipmunk with a pet duck customized his weapon. My conclusion was that there was little I could do, short of what I was already doing, to stay alive in Vietnam. I believe that was the day I started smoking.

There were times in Vietnam when I flew on pure instinct, fell back on what I was taught in flight school, practical considerations and aircraft limitations be damned. One afternoon, across the border from the A-Shau Valley, all my training and experience came together when a colleague ran out of ideas, altitude and luck all at once.

Frank was a good pilot, he just happened to be one of the company targets, a 'magnet ass.' Frank was always in the bad guys' crosshairs. From day number one of his tour he seemed to have some bad Ju-Ju. When he led a flight of four into Laos and was shot down, I was selected to get him out of his latest jam, and to pluck his crew out of harm's way as well.

September 14th 1970. Frank was flight lead on a four shipper. I was chalk two. The mission was to extract a special ops team from an LZ in the hills of Eastern Laos. The team had been compromised, and the North Vietnamese were headed in their direction. Frank found the LZ and descended to land. When he got closer he realized there wasn't room, or enough flat surface, to put his Huey down. So he hovered above the LZ. Then his crew dropped their on-board roll-up ladder so the ground troops could climb it. The ladder unfurled from Frank's ship like an overgrown Slinky, and troops clambered up one by one.

The evacuation took more time than anticipated. Then, due to the heat, wind direction and the unequal distribution of weight on one side of his aircraft, Frank began having control problems. As second ship I'd begun my approach to the LZ. On short final I realized that Frank wouldn't take off in time for my arrival, so I made a left three-sixty. When I turned back around and lined up with the LZ Frank's Huey had disappeared. When I saw where it had gone a chill ran down my back. Frank had either been shot down, or crashed—on the LZ.

I raced over and stopped, hovering directly above Frank's dying helicopter. Below me, in a twisted heap of Bell parts, Frank's ship lay on its side. The engine was still screaming, the rotor blades bent like twist-ties on a bread bag. The stench of spilled jet fuel filled my nostrils. Why there was no fire I'll never know. Gruesome as the scene was, it gave me a kind of cold comfort that the trusty Lycoming turbine was still turning after all that mayhem.

I told my crew to deploy our ladder, and it rattled out the side of my Huey. The fuselage jerked and bounced. A frightened soldier scrambled into my ship. Then another one, panting, his eyes like half dollars. More men charged up the ladder. After five of them had clambered on, I checked the gauges and saw exactly what I'd feared: engine power was tickling the limit.

Red line torque in the 'H' model Huey was fifty pounds. Beyond that limit decreasing rotor rpm was a near certainty. One more man collapsed on the floor behind me, and the torque gauge bumped up to 48. The mission was only thirty minutes old, so my fuel load was still at 900 pounds. One more man topped the ladder and bingo, the torque gauge pegged at 50. But despite all the weight, with the gauge at the red line, rotor rpm held steady. I said a quick thank you to Mister Lycoming and watched another man climb aboard.

At 52 pounds of torque my rotor rpm sagged from 324, to 320, down to 318. If it reached 310 rpm or thereabouts I was done flying for that day. Besides, the torque *was* above its book-value limit. Gauge limits are to be observed only if there's a reasonable chance that someone else might fly the machine again. If the aircraft will likely never fly again there *are* no limits. I was pretty sure the commander wanted to use my Huey again, possibly the next day, unless the war ended that night, which seemed unlikely. I had to do something right away.

The next guy coming up was a fellow named Mike who was Frank's right seater. I told my crew to have Mike hook his 'D' ring onto the ladder, and I began my takeoff. Slowly, laboriously, with all the weight on board—likely ten-thousand pounds, five hundred over the limit—the Huey inched forward. I nursed it along, using minimal control inputs to keep whatever lift I still had. Out of the blue Wayne yelled at me, his warning a year old, and brand new: "Don't wipe out the cockpit, Edgington, you'll spill all your lift!" I held the cyclic steady, wishing the Huey forward.

The helicopter dipped below the trees, the blades clipping the top branches like a giant weed-eater. I gained a few knots. I scanned for whatever low ground I could see, to drop into it, and maybe gain some forward speed. All I saw ahead was more vegetation.

I eased the helicopter ahead, almost hovering. Then the aircraft reached that balance point pilots try to avoid, the nexus between hovering and flying. It's a kind of netherworld, a spot on the performance charts called the dead man's curve. Not enough power to hover, not enough to fly either. If the engine quit right then I was along for the ride.

There was a physical, aerodynamic block at that point as well. Hovering along, I was flying in my own dirty air, the turbulent wind produced by my rotor system. I had to move into clean air somehow, move the machine forward into what's called translational lift. But that required more power, which I didn't have. I inched along in my own fouled air, power declining, trees approaching, options fading.

My pits were soaked with sweat. Hands, too. My heart slammed so hard I was sure the other guys heard it. The collective was up near my armpit, cyclic forward of neutral. The left pedal was jammed almost full forward to keep the Huey headed straight. Like watching someone else fly, and not doing it very well, I took all this in. A feeling of helplessness crept into my head, but I fought it back. What to do? There's got to be something. Am I a pilot or a passenger? The collective is way up, cyclic shoved forward. The left pedal is jammed all the way...

There comes a time in a pilot's career when he becomes an aviator. Or he stays just a pilot. I'd heard of the semantic difference before, but I always dismissed it as hangar talk, and scoffed at its puffed up purveyors. I figured such talk was meant to embellish the speaker's war story. But as I hovered forward that day, almost out of options, men's lives in the balance, I became an aviator. I didn't panic; I didn't give up; I didn't freeze on the controls and wait for the aviation god to perform some kind of miracle for me over the Laotian jungle. I considered the problem, the only option I had left, and I took it.

The tail rotor of a helicopter keeps the machine flying straight ahead, while compensating for the tremendous torque produced by the main rotor. Tiny as it is, the tail rotor uses a lot of horsepower, almost fifteen percent of available power in some cases. I did the calculations, realized that flying straight wasn't all that important right then, and let go of the left pedal. The Huey responded right away, yawing to the right like a drunken sailor against a lamp post. It slewed sideways, its tail trying to catch up with its nose like a playful pup. Like a semi skidding on ice, the Huey angled left side first, giving troops on that side a view of the trees coming at them.

But something else happened as well: I gained rotor rpm, and torque fell below fifty pounds. Moving forward faster, I felt a reassuring burble and bump as the Huey moved through translational lift into clean air. I was flying again. In a few seconds the helicopter gained thirty knots and a hundred feet of altitude.

During this adventure I was taking fire. Down the ridge to my left, 100 yards off, I heard the popcorn snap of AKs. The same hooligans who'd shot Frank down were trying to bag me. The comforting rumble of a Cobra gunship zipped past on my left.

I gained airspeed, even climbed a little. I heard an odd shout above the engine and rotor noise but I ignored it. I had some serious flying to do; it was no time for distractions. Leveling at five hundred feet, sixty knots, I headed east, and crossed the AShau Valley. Back in Vietnam I found an abandoned firebase where I landed long enough to get Frank's copilot off his ladder, and into the cabin. When Mike climbed in among the tangle of bodies I learned what the shouting had been on takeoff. When I lifted from the LZ I'd dragged him through the trees. His flight suit and chicken plate were peppered with leaves and branches. He looked like he'd been, well, dragged through trees and branches. Then *I* almost screamed when Mike told me he didn't need to unhook from the ladder. He hadn't hooked on in the first place! I'd not only dragged the man through the trees, I'd flown him several miles at five hundred feet, cold, exhausted, while clinging to the ladder *bare handed.*

Rules are a good place to hide if you don't have a better idea and the talent to execute it. That day I broke rules, exceeded limits, and threw caution out the window. But I got those men out of there.

The two ships behind me extracted all but one of those troops. One man, a Chinese mercenary, fell from Frank's ship as it crashed, and was pinned beneath the airframe. He was killed instantly. A gunship destroyed the remains of Frank's Huey so documents and armament wouldn't fall into enemy hands. Except for a burn mark on a hillside, long since grown over, it's as if the mission never happened.

The friendly fire incident is a reality of war. Take a passel of scared, twitchy young men, add a dash of self-preservation, a measure of loaded weapons, and a dose of official sanction to go forth and kill something, and the table is set for a tragic misidentification accident.

Vietnam had its share of those sad events. One of them almost had my name scribbled in the after action report. It happened close to home base, and in a reasonably secure location, which likely factored into the episode. My guard was down. But all the ingredients were in place: the frightened young soldier, the instinct to preserve his own life, a loaded weapon and the sanction floating in his nervous brain to shoot first and question later.

It was late October 1970. I took off that morning with Gil, a new-in-country Peter Pilot I'd not flown with and a rookie door gunner, a fellow I'd just met that morning. I'll call the new gunner Ken to protect his 'exotic' behavior. The mission was a simple resupply of a nearby firebase named Brick. Firebase Brick was within spitting distance of Camp Eagle. As the morning wore on, I flew in several loads of beans and bullets, mail, and assorted other items of ash and trash to the GIs on the firebase. Approaching Brick from the north for the first time, I saw a squad of American troops below. They were building a bridge across a stream a quarter mile from the firebase. On every subsequent approach to the base I flew directly over those men. It became a routine: my Huey rattled overhead a couple hundred feet above them; the bridge-builders waved; my crew waved back, and then I'd land at the firebase. The routine went on all morning, for perhaps six or eight landings.

On my last resupply drop before refuel I cruised toward the firebase, angled lower, and set up my approach to Brick's dusty helipad. I called the pathfinder on Brick to advise him by radio that we were inbound again, to see if his cannon cockers had any outgoing rounds. The tubes were cold, so I continued my approach. As I passed over the bridge builders below, for about the tenth time, I took no note of them. I was watching the fuel gauge, doing the mental math on how many loads of resupply there were before I had to dee-dee to the POL point. The radio was silent. Weather was benign. Wind was calm. Then fireworks.

As I passed over the bridge builders once again, my new door gunner's .30 cal erupted, spraying deadly rounds downward into the jungle. Bullets snapped and crackled outward, bracking like a buzz saw. The hair on my arms prickled. My heart went ballistic. Out of instinct, I wrenched the controls hard left, and jerked in power. The Huey arced over like a scalded cat. The next few seconds were a blur.

Gil screamed at the gunner. "What the fuck're you doing?"

"They're building a bridge down there!" Ken screamed, as his gun fell silent.

Gil scrambled across the cabin. He shoved Ken away from the gun, and jerked the belt out of the weapon's magazine.

"Those are friendlies!" Gil yelled.

My radio squealed, the frantic voice of the pathfinder. "Bad guys out there?"

"No bad guys," I said. My heart slammed, hoping no one was hurt. "Any casualties?"

The pause lasted maybe five seconds, the longest five seconds of my life, while the pathfinder checked with the bridge builders.

To my everlasting relief he said, "Everybody's okay...pretty shook up, though."

I apologized for the incident, and made sure Gil had the new man's weapon secured. Then I raced back to Camp Eagle with 'Ken,' and personally escorted him away from my Huey. He never flew again. I could only conclude that he'd been spooked, or had pot for breakfast, something.

For days afterward I dissected the event, wondering what I could have done to avoid it. I shuddered, thinking of what might have happened. Dead men, grieving families, official inquiries, and the ongoing component of military operations for all time—bereavement calls, chaplains at front doors, flag-draped coffins. Because some young, scared, rookie kid with a lethal weapon, a bolus of testosterone, and orders to kill something saw the 'enemy' "building a bridge."

13

Halfway

October marked the halfway point in my Vietnam tour. It also brought a change in weather, as the dry season ended and monsoon rains moved in. My schedule changed from flying every day, with a day off perhaps once every two weeks, to being grounded by weather at least once a week. By mid-November the rains came in earnest, grounding the fleet for days at a time. In some ways I looked forward to the break. It offered a chance to catch up on reading, and writing home, and it lowered my exposure to the vicissitudes of war. But as the wet season slogged on, my days became filled with tedium, the nights more so.

After Vietnam people asked what it was like. My answer often surprised them. The war in Vietnam was boring. It sounds strange to say now, but it was true. They say that aviation is hours of boredom interrupted by moments of terror. That was certainly true in Vietnam.

War movies assault us with a surplus of action till we're nearly exhausted. But Vietnam was a boring war. Especially during the wet season, when we were grounded for days, and time dragged on like a bad date. At such times the tedium was depressing. I'd read the same book four or five times, write home or to my girlfriend, listen to AFVN, with the same music selections on my battery-powered radio. I'd scour the same Playboy magazine over and over.

In my overheated twenty-year-old brain I'd bed the same centerfold again and again. It's possible that I'm married to Miss October 1970. We may have children. Likely we do.

There's no equivalent in the U.S. to monsoon rains. It's a cliché to use the term biblical, but it applies. Pouring, drenching cascades of water started Monday morning and continued till...Monday morning. The countryside became a lake. Rivers flowed in the compound. Every surface in the hooch was wet. Mildew triumphed.

Some men played cards when it rained. Some slept for days, or helped out in the hangar. Some drank themselves into a wet stupor. We'd gather at the 'O' club at three in the afternoon to start the night's drunken revelry. The club was our shrine, our watering hole, our comfort zone. When the rains came we spent whole days there.

The club was the center of our time on the ground, but it was more than that: it was our meeting place, refuge, drinking hole, and mustering point when something bad happened. When I heard about Kearsley's death I gravitated to the club; when Captain Ayers died on Co Roc I joined my colleagues there to mourn his passing. So it was beyond surreal to share a beer with George Berg the night before he crashed and burned, just as he predicted he would, then to gather at the club the following night to recognize his passing.

George arrived in country a month after I did, and he got his AC orders in sequence with me. He was a good pilot, conscientious and well liked. Enlisted crews didn't hesitate to fly with him. Had they sat around the bar with him at night, however, they may have had reservations. George was convinced he'd die in Vietnam. There was no talking him out of it; he knew he'd not go home alive. And he was right.

February 18th 1971. I was assigned to the CCN mission, (Command

and Control North) crossing the fence into Laos where we had no official presence. The mission launched from Quang Tri. I was flight lead that day at the head of a four-ship formation. Around ten a.m. my team of Hueys put troops on the ground ten kilometers west and south of Khe Sanh. Then we flew back to Quang Tri to wait, to make sure the ground unit was secure before returning to Camp Eagle. There were no calls to evacuate the ground team, so at 1700 I took off south, reaching Eagle at 1730. With all four Hueys refueled I led the flight back to our hidey-hole on the north end of the base. By then it was 1830.

Flying in Vietnam heightened my senses, my perceptions. I didn't become clairvoyant, but approaching the end of my tour I sensed the mood of the company pretty well, just by the body language of colleagues, their energy level, the way they greeted each other in the compound. When I landed at home base that evening I knew something had happened. Men passed each other without looking up. The mess hall was empty. There was none of the usual post-mission chatter. As I entered the operations hut I learned what it was. George and his crew had been killed. They'd been flying near the A Shau Valley, pulling a squad of men out of deep jungle using ropes. When George took off the ropes somehow tangled in his rotor system, and his Huey plunged into the trees. He died in the crash, with the rest of his crew and three men on the ropes. George's prophecy had come true. When I walked into the club that night his favorite seat at the bar was empty. I bought a beer, sucked down half of it and left. Then I sat in my hooch in the candlelight, and turned in early.

Every war story has an addendum, and George's accident is no exception. His right seater that fateful day was a fellow named Gerald Woods. Woodie had been in country for several months, but he'd not made aircraft commander, and hadn't pushed for it. Despite being a decent pilot, and capable of commanding his own ship, Woods declined the responsibility, electing to remain a Peter

Pilot. His death reinforced for me the importance of my own early decision to scramble for AC orders as soon as I could qualify.

We were not a subtle bunch. But we didn't wear our hearts on our sleeves, either. When a mission went bad, or the general trend of the war soured, which happened often, we retreated to the bar and drank. Simple. Straightforward. It's what men do. When the going gets tough, the tough crack a beer. Because of George and Woodie's death or not I can't say, but that night or the next we played with fire in a rather less humane way.

There were rats in the compound. Big rats. The rodents left us alone, and we left them alone as well, mostly. But they did get out of hand on occasion. More than once I awoke to a rat skittering across my blanket in the night. Startled, I'd swat in the dark, and sometimes make contact with the furry thing. The animal would hit the floor of my hooch with a squeak, and then scamper away. I'd lie awake wondering if it had relatives.

Shortly after George and Woody died, one of my colleagues saw a rat near his hooch, and he cornered it. Then he took a can of lighter fluid, sprayed the rat with it till it was soaked, and flipped his cigarette, a direct hit. The poor animal poofed up in yellow flame. Squealing in pain, it raced from its corner, scrambled in circles for several seconds, flame licking, smoke curling like a circus hoop. Shameful to admit, as I said, we watched the poor thing in its agony and, as with the mess hall fire, we laughed like idiots. The rat bumbled along, a shish kebab with legs, fire licking its fur, smoke trailing behind. We roared like a coven of sadists, with tears in our eyes from the rat's hopeless situation.

Then our mirth turned to concern when the immolating rat spied an escape. The flaming animal scampered toward the only dark spot it saw. Straight as an arrow, it raced directly under my hooch! Flames spitting off its back, the rat seemed to be sabotaging whatever it could before dying. Like a suicide bomber it nestled under the bone-dry floorboards. Smoke wafted out. I looked under, but couldn't see the animal. It must have been dead, the fire extinguished, or, like the mess hall, the building would have gone up in flames. I would have gotten another chance to see Camp Eagle's Pygmy Pyro specialists in action, but I would've lost all my stuff, too. Nothing funny about that. Afterward, I slept under the covers, and left the rats alone.

My exposure to the way the world works started pretty early. As second of ten kids I grew up crowded. I was forced to learn how to get along, to grab for groceries when available and to take nothing, like an evening meal, for granted. When my ambition to become a priest was jerked away I learned another lesson—that dreams can die. When I lost my deferment in college, and was drafted, that lesson told me there are classes outside college, too, social classes. And in this culture the higher social classes will have their way, come hell or high altitude. It's not a rant; it's reality. I grew up a (reasonably) poor lower-middle-class kid on the wrong side of the tracks. I knew that growing up, when schoolmates with new bikes every year, and after-school activities like tennis and horseback riding wondered why my sibs and I didn't partake? So it wasn't a shock to see class differences manifested in Vietnam. Indeed, it was something of a shock to see men from society's upper echelons, the tennis and equestrian set over there at all. The elites of society were back in the college classrooms I'd been ushered out of.

I flew with a fellow one day who represented that upper class. These days he might safely be called a member of the 1%. Nice enough guy, just way out of his element. I flew with him on a resupply mission near Khe Sanh in November. We took off at first light, Gil and me, the Captain in my right seat, and John at the door gun. The Captain was from 101st Airborne Group headquarters. He'd given up his desk for the day to fly with me, I suppose, so he could tell folks back home in Westchester or Bloomfield Hills that he'd flown in combat. It was obvious by his apprehension, his disinterest in learning the particulars, and his starchy-new flight suit that he'd been posted to Vietnam to fly a desk. In the GI lingo of the time the good Captain was a REMF, a Rear Echelon Mother Fucker.

At eight a.m. my crew and I arrived over Khe Sanh. We found the first of several LZs where troops needed resupply, dropped stuff off, and climbed back into the sky. We flew into Quang Tri, loaded beans and bullets, flew the stuff out to the troops near Khe Sanh. Then back to QT we went for more war materiel, courtesy of American taxpayers in Toledo and Tulsa and Terre Haute. The mission went on in similar fashion all morning.

Then a glitch. I couldn't find the last LZ. For several minutes I tried raising the ground commander on the radio, but got no response. I switched frequencies. No answer. Since the radios worked on a line of sight basis, I decided to climb. The new Captain was on the controls, so I told him to take the ship up to four thousand feet. He lifted the collective, and up we went. Soon we were floating in a lazy oval pattern directly over Khe Sanh. I made several more tries to contact the unit. Out my windscreen, across the DMZ a few miles away, the hazy green foliage of North Vietnam stretched as far as I could see. To the west lay the rolling hills of Laos. Directly south was the AShau Valley, its northern end a few klicks away. Ten klicks or so further along, forlorn and abandoned, a ragged brown spot at the north end of the AShau was a mountain-top spot called Dong Ap Bia, otherwise known as Hamburger Hill.

I heard reports below, rat-a-tat-tat like popcorn on a stove. It was the unmistakable sound of AK-47 fire. I checked my altimeter. Four thousand feet. Khe Sanh sat at around twelve hundred feet above sea level, so my Huey was still almost three thousand feet off the ground, well above the effective range of an AK.

"Hey, Gil." I opened my intercom in the chill air.

Gil read my mind. "I see it, sir." He pointed down, at the spot where the sound was coming from. "That's funny."

Together we watched yellow prickles of light, like sparkles on water, muzzle flashes of small arms fire.

"I've been watching it, too," I said.

"Their commander's gonna be pissed at them for using up ammo," Gil said.

"And for giving away their position," I said.

In the right seat, the Captain's curiosity piqued. "What's that?" he asked.

My answer did not reassure him. "We're taking fire," I said.

Silence. The fellow's jaw sagged. "Taking..?"

"Yeah, a little AK fire down there. I think we're okay." I motioned for him to bank hard left, which put the helicopter directly over the pinpricks of light. "Look down there. See it?" I tried to get him a view of the 'danger' we were in. It was the least I could do, since he was in as much *danger* as I was.

He wanted nothing to do with danger. His interests lay in getting away from that sort of tomfoolery and back to White Plains in one piece. "Shouldn't we call for gun support?" he asked, thinking like a true warrior.

"By the time the gunnies get here they'd be long gone," I said. "Besides, they can't touch us up this high."

I managed to raise the lost unit on the radio. We landed, offloaded our cache of supplies, and completed the mission. Then we flew back to base, and wrapped up for the day. The Captain departed, back to his desk at HQ. I never saw him on the flight line again.

The conflict in Vietnam convinced me of several things: that war is basically stupid—a failure of human imagination; that wars are always about money; that they will cease only when men refuse to fight in them. One thing Vietnam did very well was reveal our true personalities. Since we took off every morning unsure if we'd land that night, even at twenty-years old we got a bit philosophical. Especially when the beer flowed like water, in other words every night, we'd often engage in morbid and/or fatalistic conversations. If there were men in my unit who believed in the war they were awfully quiet about it. Mostly we knew it was the Vietnamese people's war to win or lose. We were the Redcoats in a revolutionary effort to unite North and South Vietnam. Our primary goal was to not die.

I sensed pretty quickly that the war was a lost cause, and that opinion factored in to every mission. I took no chances. I did what was necessary, and no more. I was fiercely protective of my crew. Gil in particular. His brother had been killed in Vietnam before he arrived. For that reason Gil had dispensation from serving in Vietnam, but he elected to go anyway. When he flew with me, Gil and I looked out for each other always, and I'm happy to report that he made it home to El Paso a few months after I left Vietnam. He stayed in the Army, and last I heard he was no longer a spec 4 enlisted guy, but a Colonel.

There were men who believed in the war, and refused to see the writing on the wall. Many high-level officers charged on, deeply involved in what psychologists call cognitive dissonance, convinced that we could salvage a victory in Southeast Asia despite indications otherwise. Toward the end of my tour I saw an example of just what that tension can do to a man. The event involved my dustup, no pun intended, with a Colonel. It was the most peculiar episode in my time in Vietnam, and it happened on the ground.

February 1971. The Lam Son 719 operation was a last desperate test of the concept of Vietnamization with a baptism of fire exercise, an invasion of Laos.

As American troop strength waned, the ARVN were forced to defend their fragile country. The endeavor was not going well. The

South Vietnamese wouldn't 'stand and fight.' American commanders tried to make them do it anyway. In Laos, the effort reached an impasse. During Lam Son, helicopter pilots learned right away not to land in LZs to pick up frightened ARVN troops. Desperate to escape the fighting, those men flooded aboard, making the aircraft too heavy to fly. Pilots had to hover at three or four feet. Only the most agile ARVN troops could grabble aboard, a kind of Darwinian test in the Laotian jungle. Several ARVNs grasped the skids of departing helicopters, only to fall to their death from altitude. This and several other insanities of the ill-fated Lam Son operation may explain why, in his frustration, the Colonel in my story went high and right on me.

I'd been tasked with flying a different Colonel around to visit his units in the field. This fellow bade me land. Then he'd jump out, give his troops a pep talk, board the helicopter and off we'd go to the next stop. This went on all morning, till we'd visited nearly every LZ in northern I-Corps. At noon the Colonel decided to have a proper lunch, so he told me to fly him back to Khe Sanh, which I did.

Circling over the base, eyeing the reddish dustbowl plateau that was Khe Sanh, I asked the Colonel where he'd like me to land. "There," he said, indicating a spot adjacent to a tent rather more large than the others. Obedient Warrant Officer that I was I powered down, and landed in a cloud of reddish, rotor-blown Khe Sanh dirt, precisely where the Colonel told me to. I put the pitch down. He leapt off the helicopter and disappeared.

The next few minutes are a blur. Suffice to say that, in a very short time I came as close to being injured in Vietnam as I had at any time during my tour, and I had only a month left in-country.

The Colonel departed for lunch. I was cleaning up the cockpit, shutting down systems to wait for his return so I could get on with the mission. In my peripheral vision I noticed a figure storming toward my Huey, clearly in some distress. The fellow practically hovered across the thirty yards between my aircraft and the large tent close by from which he'd recently come. It turned out that the tent was the 101st Airborne group HQ. The fellow charging toward me like a runaway beer truck was the Colonel in charge. And he was not pleased.

An important point is this: the military observes a gentleman's agreement that officers are not to touch each other unless given permission. Technically, if a Major saw a deadly snake on a Warrant Officer's neck he had to first ask permission to swat the damn thing. The snake, not the Warrant. So what the Colonel did to me at Khe Sanh was particularly bizarre, and downright amusing. I opened my door to greet the red-faced Colonel, and to ask if I might be of some assistance to him. I never got the chance. His eyes on fire, the Colonel tore open my door, snagged my coat collar and dragged me out of the aircraft. So much for asking permission.

We shared thoughts—or he did. Sputtering and spitting in apoplexy, he raged at me for landing near his tent. "You %$#@&, you Goddamn near blew my &%#@ briefing tent away!" He jabbed my chest with a fat finger, and expended yet more venom. His out of control rant even included an unequivocal reference to my parental lineage, with the possibility of canine interaction. "You're finished, mister," he screamed. "I'm calling your commander to have him fly this %$@! helicopter out of here. You're through!" With those words the Colonel released me. He spun around, and with a nasty backward look for good measure, he stalked back to what was left of his tent.

Dazed and amazed I watched him go, processing what he'd said, wishing I'd had the chance to explain that I was just following orders by landing there. But it's funny how your mind works, especially in times of relative danger. One thought that flashed across my brain was the fervent hope that he'd been serious. Finished flying in Vietnam? Did he mean it? Can I go home now? He *was* a Colonel, after all. In that capacity he could make it happen.

Unless he wimped out, I could be on the Freedom Bird that night. An hour to pack? What's the other fifty-five minutes for?

The second thought followed close behind; when the Colonel jerked me out of the aircraft I wished I'd fallen and 'injured' myself. I could have gotten a purple heart out of it, although it would have been a trifle embarrassing explaining to the grandkids that papaw got an award for being pummeled by a Colonel, one supposedly on our side.

My happy fantasy was short-lived. I wasn't 'finished,' exactly. And there was no purple heart in it for me. But, true to his word, the Colonel ordered my commander to fly to Khe Sanh—a 30-mile trek—to move my Huey 100 yards, stirring up the dirt once again, of course. As Dave Barry says, I am not making this up. My commander wasn't the least bit upset. He moved the helicopter, gave me back the keys, explained that the good Colonel was under a lot of stress, and he split. The original Colonel returned from his noon meal to find the helicopter had been moved. He boarded without a word, and I finished the mission, not finished flying in the war after all.

A month later I was *officially* finished flying in Vietnam and more than ready to catch the Freedom Bird back to the world.

By the time my tour in Vietnam ended I'd fallen into the same pattern my former colleagues had. To wit, the closer my departure date the higher I flew. Starting in February 1971, any time I took off, which was less and less often, I headed up to nosebleed country. I needed oxygen a few times. Once or twice I flew so high my crew wondered, as they shivered in the back of the aircraft, if perhaps I was trying to see Ohio? They even asked a time or two if I'd pretty please crank on the heater? But, like every other perversity of war, my high-altitude evasive tactic nearly did me in. The event happened, once again, over sunny Laos. And it happened two weeks to the day before I left for the States. This particular fact was, to me, significant: during the terrifying episode, thoughts of Tom Kearsley and his dead crew raced through my mind. Kearsley was killed two weeks to the day before *his* departure for home.

On that day I was number three ship in a four shipper. The plan was to insert a recon team onto an LZ across the fence, west of Khe Sanh. I'm not sure where the LZ was because we never got to it. The North Vietnamese spoiled our plan. Our leader, a fellow named Jim Collins, had the flight up at five thousand feet thinking we were perfectly safe at that altitude. (Yes, Jim was a short-timer, too.) It was mid-February, and pretty chilly up that high. But the option was to be down in the tulips, zig-zagging around. We knew the enemy was there in strength, and we didn't wish to give him an easy target. Down in the tulips would have been a better choice, as it turned out.

Flying along fat, dumb and silly, I watched the lush greenery of Eastern Laos slide by under my Huey. Two aircraft in front of me bobbed and bounced in the morning sky. I looked forward to finding the landing zone, depositing my troops on it, and hightailing back to Quang Tri. Then, for no apparent reason, the Huey in front of mine did a funny kind of whifferdill. The odd jinking movement got my attention right away. The pilot of that ship was a fellow short-timer named Jack, from Philadelphia. As I watched in fascination, Jack's Huey took a sideways dive, nearly flipping onto its back. It was not a typical maneuver for Jack, even if he was from Philly. Then I saw why Jack had evaded the way he had. Like a bolt of lightning crackling up from the ground, anti-aircraft tracers lit up the sky around his ship. I watched, dumbfounded, as Jack's Huey dove out of the way, down and right, dropping like a homesick brick.

Then it was my turn in the crosshairs. Like burning basketballs, tracers erupted all around my cockpit. Those demonic flares flashed past me, crackling in the high ether of five grand. Like pistol shots, rounds snapped all over, a fireworks show worthy of the 4th of July. From pure instinct I yanked the stick hard left, opposite the direction Jack had gone and bottomed the collective. The Huey dove like a footlocker full of paperweights. My altimeter unwound like a crazy clock. The airspeed went God knows where. My knees shook from fright; I couldn't stop their quivering. Passing five hundred feet, I wrestled the ship under control. Gil and the rest of my crew were silent as monks, and it wasn't from the cold. I leveled off and headed for Quang Tri, my knees still quaking.

Zipping along on a random course toward home, down in the daffodils where I should have been in the first place, I regrouped with the flight. The radios were dead silent. There was none of the usual banter and bullshouting that hissed in my headset to and from an LZ. It was as frightening an experience as I'd ever had in the cockpit. The flight of four limped back to base, the mission unfinished, unless staying alive was the mission. My mother said she always knew I'd return from Vietnam in one piece, that I had something else to do. I was beginning to think Momma was right.

The upshot of the story is that I'd escaped a highly dangerous situation once again. For nearly twelve months, flying almost 1,200 hours of combat time with the unit, in all manner of lousy weather, innumerable perilous missions and near misses, I was unhit. I'd flown onto LZs where my colleagues took hits, and left those landing zones unmolested. My crew would examine the Huey after hostile missions, certain that, finally, Major Edge had taken at least one enemy round. It never happened. Hovering for almost five minutes while Frank and his men scrambled into my aircraft that day in Laos, I took fire the entire time. Not one hit.

By the time my tour ended all the enlisted crews wanted to fly with me. I'd led a charmed existence. I seemed invulnerable. Instead of feeling grateful, it bothered me. I couldn't decide whether I was ripe for a real takedown, or lucky, or what. Didn't know whether to feel guilty or glad. It was uncanny.

Very few pilots finished a flying tour in Vietnam with their 'cherry' intact. I was one of them. It was a strange kind of distancing feeling. Despite all the flying I'd done with my colleagues, I was somehow removed from them. Taking hits was a mark of distinction, proof that we'd flown in harm's way and survived. I'd been in harm's way, too, many times. But I lacked the proof. My conclusion was that, if it meant anything at all, I'd discover what that meaning was at some point.

DEROS: Date of Expected Return from Overseas. Another definition: Going home. March 15th 1971 was my last day in the unit. I woke early, showered and shaved, dressed, and prepared to leave the war behind. I took a crayon and filled in the last number on my short-timer calendar. Then I schlepped my duffel bag to a waiting Huey, destination Phu Bai airport. From there I caught a C-130 ride to Cam Ranh Bay for out-country processing. I waited at Cam Ranh a day and half for a seat on the Freedom Bird. After 1200 hours of combat flying, and twelve months in Vietnam, I clambered aboard a blue and white Pan Am 707 on March 17th 1971. When the big Boeing left the runway at Cam Ranh the cabin exploded in a roar of jubilation, an eruption of noise that was likely heard in California. And that was just me. There were 150 other men equally enthused. That plane would have flown without wings. We landed at Yokohama for fuel, then passed over Anchorage, then touched down at McCord Air Force Base near Seattle. Inside of 48 hours I was out of the Army.

My feelings about Vietnam and our involvement there are (still) mixed. I was more grateful than I can say to have survived the war when many of my colleagues didn't. Their sacrifice may have been in vain. I believe our cause in Vietnam was ill advised, and poorly conducted. Some of my colleagues don't subscribe to that opinion. I'm convinced that the war was not winnable, at least not by the common metric of sweeping the enemy from the field of battle. In some ways our efforts were quite honorable. We saw a people vulnerable to the ravages of communist one-party rule and its depredations, and we intervened. That intervention was initially at the behest of the Vietnamese government, as unpopular as it was. Over a course of years our presence came to be onerous and hurtful, and we Americans did indeed become 'The Redcoats' in the Vietnamese people's revolutionary war. Politics aside, and looking back with the luxury of forty years, it appears that our original plan was a good one. We just refused to allow the Vietnamese to take on the war, regardless of its outcome, and make it their own. It was obvious to me from early in my tour, from the hesitation the ARVN displayed, to the disdain the Vietnamese people showed for us GIs, that we'd overstayed our welcome. When an Army isn't safe in the villages it's trying to liberate, that Army should go home. The awful truth of it is, that many fine men and women died in Vietnam in dubious battle. It was a long year for me, and it was finally over.

The airplane banked away from Cam Ranh, and soon the coast of Vietnam receded and disappeared. Twenty-four hours, a lifetime, a war and a world later I landed at McCord. A day later I was out of the Army, en-route home to Columbus, a free man. The shock to my system was almost breathtaking; mere hours before I'd been in a dangerous, war-torn, third-world country. In an instant, it seemed, I was in the land of shopping malls, safe streets and flush toilets. People strolled on sidewalks without fear of ambush, or of taking fire from a treeline. People in casual clothes, not camo, drove cars, stopped at don't-walk signs, snoozed on park benches. Kids rode bikes instead of water buffalo. They climbed trees instead of hiding behind them. Instead of rice paddies and concertina wire there were parking lots, and open, grassy yards. I could close my eyes and imagine that I'd made the war up; that Vietnam had been an exotic dream, a product of my overactive imagination.

Looking at civilians going about their business I thought of my flight to Phu Bai in the helicopter just three days prior. Below me, as I flew over Vietnam's Highway 1, there were no don't-walk signs, no newsstands, no bucolic parks with benches where people slept in the morning sun. I knew we'd lose the war in Vietnam. Few of us who fought there doubted that our presence was temporary; that North and South Vietnam would unite, that our side would not prevail. Watching people in Seattle go about their business unmolested I hoped for the Vietnamese the same things: safe sidewalks, sleepable parks, smooth bike paths, the simple things that only peace can provide. I hoped those things for them regardless of who won.

Like all wars Vietnam was a Darwinian experience. I say that with a degree of humility because there were excellent pilots, much better qualified than myself, who were killed there in spite of their superior flying skill. I left Vietnam in March 1971 having come damned close a few times to a ride home in the refrigerated plane, but I survived nonetheless. Those few close calls made me wonder why I got through the war, when some of my equally competent aviator friends did not? Why did Kearsley and Mattingly crash and burn that night? Why did George and Woody die in Laos a month before I came home? Why did Captain Ayers die on Co Roc mountain on his first mission with the company? And why did I fly for a year, dodging one bullet after another, missing one scrape after the next? Maybe I was destined for something else? Maybe I was smart enough to know how dumb I was?

The war in Vietnam lasted four years after I left, ending in April 1975 as North Vietnamese tanks clanked into Saigon. Watching that event on TV at home in Ohio I couldn't help thinking of all the troops, on both sides, lost for no reason. The silver lining was that the experience gave me a career that would take me to retirement. I spent the next 35 years in a state of suspended aviation. My war was history. It was time to make some kind of a living.

14

Home from the War

The airplane landed at Port Columbus and taxied to the gate. It was a full flight. I was seated two-thirds of the way back, in coach. In order to use my military free travel option I had to be in uniform. So flying home I wore my dress greens, which were at that point festooned with medals: Army Commendation, Good Conduct, Air Medal with 24 oak leaf clusters, Vietnam Service, Vietnam Campaign, Bronze Star and Distinguished Flying Cross. Though I was very far from it, according to the decorations on my chest I looked like a damn war hero, Vietnam's answer to Audie Murphy. My fellow passengers on the airplane that day must have thought so. Their courtesy to me is something I've not forgotten. The plane stopped at the gate, and the seat belt sign chimed. But unlike the typical frantic scramble of panicked passengers grappling for overhead bags, elbowing each other, scrapping toward the exit, no one moved. Instead, people turned in their seats, looked at me, and waited. Not one of them stirred, or stood.

I stared at them a bit dazed. Then, understanding what they were offering, I got up, grabbed my carry-on and walked off the airplane. It was an odd, but gratifying experience. I still see those people waiting for me, their deference to a returning soldier obvious in their gracious behavior. When I hear about rude and dismissive acts against returning Vietnam vets I think of those people on my

LA to Columbus flight that day. And I thank them again. They didn't have to do that, but they did.

Years later, during the height of the conflict in Iraq, I had a chance to return the favor. On a flight from Columbus to Dallas two troops were seated about where I'd been all those years ago. I asked the flight attendant to make an announcement, which she was happy to do. When the plane stopped at the gate in DFW we civilians waited for those men to deplane. I watched them shuffle up the aisle, desert-camo fatigues, sand-colored boots, small duffels in hand. I knew just how they felt.

Because I missed flying, I joined the Ohio National Guard aviation section in September 1971. With a glut of helicopter pilots leaving the military, and few seats available in the commercial flying world, the Guard was the only place I could take a helicopter into the air and get paid to do it.

My refuge was the cockpit. Flying was the only time I felt truly at peace with my world. When I heard people mention the dangers of helicopter flight I dismissed it as nonsense. I felt safe in the sky. Off the ground I was whole and competent, satisfied with the direction my life was going. Once I was aloft, my navigational skills counted for something. On the ground I was always lost to some degree. Only in the sky did I feel completely at ease.

So I joined the Ohio Guard, and put my zoom suit back on. An incident in the Spring of 1972 closed a gap for me, expanded the insight from a stormy day almost a year before when I'd questioned my own humanity and compassion. The closure also restored my corroded self-esteem in a way I never imagined.

In the mid-seventies, before commercial operators filled the role, The Ohio National Guard fielded an emergency rescue Huey called the Medicopter. The aircraft was a flying emergency room, and the first helicopter so equipped in Ohio. Every Friday night, into Saturday morning, peak time for trauma, the Medicopter was available for immediate liftoff from the Guard hangar in Northwest Columbus.

I was on Medicopter duty one Friday night in the spring of 1972. The staff consisted of two pilots, two crewmembers, and two civilian medical personnel. The doctor that night was a fellow named Stuart Roberts, a member of the ER staff at The Ohio State University (now the Wexner) Medical Center in Columbus. That night, the Medicopter crew was in the ready room, eating pizza, telling war stories, waiting for an emergency call. I sat across from Doc Roberts who was chomping pizza, listening to one tall tale after another. "There I was," and "Listen to this" and "This is no shit..." War stories passed from one veteran to the next.

When it was my turn, I began describing a rescue mission for a pregnant girl in Vietnam. The tale included a warning from my commanding General to be on the ground by five o'clock, a flight down the coast, then back to Hué in buffeting winds and punishing rain. Holding forth, I told my story. When I finished, something came full circle. Something balanced out.

The little village was fifteen-minutes by air from Hué, I told my colleagues. I battled a headwind flying down, but that was a comfort. I'd have a tailwind flying back. I found the village, landed and watched the frightened girl board my Huey. My crew buckled a strap across her as she lay on the folded canvas seat, and we lifted off with her at ten minutes till five. The storm was on top of me. Wind gusted to forty knots. Dollops of rain like half dollars smacked the windscreen. The sky looked like a day old bruise, and the wind was on its hind legs. Thunder rumbled like a kettle-drum, and whips of lightning chased me up the coast. In a heartbeat, danger and difficulty had cancelled my easy, carefree day. Then it got worse.

Medics at the hospital in Hué wouldn't accept the girl. The

orderly waved his hands, frantic. "No room," he yelled. "No room!" With one eye on the pregnant girl, one on the fuel gauge I pleaded with the man, but he wouldn't budge. When I ran the throttle open a yellow light blinked on: Low Fuel.

While my crewmembers downed pizza in the Guard hangar, I continued my war story:

The storm stronger by the minute—inside the cockpit and out—I took off and flew to the ARVN military hospital, where the gatekeeper demanded that I get off his helipad. They didn't accept women, much less pregnant ones. He shouted for me to leave. Angry and desperate, I lifted toward Phu Bai and the American military hospital, the 85th Evac. I radioed ahead, then waited. The radio buzzed with static. A full minute dragged by. Then the fellow responded. "Bring her in," he said. I landed, and idled the engine. An orderly helped the girl off my Huey and wheeled her inside, where she vanished in the drowning rain.

Gas gauge on empty I took off, headed back to base, and landed. When I walked into operations the phone from HQ buzzed. Sergeant McKay grabbed the receiver, grunted, handed it to me. "Walsh at battalion."

I sucked in an anxious breath. Here it comes, I thought. It was five thirty. I was half an hour late for the General's down time. "Go ahead."

"Mister Edgington, welcome home. I have one question. Was it a life-or-death mission?"

"Yes, Bill, it was."

"That's all I need to know."

My voice breaking with emotion, I told my Guard companions about the flight, and its effect on my feelings about the war and my place in it.

Doc Roberts had been posted to Vietnam on a medical leave. All I knew about his duty there was that he'd been in country about the same time I was, but I didn't know when or where. He sat forward, brow furrowed, listening to my story about the pregnant girl. Leaning my direction, Roberts put his pizza down and interrupted me. "Was that August of '70?" he asked.

"Yeah, Doc. Why?"

"Girl from Vinh Mỹ, down the coast a ways?"

"Yes..."

"Big storm that night?"

"Big storm," I said. "...in fact, I was late getting..."

"I delivered that kid," he said.

"You delivered..?"

"I remember you landing on our pad with her. I thought you were nuts to be flying in that weather, but..."

Chills peppered my arms. "You delivered that baby?"

"Yep. Baby boy. Mom and kid did fine. We made junior a crib out of an empty rocket box, and they went home the next day."

Tears pooled in my eyes. I couldn't speak. The room fell silent. A guy cleared his throat. I thought back to that August afternoon, the girl, the weather, the mission and my own inner conflict that almost turned me around. Ripples spread in all directions. I'd accepted the mission, rescued the girl, then a doctor named Stu Roberts took over from there and saved two lives. Maybe three. I saw that angry pilot who'd made those choices, saw him battle his harsh, judgmental self. I watched him make a decision that might have been his reason for deciding to fly in the first place. At that moment I began to like the fellow in the mirror again.

15

Guard Aviation

I felt good about flying once more, even if Olive Drab wasn't exactly the fashion in the fall of 1971. Slightly used Vietnam Hueys were being parceled out to various National Guard units across the country, and our unit started getting them.

When I joined the Ohio Guard the unit was housed in two rickety buildings at Don Scott (OSU) Field in northwest Columbus. With its decrepit shacks, tin roof hangars and grass pads the place looked like the pretty good OD flying club. When I first joined it, the unit had exactly one Huey. Most of the flying inventory was Bell H-13s, helicopters familiar to anyone who watched M*A*S*H on TV, the very type of same aircraft that had landed behind my house when I was a ten-year-old. Korean War vintage machines, the newest H-13 on the flight line was likely fifteen years old. But they flew. And the unit needed pilots.

Aching to get into the air again, I looked the unit over, raised my right hand and swore allegiance to the Governor of Ohio.

The National Guard differs from the active military in significant ways. The majority of Guard personnel are part-timers, weekend-warriors. The Guard has very few full time members. Units are comprised of local men and women rather than a conglomerate from around the country. This creates a more cohesive, neighborly atmosphere. Some weekend drills looked more like family reunions than military events. Often there was potluck. So after two years of full time, war-zone Army, the Guard was an adjustment for me. For one thing there was little deference paid to military pomp and protocol. We had the occasional formation to count heads, the odd inspection of equipment, and a visit once in a while from an officer above the rank of Major. Mostly, the Guard not only looked like a flying club in those days, for all intents and purposes it *was* a flying club, one where everyone had the same tailor.

There were scheduled flying nights. Wednesday evenings I'd drive to the airfield, grab a set of keys and a logbook, and take a helicopter up for a spin. I'd check in, scribble a quick flight plan, grab my helmet, a logbook, and a co-pilot, and off I'd go into the evening Ohio sky. The only restriction on flying was whatever range a bag of gas allowed, and how long before I had to pee. The H-13 carried enough fuel to fly about 2 hours, at a blazing speed of 100 knots, so I couldn't fly to Chicago and back. But I could range around central Ohio, landing at small airfields, and at locations where Guard-friendly citizens allowed us to use their property.

The Guard's mantra was (and is) training. Every turn of a rotor blade is expensive, so every hour spent in the air must be justified to the taxpayers. Training was the catchword. Our flying usually satisfied that contingency, even if some of it was a bit, let's say, casual. My colleagues and I sometimes raised eyebrows by buzzing girlfriends' homes, flying to golf outings, or to the hottest Mexican food joint in a town a half hour away. There was a decided lack of oversight back then. In time we sensed that our days of nonchalant cruising around Ohio were short-lived.

And we were right. As the old H-13s flew off to the boneyard, and the Hueys filtered into the system, our flights to secluded fishing spots quickly ended. For one thing, with its signature wop-wopping blade sound the Huey can be heard miles away by all but the blessedly deaf. There's no sneaking up on anyone in a Huey, no buzzing Betty Lou's house. So when the unit acquired UH-1s we began doing legitimate training on every flight.

As much experience as I had flying them, I needed continual training updates in the UH-1. Hueys are more sophisticated machines than the old two-seat, piston-driven H-13. It had been more than a year since I'd flown a Huey, so I had to get back into the books, re-learn the limits, and know the emergency procedures. One particular night flight in a Huey took me past a limit, and led me into the commander's office with my tail between my legs.

The aircraft I'd flown in Vietnam was an 'H' model Huey. The latest iteration of the venerable UH-1, the 'Hotel' model had a thirteen-hundred horsepower turbine engine, improved transmission, and a fuel tank capacity of 209 gallons, enough 'go-juice' for two-and-a-half hours of flying. The 'H' model was a big improvement over one of its predecessors, the 'B' model. The UH-1B was a good helicopter, it just didn't have the bells and whistles, nor the endurance that the 'H' did. The 'B' model's fuel tank held 164 gallons, enough for two hours of flight.

The night in question I'd been assigned to fly a 'B' model. I took off at seven p.m., flew the training period, and landed back at base. I shut the engine off, put the aircraft to bed and walked into operations, where the commander was waiting for me. He was not happy. He called me into his office, and read me the riot act, parts one through four.

"Mister Edgington you flew a 'B' model tonight, correct?"

Heels locked, standing at attention, I responded in the affirmative. "Yes, sir I did."

"The 'B' model Huey's tank holds how much fuel?"

"Uh, it holds 164 gallons, sir." My instant recall of the aircraft systems made me feel proud. For perhaps five seconds.

"And how much flight time does that allow?"

"Well, er, about two hours, sir, why?"

His knowledge base somewhat broader than mine, he refined the answer for me. "Two hours and two minutes, according to the Dash-10," he said. Thus the reason he was the commander and I was not.

"Uh, yes sir," I stammered.

He produced the flight plan I'd completed earlier that evening. The ETE block was circled in red ink. "Then why did you flight plan for two hours and *thirty* minutes?"

"Well, sir, I uh, er, eeep," I responded brilliantly. "Sorry, sir. I'll be more careful."

"See that you are," he said. "That's all."

I left the office chagrined and embarrassed. Complacency had killed more than one pilot. I sucked it up and renewed my intention to be more cautious than I needed to be.

The high point of the National Guard training calendar was two-weeks of summer camp, called Annual Training. Depending on where we deployed for it, A-T was two weeks of camping out in somewhat more primitive conditions than I'd experienced in Vietnam. It meant flying airborne tactics designed to win the previous war, with equipment that would never again see military action, we hoped. In other words a retrograde operation. But A-T kept my flying skills up, and padded my logbook, so I looked forward to it.

My ultimate goal was to log enough time to be marketable in the commercial flying business. For that I needed at least two thousand logged hours. I left Vietnam with 1,400. Through interaction with other pilots, some of whom had managed to land commercial jobs, I began to see a chance to fly for a living. There were few opportunities in the early seventies, but more all the time it seemed, so I kept piling up flight hours, the metric employers look for in the hiring process. I needed a commercial license, too, and I acquired that from the FAA.

By the end of 1975 I'd reached the magic 2,000 hour milestone, and began actively seeking commercial employment. It would take another five years to land my first flying job, with a new charter operation in Toledo. After the Toledo experience jobs came a bit easier, because I learned an important lesson. It's good to buddy up with a helicopter salesman. Helicopter buyers are almost always looking for a pilot, and for recommendations. I landed my first two flying jobs because Steve, the local Bell Helicopter salesman, was a good friend, and National Guard colleague. Steve recommended me to the Toledo folks, the ones who eventually fired me, but Steve and I stayed friends anyway. It's a very small business. For details on my ejection from a company named Fly By Helicopter, (I'm not making this up), keep reading.

Byron H. Edgington

The TH-55
I learned to fly in one of these

"I learned to fly back when sex was safe and flying was dangerous." It all started at Fort Wolters Texas in June 1969. I soloed June 27th, went on to advanced training at Hunter Army Airfield, Savannah Georgia graduating in February 1970. A month later I arrived in Vietnam assigned to the 101st Airborne Division at Camp Eagle. After 1,100 hours of combat flying I left Vietnam March 17th 1971 from Cam Ranh Bay. Forty-eight hours later I was a civilian.

The Comancheros in formation Vietnam 1970

I'd fly a Huey today if they ...

W-1 Edgington & Miss America 1970

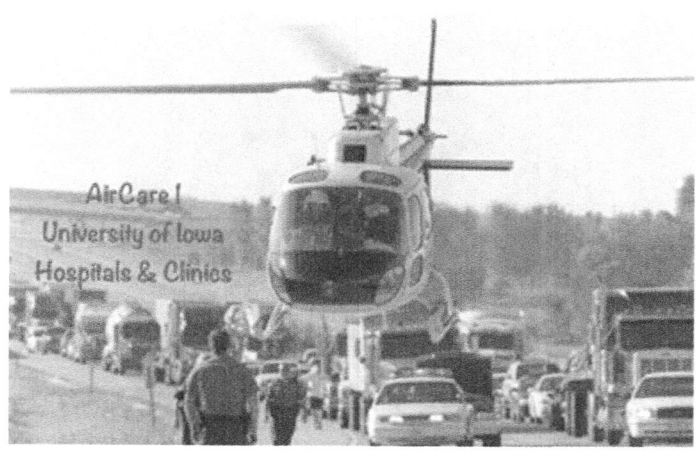

Air Medical: Iowa City 1983

3,200 patient missions

Byron H. Edgington

Bell 206-L1, a true pilot's helicopter

NaPali Coast of Kauai: 2005

With Friends from Iowa post-tour

16

First Commercial Jobs

In my pursuit of a commercial seat I took an assortment of odd, exotic, often ill-fated flying jobs, some of which I was fortunate to survive. I went to Panama to spot tuna offshore in the Pacific, the only job I ever walked away from. The equipment was shabby and poorly maintained, the mission dangerous, and it required me to leave my family behind and out of touch for an indefinite period. The less said about that foray the better, except that I did have the good sense to quit early and hightail it home before I killed myself. After I left Panama my replacement, a pilot I'd met only briefly, had an engine failure in the machine I would have flown. He plunged into the Pacific, the helicopter sank and he barely escaped with his life.

The summer of 1980 I went to Alaska to fight forest fires. There are no roads in the interior of Alaska, so folks up there need helicopters with water buckets to tamp out lightning-generated fires. I landed in Anchorage in June, and checked in with the company. SeaAirMotive had several contracts with the Bureau of Land Management, including survey work, reclamation, critter counts and firefighting. It seemed odd to me that in Alaska, where people take great pride in self-sufficiency, that so many of them rely on the guv'mint for a paycheck. The BLM seemed to be everywhere. Likewise the Bureau of Indian Affairs, the Office of Aircraft Services, U.S. Forest Service, Bureau of Mines, the EPA, USGS and U.S. Coast and Geodetic Survey. In the land of rugged individualism it seemed like everyone was nuzzled up to the Government trough. The only Federal agency that didn't seem to have much presence in Alaska was the FAA. Because of the State's vast distances, lack of roads and peoples' general attitude of self-reliance, a lot of Alaskans fly their own aircraft. That doesn't mean they have a license to fly them. Oversight by the FAA seemed to be relaxed at best. I got the impression in Alaska that whatever it took to get the job done was done, and no questions asked.

The company airplane flew me to my outpost 100 miles west of Denali, to a smudge on the great map of Alaska, a fishing village called Lake Minchumina. The helicopter I flew, a Bell 205, was a civilian version of the UH-1, essentially an 'H' model Huey. The only differences were that the aircraft was not olive drab, but red and white to make it easier to find on the tundra should a pilot ditch somewhere. It had one set of controls, in the right seat, and civilian radios. It seemed odd to be back in the right seat of a Huey again, but in the commercial helicopter world that's the pilot in command side of the front office. The other difference involved the one between military and civilian flying. It became obvious right away in Alaska. Indeed, my adjustment from military to commercial flying was hard, and hardest when it came to maintenance issues.

Imagine my surprise when one of the aircraft's two fuel pumps malfunctioned on an early flight, and the company refused to fix it right away. I had to fly the machine for almost two weeks with a yellow caution light glaring at me from the panel, getting brighter, it seemed, by the day. I assumed any squawk would be fixed overnight. I was mistaken.

In the Army, when something broke on my helicopter I wrote the malfunction up in the logbook, and a mechanic fixed it that night. In the commercial world, not so fast. Naïve as I was at the time to real world flying, I failed to understand the financial aspects of taking a helicopter into the air, while trying to make money doing so. Flying in Alaska, three hundred miles from company headquarters and the nearest mechanic, I began to understand the necessity of ignoring the loss of aircraft systems to keep profits coming in. The FAA isn't happy about such practices, but to make money and keep flying often required me to 'discover' deficiencies, non-safety related ones in any case, on shutdown, or just as parts magically arrived to fix them. I never once flew a helicopter with a safety-of-flight item inoperative, but I abandoned the habit of reporting every little hiccup or twitch in the system, too.

The fuel pump failure on the 205 was a good example. When it failed, I called the company to report it. At the altitudes I was flying the pump wasn't needed, so the company rightly postponed fixing it until something else malfunctioned. Two weeks later I called them to report a broken latch on a door that required me to lock it shut. The mechanic flew in from Anchorage the next day, at considerable expense, to fix both items. The lesson was clear: if it's flyable and safe, fly the sucker or be out of business. My kid-gloves treatment of mechanics in Vietnam served me well in this regard; when something broke, I always considered the wrench-benders, and how it affected them. Years later, when something broke in the middle of an Iowa winter night, the safety-factor of the item often dictated my phone call to the mechanic-or not.

Speaking of lessons, I soon learned my first about Alaska from one of the locals. Don't call the big Mountain *McKinley*. To the natives, it's Denali, The Great One. Its other namesake, to those of us in the lower forty-eight at least, was America's 25th President, William McKinley. The upshot of the story is that our 25th President never saw the mountain that was named for him, because he never went to Alaska.

Something else I learned is that Alaskans learn to fly like teens in the lower forty-eight learn to drive, minus perhaps the parallel parking part. There are more licensed pilots in Alaska per capita than anywhere on earth. There's a reason for that. Lacking roads in the interior, people in Alaska use airplanes for the most mundane trips. For instance, at Lake Minchumina where I was stationed, folks lined up each Saturday morning on the airstrip. At nine a.m. the grocery plane arrived and taxied in. The port side engine stopped, and local people boarded. The plane then took off, destination Fairbanks an hour away. At two p.m. it landed again, and folks got off, their arms filled with grocery sacks. It was a weekly ritual. Imagine boarding a plane to go to the Big Save in Buffalo.

Lake Minchumina Alaska, population 32, was home for the summer of 1980. Minchumina's hearty souls survive on what vegetables they grow in the ten-week Alaskan summer, and on racks of fish that hang on clothes lines everywhere like an insane collection of drying socks. The outpost was a smattering of huts, an abandoned FAA weather station, too many mosquitoes to ever count in a zillion years and not much else. The lake teemed with northern pike that seemed to stand in line to grab the next hook, so they could wind up hanging like drying socks.

And there were bears. One afternoon I met one of them. He (or she) was a fat bundle of fur with an attitude. Mister bear smelled food, and he/she made a bee (or bear) line for it.

Bears are highly intelligent animals. They know that where there's smoke there's, well, food. They know that when smokejumpers set up camp they always bring provisions. So when a fire breaks out bears head for the nearest column of smoke for a yummy lunch. When Mister Bear arrives in camp, smoke jumpers jump up a tree, leaving the fire untended. Smokey may not approve, but bears gotta eat.

I dropped my motley crew off one afternoon at a small fire ten miles from base, and then flew back to Minchumina. The fire didn't amount to much, but it had the potential to spread, so the six-man crew attacked it. They almost had it under control when Mr. Bear shlepped into their midst for a bite to eat, effectively stopping the fire-fighting operation. The crew boss called me back on scene, and shortly I was in the air headed their way.

When I circled overhead what I saw was rather comical. All six men were in trees, as the bear wandered through camp, picking their packs and provisions apart, taking his sweet time to satisfy his hunger.

I radioed the crew boss to ask if everyone was okay, and he assured me they were. Then he asked me to do what I could about their ursine visitor. I approached the ridge, slowed the helicopter and drew a bead on the pesky but hungry bear. Like a flying shepherd I hovered close to the fellow, ten feet off the ground, closing in on him, as he watched me with some interest. When I got within a hundred feet of him he gave me the once over, but continued munching his lunch. At fifty feet he stopped munching, looked at me hovering toward him, sticks and weeds flying his direction and he paused, mid-munch. When I got within twenty feet he got the message. But because I'd interrupted his repast his back was up, and he did what bears do; he stood his ground, all seven feet of him, daring me to come closer. Like a menacing stuffed statue in a sporting goods store, he stared me down, furry arms, fists full of claws, daring me to come closer. If he could talk he'd have said 'bring it on!'

I was at the controls of nine thousand pounds of earth-shaking, blade-whipping, wind-blasting helicopter, so I knew Mr. Bear would eventually decide that running was in his best interest. But I must say it took somewhat longer than I'd expected. I hovered close enough to see the alarmed expression in the fuzzy fellow's yellow-gray eyes before he finally bolted. The bear swiveled, dropped to all fours and scampered up the ridge. Black fur wobbled on his back, and branches shattered in his wake.

I chased him half a mile up the ridge, just to be sure he'd stay away. He may have shot me the bird when I turned, though I have no memory of that. I hovered back to the fire crew, landed and checked to see if they needed anything. They didn't, so I flew back to base. I should have stuck around. Within 30 minutes the bear was back in camp. The crew boss finally had to kill him. He did all he could to avoid it, but his men were in danger, and the fire was spreading. He dropped the bear with the rifle that was standard equipment on any trip into the Alaskan bush.

When I heard of the bear's demise I envisioned Smokey going over to the dark side, fanning the flames, and having to be put down. School kids everywhere would be alarmed about that, I thought. It would be like finding out that Superman was a peeping Tom, or that Santa beat his elves when they tried to organize. But another lesson came from the bear tale. In Alaska, locals are allowed to shoot the animals as long as the bear is a threat to people, and as long as the bear's head is then delivered to State wildlife officials afterward. It seems those folks study the critters for signs of disease and parasites, the better to be proactive about their health in the wild. This legal injunction also precludes arbitrary hunting of bears for trophies and mantel art, so a good thing.

As for my Alaskan venture, not many pilots can claim on their résumé that they've 'herded bears.' For what it's worth, I can. Everybody needs a gimmick. Employers are always demanding just one more item, another five hundred hours of flight time, a checkout in the newest equipment, at least one space shuttle landing, something to make us stand out... I stuck every item I could in my logbook, no matter how trivial. Herded bears by air? Yep, done that.

~*~

I left Lake Minchumina in mid-August, flew to McGrath, and spent the last two weeks there before returning to Anchorage. McGrath is fifty miles west of the Alaska Range. It's not the end of the world, but on a clear day you can see Vladimir Putin from there. The only thing McGrath had going for it is a damn good roadhouse, and regular visits by Wien Air Alaska.

There were no fires to put out around McGrath. Late August is nearing the end of fire season in Alaska, indeed, the end of summer. The interior of the State had been quite rainy, and there were few fires to put out, so the company ordered me back to Anchorage. On August 26th I packed my bags, loaded the helicopter, and left McGrath headed southeast. My return route took me across the Alaska Range, the mountainous spine of the Last Frontier. That flight was one of the most memorable in my aviation career. It showed me just how privileged I was to be immersed in beauty that most people never see.

To cross the Alaska Range I had to locate Rainey Pass, about 100 miles from Anchorage. I left McGrath headed southeast. The weather was clear and, as I entered the pass at five thousand feet, the stark beauty surrounding me was astonishing. Out both sides of my cockpit an almost overwhelming view of rugged, untouched wilderness stretched east and west as far as I could see. To my right the Aleutian Chain and Lake Clark—to my left Denali and beyond. The Great One was 200 miles away, but visibility was such that the mountain looked close enough to land on. Crowning the Alaska Range, Denali's crest stands at 20,320 feet, the highest point in North America. Skimming the Alaska Range, I was looking at wilderness that had never been explored, great swaths of woods, snow-covered tundra, and crystalline rivers that only the eagles and hawks had ever seen. It was such rugged, inviolate country that its magnetic draw activated some inner yearning I always knew was inside me. Having seen that wild, unmapped wilderness I understood why men have always had an obsession with the unknown. It isn't curiosity, or avarice, or pursuit of monetary reward. It's because we can't resist the power of the wild. Like Odysseus, or Marco Polo, or Columbus, I could have landed somewhere among those valleys and craters, left all behind, made provisions somehow for shelter and food and never looked back. I understood why some men did just that, even if it meant dying among the frigid, the harsh and the savage beauty that overmatched them.

As I exited Rainey Pass I looked at the gas gauge, snapped back to reality and pressed on toward Anchorage. Looking at the chartless wilderness behind and below me was a bit sobering. If I'd had to put down there it would be a very long time before anyone found me, if they ever did. There are tales in Alaska of pilots disappearing, never to be seen again. Crossing Rainey Pass that day I understood how it might happen. But I sensed that, as with certain other Alaska lore, and given the remote and awesome beauty of that part of the world, some of those pilots may have elected to land on purpose, to take their chances surviving in the wilderness. I understood it.

Just as Anchorage loomed ahead the fuel god whistled for my attention. I crossed over the city, and landed at the airport, my Alaska adventure nearing an end. One more mission loomed, and that mission showed me why folks who live in the Great Land must be hearty, self-sufficient souls, able to do almost anything with nothing. The last week of August I encountered a snowstorm in the mountains above Anchorage.

They say there are only three seasons in Alaska—Summer, Fall and all Winter long. Without a deep desire to be away from everything, left alone, free in an almost antisocial way, you likely won't take to Alaska. What's left to say about a place where moose wander downtown and people ignore them?

My last mission was again for the BLM. I was to fly north of

Anchorage, into the mountains above the rugged Matanuska Valley. Matanuska is famous for its 12-pound tomatoes, world record 135-pound cabbage, and pumpkins as big as a Smart Car. I took off on the mission, cruised across the Valley and turned right. My passengers were two BLM workers, weathermen who had to fetch equipment off the mountain before winter came. Their timing was excellent.

The equipment consisted of three temporary weather stations. These portable stations had been set up in the mountains to record and report conditions too remote to get to otherwise. The BLM put them there in the Springtime, mid June in Alaska, and then dismantled them in the Fall, late August. If those seasonal dates seem odd, keep reading.

My job was to fly the two-man team into the mountains, find those stations and bring them back to Anchorage. I landed at each site, then waited while the team took them apart, and loaded them aboard the helicopter. Then I'd fly the whole kit and kaboodle back to their headquarters. The mission was slated for three hours. Lucky for me the snow held off for two of them.

I found the first station, and landed. The team took the portable rig apart quickly, and snugged it inside the aircraft. Then it was off to the second site. We had a bit of trouble finding it, because the haze had turned to a kind of dry, frigid mist found only in Alaska. It wasn't fog, exactly, but a close relative. Call it snog. The temperature had been dropping all morning, and by eleven o'clock, just as we found the second site, it was a chilly thirty degrees. Keep in mind it was August 28th. Number two station was soon secured, and I took off again.

At the third station, I landed and shut the engine off. The team dismantled the equipment, stowed it aboard the helicopter, and I fired back up. By that time the snog had changed to a weather phenomenon somewhat more familiar to me in mid-December Ohio. I called it snow. As I lifted off to return to Anchorage thick flakes swirled around the cockpit. I dove off the mountain, dropping into the valley to maintain visibility. Fortunately the Matanuska was directly under me, and its contours guided me back into Anchorage.

Alaska is more than a place; it's an experience. But having spent a few months there I knew I'd always be a cheechako, someone who's never over-wintered in Alaska. I have a lot of respect—or is it pity?—for anyone who chooses to live in that environment. I landed at SeaAirMotive headquarters, turned off the helicopter, signed off and packed my stuff. Soon I was on a flight to Seattle to meet my family.

I've said that Alaska is a forbidding place. It is that. It's also haunting in its beauty and allure. Something else the locals say about Alaska: once you've been there, you never fully leave it behind.

17

Fly By Helicopter

Back in Ohio I landed my first stable, long-term—I thought—commercial flying job. The position was with a start-up company in Toledo, with a brand new helicopter, and the promise of an experience many pilots never have, the chance to start a flight operation from the ground up. It was also the first time I got canned.

Inexperienced as I was in commercial aviation I should have listened better, or more, or to different veterans when I heard them rate my chance of success. Long-time commercial pilots told me that a helicopter charter business based in Toledo Ohio would never fly. That the overhead, aircraft acquisition costs, lack of a backup aircraft, unknown clientele and on and on would never allow the operation to get off the ground, much less thrive and show a profit.

But, taken in by the prospect of a new company, new aircraft, and a real job instead of chasing bears in the Alaskan bush, I chose to ignore all that to chase a pipe dream instead. In the winter of 1980 I packed up my family and we moved to Toledo Ohio. Just before Christmas I flew to Fort Worth Texas, home of Bell Helicopter, to test fly and accept a brand new out of the box Bell LongRanger—a half-million dollar jewel of an aircraft. On December 24th I flew it back to Ohio with the boss aboard. The fact that my boss, a fellow named Don, decided to schlep along to Texas and back to Ohio with me in the middle of the winter should have told me something: Don didn't trust me. One problem was that it wasn't his money. Funding for the new company—Fly By Helicopter Inc.—came from Don's old, eccentric boss, a fellow named Knight. Mister Knight had wanted to name his company, what else? Fly By Knight, until family members convinced him how unwise that might be.

To further sandbag Fly By's chances, the old man's family was alarmed at dear old Dad's latest money-losing scheme, and they were quite vocal about it. A brand new helicopter, spendy office space, letterhead and advertising and a salary for the likes of me were all part of the family inheritance. As it trickled (hemorrhaged) away, I understood their concern.

The immediate tension came because Don didn't trust me, or anybody else for that matter. Don had heard the very same odds against our success that I had, and he was as nervous as a burglar with Tourette's. Old Mister Knight appointed Don official Fly By Helicopter chief honcho and book-cooker. Don said more than once that if the company went under it would be his "ass on the line." Indeed, Don had little trust in the aviation business. An incident in Fort Worth at the Bell plant did nothing to alleviate his mistrust.

At the factory, I'd flown the aircraft, checked out its systems, made sure everything worked as advertised. Don handed the Bell cashier a big fat check, exactly $573,478.00. How do I remember that almost 40 years later? I still see Don handing it over with a bit of hesitation, right after he slipped it out of his briefcase and showed it to me. You don't forget a sight like that.

In any case, when we prepared to depart back to Ohio, our new half-million dollar bird developed a glitch.

Don and I were preparing to take off, destination Toledo Ohio. I climbed into the cockpit of our new LongRanger, FAA registration N5752F. I zipped through the checklist, mashed the start button, and spun up the blades. Everything appeared to be fine, until just before I lifted the collective. Then a single yellow caution light flickered on the panel. FUEL BOOST. One of the two fuel pumps had malfunctioned. I shut the engine off, and stopped the blades. The Bell guy wandered out to see what the problem was, and I pointed at the yellow light. He nodded. "Back in a second," he said.

Don and I waited. The Bell mechanic returned. In his right hand he held the right tool to fix our errant fuel pump. It was a hammer. In his left hand he had a small section of two-by-four.

The fellow told me to switch on the battery and fuel pump, which I did. Then he crawled under our shiny new, half-million dollar helicopter. He placed the two-by-four against the belly of the machine, and took careful aim. What happened next convinced Don that he needed to update his resume. The Bell mechanic landed three solid wacks with his hammer, smacking the two-by as hard as he could against the underside of the helicopter. Bam-Bam-Bam—he assaulted the belly of our new half-million dollar machine with his buck-forty board, yelling as he did so. "These filters—bang—get—bang—shit in 'em—bang, till they settle down. There, that ought'a fix you right up." He stopped hammering, and yelled again. "Check it now."

I looked at the caution panel. The boost light was indeed out; the problem fixed. I looked at Don, who studied the ground around his shiny Oxfords, the flight to Toledo stretching in front of him. Needless to say, despite the fact that my flight plan had us headed north out of Texas, things went downhill from the time we left the Bell plant.

The upshot of the tale is that, given the financial hurdles in the flying game, Fly By Helicopter was doomed from the start. The way to make a million bucks in aviation is to start with five million. And the quickest business model to make that happen is likely the very one we had: a helicopter charter service, using new (very expensive) equipment, with no backup aircraft, no idea who our customers were, based in Toledo Ohio. We incorporated at the end of October. By mid-March it was obvious that we were taking on water, and the bilge pumps couldn't keep up. The fact that there were no customers was the least of our concern. When we did the financials we realized that, even if we *had* clients, which we didn't, we'd need to charge them a minimum of $500 per flight hour just to break even. That wasn't fantasy; it was harsh reality.

Oddly enough our first obstacle wasn't a lack of customers, or bad weather, or ill will from the boss' family as they watched their legacy skittering down a rat hole. Our first bit of turbulence came courtesy of the FAA. Instead of helping, guiding and promoting our new venture, the Federal Aviation Administration made it as difficult as possible for us to open for business. Our first indication was the application process for an Air Taxi Commercial Operator's permit. The FAA required this document's (accurate) completion before allowing us to conduct charter flights. Don was an attorney; I was a pilot. Between the two of us we should have been able to figure the sucker out. Don and I pored over the FAA ATCO application, a ten-page dossier. We filled in information, checked data, scribbled every jot, tittle, underline, overline, strike-through and iota—using the FAA's very own guidebook to do so—only to have the application rejected not once but three times! We'd fill in a needed change; the Federales would send it back. We'd make the new change; they'd send it back again. A full month passed with no chance to fly, therefore no opportunity to make money. Don was incredulous. He threatened to sue everybody from Ronald Reagan to the Wright brothers.

At one point we contacted the FAA office in Cleveland by conference call to make sure the form was right. Finally, we received our so-called ATCO certificate. We framed it nicely, and hung it on the office wall just so, where the FAA said it had to be displayed at all times. Then we sat in the very same office, staring at our nicely framed ATCO certificate, and at each other, waiting for the phone to ring. We waited. And we waited a bit more. Silence. Utter, deep, expensive silence. What's that C&W song? if the phone don't ring you'll know it's me? Well...

Don scared up a flight or two using his (meager) business connections in Toledo. Those short hops were freebies to get us out and about, and a bit of ink here and there. There was a five-minute flight to a downtown hotel to meet with a group from the Toledo Chamber. Another very short flight to check out a possible site for a helipad, in case we had to land near the center of town. There was precious little need for a helipad; the blessed phone appeared to be disconnected. We knew it *would* be too, and reasonably soon if cash didn't start flowing. Old Mr. Knight had written a check for a million bucks. Half that dough went into the aircraft, and the other half was evaporating in office space, advertising, hangar rent, insurance, salaries and paper clips. I understood why the family was anxious. So was I, and the only thing I had to lose was a job.

That job was in jeopardy from the day I met my new boss. Our styles were opposite; I wanted to fly; Don wanted to stay on the ground where it was safe. Our flight together from Fort Worth to Toledo showed me that he and I had little in common, and worked together poorly.

Don's appointment as CEO of the company had less to do with his legal skill than with his passing acquaintance with aviation. He could identify a helicopter seven out of ten times. He'd been a jet pilot in the Air Force during the Korean conflict, though he never left the country. Don was the least likely person I ever met to be a jet jockey, or a pilot of any kind. The man looked both ways crossing a one-way street. He got sweaty at card tricks.

One incident with Don that showed his lack of trust in my flying skill happened early. I landed at our hangar one afternoon, with Don aboard in the left seat. The pad at the hangar was built specifically for helicopter use, so the dimensions had been tweaked to a skeeter's ass. I knew exactly how much room I needed to land, so I approached the hangar pad, and stopped at a hover. I was about to set the aircraft down when I noticed Don cringing about something, I didn't know what.

"Aren't those blades too close?" he asked, his voice shaky.

There was a ten-foot clearance with the hangar if there was an inch. I tried to ignore Don's comment, pretending he was joking. But I knew a bit of tact was needed; he *was* the guy who signed my checks, after all, teeny as they were. "Uh, well," I stammered. "If you want me to move further away..."

"No, if you think we're okay..."

"I believe so," I said. "We'll look after I shut down."

When everything stopped, Don eased out of the cockpit. He looked up at the rotor blades, which were ten feet away from the hangar, and he shook his head.

One afternoon I flew to Detroit airport to bring Senator Dick Lugar to Toledo for a political event. The flight put another rip in the tattered fabric between Don and me. As I prepared to land with Senator Lugar and his aide, I saw that someone had circled the pad with yellow police tape. It was weighted down, so I knew it would stay put, still... When I landed, without incident, I saw Don in the crowd, and damn if he wasn't cringing again. He told me he was sure I'd stick my tail rotor into that yellow tape and crash. The guy was a bag of snakes.

But our biggest difference was in promoting the business. Don's idea of advertising Fly By Helicopter was death-by-powerpoint in front of groups of business people, showing them pretty pictures of the aircraft, telling them what wonderful things it could do for them, blah-blah-blah, next slide please.

My idea was to put their butts in the seats of the helicopter. I'd fly them where they needed to go—for free. Then I'd pick them back up, another freebie, and maybe even give them a tschotske of some kind emblazoned with the company logo. I wanted to dazzle those executives by doing all this free flying at rush hour, a couple hundred feet over stalled traffic on I-465 to show the benefits of zipping along unimpeded. Some of the big-ticket business people in that room were bringing down the equivalent of a thousand bucks an hour. Sitting in stalled traffic was their idea of a nightmare.

Don's nightmare was the thought of flying them for free. We couldn't be flying the machine around at no charge, even though that's precisely what we'd been doing since we left Texas. We shared thoughts about this, but I knew I'd lose the argument.

One day the Toledo newspaper sent a reporter to do a piece on the new helicopter business in town. The reporter asked Don and me to pose for a photo to accompany his story. The camera guy put us by the hangar, with the helicopter behind. Then he asked if we had something to hold up, a prop of some kind to make the shot more interesting, perhaps a map, or an aviation book? With my usual snark, and much to Don's displeasure, I suggested we hold up our empty wallets. In the photo the following day readers might have noticed a snarky pilot standing next to his disgruntled employer. It would not be long before that pilot left the picture.

Then one day in March we got our very first revenue call for an actual charter flight! Old Mister Knight's daughter called. She and her family were traveling to Colorado for vacation. They were departing from Detroit. Could I land in their back yard in Toledo, she asked, fly them to Detroit Airport, and on their return from out west, fly them back home to Toledo? It wasn't much, an hour flight perhaps, but it was business. I pictured old Mr. Knight's daughter essentially writing a check to herself, but the flight would be in the books, so what the hell. I assured her that we'd be happy to make it happen. Half of it did happen. My logbook will always show half a mission, with the second half missing.

I landed the helicopter in the Knight family backyard, piled on the wife, the husband, and the three lovely kids, and promptly flew them to Detroit Metro Airport. Mission half accomplished. They were in Colorado for a week. Back at Detroit airport from their ski trip, the family called for me to pick them up in Detroit, fly them home to Toledo, and land once more in their back yard. It was such a simple thing really, what could possibly go wrong? I took off that Friday evening at around four to pick them up, and half an hour later I landed at Detroit Metro. I gassed up, met the happy returning vacationers, and off we flew, back to their suburban Toledo home—or so I thought.

In that part of the world, near Lake Erie with its peculiar weather patterns, the likelihood of fog is pretty high. For that reason, and because I always did anyway, I checked the weather forecast prior to flying the mission. The weather guessers in Toledo assured me that all was well. Weather was cold but clear, with nothing in the forecast to set off my alarm bells. But one thing pilots learn early is that forecasts are basically horoscopes with numbers. In what other occupation besides weather person and designated hitter can someone be highly paid for being right less than half the time? Imagine if surgeons only got it right that often. Lawyers would love it; patients, not so much. I suppose that's why they call it *practicing* medicine.

I wasn't practicing anything; I was flying the company owner's daughter, his son-in-law and his three precious grandkids home at Christmastime. No pressure. When I departed Detroit Metro weather was what pilots call CAVU: Ceiling And Visibility Unlimited. A delightful night to fly. At six-thirty, with the owner's family aboard, their eleven-year-old son ensconced as honorary copilot in my left front seat, I took off, expecting to land the family at their home by seven p.m. Flying along fat, dumb and gleeful I glanced ahead into the dank winter sky, expecting to see the Toledo city lights straight ahead at any moment. Ten minutes passed; no lights. Ten more; nothing but darkness. I checked the clock. I should have been seeing lights in Toledo by then. There were no lights, only unremitting darkness. It was the first sign of trouble, followed quickly by the second.

The Detroit radar controller handed me off to the Toledo controller, the air traffic folks whose job it is to guide pilots back and forth without running into each other and thereby making a racket. I thanked Detroit ATC for their service, and dialed up Toledo Express Airport for weather information. What I heard made the skin on my neck prickle. Toledo airport visibility was half a mile— in fog! That explained the lack of city lights. I dialed in the frequency for Toledo radar, and the first thing I heard in my headset was a pilot calling for a missed approach at Toledo because the weather was too bad for him to land. Interesting, I thought.

I took a breath, checked mister gas gauge, and decided I had enough go-juice to continue. I'd try for Toledo once. If I couldn't land, I'd have enough petrol to return to Detroit—barely. I called the controller, asked for the instrument approach to runway 2-5, and told the boss' family I couldn't take them home, exactly. Unless they had an instrument approach in the backyard, landing there was out of the question. The boss' daughter was very gracious, accepting my judgment for the task at hand.

I angled onto the ILS approach at Toledo, dropped to the appropriate altitude and flipped on the autopilot. I set up the cockpit to maximize my chances of a successful instrument approach, including turning down the cabin lights so I'd be sure to see the 'rabbit,' the sequential lighting that would—hopefully—guide me onto the runway at Toledo airport. When the ILS signal came through, the appropriate needles centered in the gauges, and the autopilot latched onto the glide slope. The cockpit looked good: needles centered, descent rate perfect, airspeed conducive to finding the runway and not overshooting it. I didn't have enough fuel to fly the approach twice. The first one had to work, or back to Detroit I'd go.

I asked Toledo tower to check Detroit weather for me. To my

relief Detroit was holding steady. Down I went, into the murk and fog at Toledo, down further, looking for the runway that the gauge said was directly in front of me. As for altitude, the magic number, the so-called Decision Height on that runway, was 884 feet above sea level, in other words 200 feet above the cold, hard ground in Toledo Ohio. If I reached that altitude and didn't see the runway, I had to abandon the approach and schlep back to Detroit. The altimeter passed through 1,000 feet. Nothing but dark, opaque fog. Down, down, down, 950, 900. Nothing. Then, at the last possible second, the flashing lights of the rabbit strobed ahead, guiding me onto the runway. Except for the inside of the freedom bird leaving Vietnam, that murky, fogged-over runway was the most beautiful sight I'd ever seen in aviation.

I landed at the terminal, shut down, escorted my passengers inside and called the boss to tell him of my diversion. Don was gracious on the phone. He jumped into the company car and taxied the Knight family the rest of the way home.

Two days later I was fired. The premise was a maintenance issue I'd mishandled. I turned in my uniforms, cashed my severance check before the ink was dry, and started looking for another seat.

18

Coal Miner's Pilot

My next job wasn't long in coming. Within a week of my dismissal in Toledo my pal Steve, the Bell Helicopter salesman, put me in touch with a construction company/coal mining concern in Evansville Indiana. Steve had sold them a LongRanger, the same aircraft type I'd flown in Toledo, and the company, Koester Contracting, was looking for a pilot to fly it. So off to southwestern Indiana I went, my wife and our young daughter tagging along. Toledo looked awfully good in the rearview.

Evansville Indiana is a placid, some would say backward little city on the Ohio River upstream from Paducah Kentucky. I spent two years in Evansville, flying the boss of the construction/coal mining company and his cohorts here and there, from one job site to another. It was corporate aviation at its best—and worst. For long days I sat in the back of the helicopter waiting, twiddling my thumbs, daydreaming while the company principals did whatever it was they did. Then I flew them back to the shop in Evansville. I felt very much like a glorified taxi driver, and that's pretty much what I was. Many times I'd land the fellows at a work site at eight-thirty in the morning, sit, sit, sit some more, take a nap, wake up, then fly the boss and his cohort home at four p.m. It's a wonder I didn't go stir crazy, and perhaps I did to some extent.

The position demanded a fair amount of versatility. That's my euphemism for the humility I had to acquire to keep working there. The job description contained those four magic words familiar to a lot of corporate pilots: Other Duties As Assigned. My position as company pilot was well compensated, highly specialized and very high profile. My office was in the main part of the building, right across from the bean counter's. At first I thought being in the main office was dandy; I could mix with the big boys, tag along with them for lunch, become a fixture in the company, which appeared to be a first-rate operation. My limited understanding of business people didn't allow me to see the downside of all that visibility; there's a reason they call them bean counters. They spend entire days scouring the bottom line looking for nickels and dimes to pinch. When they see dollars to be saved their eyes light up like in Vegas.

As a pilot, I considered visibility a good thing; clear days were always better than foggy days. But sitting in my Evansville office, in full view of the number crunchers, my feet up, whiling away the hours between flight assignments, proved to be way too much visibility for those concerned with personnel efficiency. The upshot is that, before long the HR, Humiliating Resource people, found things for me to do when I wasn't flying. My training, experience, unique responsibility in the cockpit, and my facility at getting the bosses where they needed to go, and doing it safely, didn't mean I could sit around collecting a paycheck when the blades weren't spinning. Oh no.

I was in my office one morning, third week on the payroll, when the boss came by and told me to follow him. I was sure he had a bit of flying for me to do, a trip somewhere, to retrieve a part perhaps, or to fly one of his minions to a job site. I was mistaken. He led me onto the noisy shop floor, where men were repairing company machinery. In the middle of the shop, next to a water hose and bucket, sat a newer model Lincoln Continental that belonged to the boss's wife. The big Lincoln looked pretty clean to me, but what did I know from dirty cars?

The boss handed me two sets of keys. "Here you go," he said. "Wash Betty's car. When you're done, bring mine around and wash it, too."

He wandered back to his office. I fingered the keys to Betty's Lincoln, imagining what emancipation might feel like. I tried to suppress the irritation rising in me, my ego asking what I'd gotten myself into. I'm a pilot, fer Chrissakes, not a car wash peon. I didn't spend all that time in flight school, then getting shot at in Vietnam so I could wash the boss' wife's Continental. Staring at that car, knowing my assignment was make-work nonsense, I saw all those crude men watching me. I'm sure they were amused at my predicament. I thought about what my aviation colleagues would say if they saw me scrubbing hubcaps. It was mortifying.

Then I thought about my wife. She'd enrolled in college there in Evansville. I thought of my four-year-old daughter who was having fun going with mom to the day care we'd found for her, which she loved. I thought of how my pursuit of a flying job had disrupted their lives for the past two years, and how I owed them a bit of stability. The tension in my family over my peripatetic life in the sky lay just under the surface. My spouse was a smart, stable, patient woman. She'd done the good wife thing, uprooting for my pursuit of a flying career. It had not been easy for her. In the early eighties the feminist movement was still very much a guiding force for us, or so I claimed. She and I had been strong advocates of its principles. I promoted women's rights, equality, the ERA, all the hyper-partisan male/female dialogue that defined that movement. When our daughter was born in 1978 my conviction only got stronger. I looked forward to a day when my woman child had equal access with men to all that life offered.

So it was hard to look at the reality of what my job search had entailed for them. I'd been ruthless in my chase of one flying job after the next, dismissing my family's needs and desires to pursue my career. It was hard to look at the reality of the male prerogative, the incessant demand to take a job, regardless of where or what it was, to be the breadwinner. As I stared at the water bucket, the hose, the rags hanging next to Betty's car waiting to be washed, all that ideology and those high-blown pronouncements clashed together.

I grabbed the wash bucket, and started scrubbing Betty's Lincoln. By the time I'd polished Bill's Mercedes I was getting pretty good at car detailing. Before long I was in charge of cleaning Bill's daughter's car. When I wasn't flying I stocked parts in the tool bins, ran errands for assorted mid-level managers, collated in the office. Then the ultimate distinction: I was given responsibility for keeping Bill's boat shipshape.

The job paid very well, $500 a week, at that time a good salary. Benefits and schedule were excellent, equipment superb. There were no nights or weekends. No on-call time. It was an ideal job. I hated it.

There were a few incidents of note while flying in Evansville. One Friday evening I was dispatched to a job site on the Tennessee River a hundred miles away to bring the troops home. It was a three-hour drive, and those men had been away from home for a week, so the boss took pity on the poor guys and offered to fly them back. Among the crew that evening was the boss' son, Danny. The lad was twenty, and recently married, which may have been why the hurry home. I put Danny in the left front seat of the aircraft, secured everyone else inside and off we went, destination Evansville forty minutes away.

As I said, the crew was pretty tired from a long week of work. I leveled at a thousand feet. Just as I did, Danny dozed off. Since he was strapped in, this didn't appear to pose a problem, but it did, and right away.

The collective stick is directly to the left of the pilot's seat. It's attached to the floor, and it's unguarded. There's another collective just like it next to the passenger seat. Leveling off, I punched on the autopilot, prepared for a simple, carefree flight home. Just as the autopilot took over, Danny lapsed into la-la land, and his left arm dropped onto the collective, ramming it almost full down. Like it had been shot out of the sky, the helicopter plunged toward the earth. We dropped a couple hundred feet in a few seconds. Four guys in the rear yelped, convinced that they were soon to be dead entirely. Danny snapped upright like he'd received an electric shock. I yanked the collective back to its rightful place, and leveled off. Those previously drowsy employees didn't close their eyes again the entire flight.

From the time I began flying in Evansville I understood that, in that part of the world, certain things are chiseled in stone: people are different; people of color are *way* different; non-Christian, non-white, non-males, all are suspect and best avoided. In the far southwest corner of Indiana there are folks, even today, who believe that George Wallace fellow got a bad rap, even though he was kinda liberal. Evansville Indiana was once the site of a prominent base of the Ku Klux Klan. People I worked with, people in line at the grocery store, people on the streets of Evansville used the 'N' word with impunity, and this was 1981. In Evansville, it could have been 1881, it seemed. As an extension of this prejudice my employer went out of his way to avoid hiring minority workers, to the point of endangering his company.

In the spring of 1982 the company was in financial trouble. The bottom fell out of the coal market, the company bread and butter, and things looked bad for all of us. Bill told me to report to work only three days a week. Jack, the company bean stalker hinted in no uncertain terms that I should look elsewhere. "You should look elsewhere," Jack said. It was very subtle. I did as he suggested, polishing my resume' and sending it hither and yon.

Then a call for bids came in, for an earthmoving contract with the potential to move the earth for the company, and to turn things around. The work required expertise the company had in depth, moving dirt in large quantities. The contract offered long-term, lucrative proceeds, and the job site was nearly in our backyard. Officials familiar with the offering said that the work was ours for the taking. Just one hitch. As a government contract, it required minority hiring.

Incredibly, faced with bankruptcy, and possible business failure the bosses declined to bid on the project! I was astonished. Clearly, no one else was; it was business as usual. Not long afterward I wandered into work on a Monday morning. As I came through the door Bill called me into his office. Great, I thought. Here it comes. Sure enough the first words he said to me were exactly these: "How much do you think we can get for that helicopter?" Funny how our minds work. I was hoping he'd ask me to wash Betty's car.

In a week the aircraft was gone, brokered for sale by a company in Janesville Wisconsin that, in an interesting twist, I'd wind up working for. Another aviation lesson: if the aircraft is sold, fly it to its new home. I flew the helicopter to Janesville and parked it on the ramp. I stashed a copy of my resume under the pilot's seat so a new owner might see it, and give me a shout. Yet another lesson about the flying game: always keep your options open.

Leaving Evansville was a very good thing, for a number of reasons. I'd met a fellow pilot there named Jack Cunningham. Jack was putting the Air Medical program together at Deaconess Hospital in Evansville. I'd given Jack a copy of my resume' months before. When he heard I was looking for a seat he mentioned an opening for a pilot in Iowa City, wherever that was. It was an Air Medical job at the University of Iowa Hospitals and Clinics. I looked the job over, gave it about thirty seconds of consideration, and off I went. I wouldn't leave Iowa City for twenty years.

19

ER In the Sky

He was a farm kid doing a man's work. The machine caught him, tossed him around like dirty laundry, chewed him up and spit him out. Farming is dangerous, unsentimental work. The boy was seven. It seemed likely he'd never see eight.

When I took off from Elkader hospital in Northern Iowa that February night in 1984 I couldn't help looking at the youngster on the cot beside me. From my seat in the cockpit he was three feet away, a flimsy Plexiglas partition between us. I could reach across the panel and touch him, and I did. I put my left hand on his bloody, tattered sheet. I touched his shoulder, careful to avoid the IV line snaked across the linens into his arm. The flight nurse hovered over him, her face glowing in the lights of the instrument panel. Two IV bags swayed with the movement of the aircraft. The heart monitor showed the boy's craggy sinus rhythm, heart rate frantic and rapid because of his low fluid volume. I went back to my flying. At two thousand feet, snow covered farm ground passing below, stars painting the sky, I aimed the helicopter for Iowa City.

The thought forced its way forward, one of the reasons Air Med flying attracted me so. He could be my kid. My own child hit by a car, injured in a fall, critically ill with some unsentimental childhood disease. Beyond that, he could be a family member, a father with a heart attack or cancer, mother with a blood disorder, diabetic crisis, a stroke. He could be a brother after an accident on the freeway's icy surface, a sister in the middle of a pregnancy crisis. This child could be someone I know and love.

I had a seven-year-old kid at the time. My daughter was the boy's age. As I raced across the night sky she was safe at home in her bed under clean, dry sheets. She had no life-threatening injury, no traumatized body and no IVs or blood-soaked linens. My child was safe and warm that night, protected from the harsh reality of brutal work that farm kids do as soon as they can walk it seems. So I couldn't help thinking of my own, and from there to the next clear thought. This is someone's child. As is everyone.

The helipad lights gleamed atop the hospital. I landed. The offload crew met the helicopter. With the flight nurse directing, they eased the boy's cot into the frigid night, and wheeled him inside to an OR, and then into intensive care. The piece of equipment he fell into, a grain auger, had grabbed him with its razor-sharp blades, and banged him around in its maw. His legs were sliced open, arms broken and bruised. His skull was fractured. He'd lost a lot of blood. His prognosis was poor enough that his parents were told not to get their hopes up.

My life saving machine scooped him up, flew him as fast as possible to a trauma center, and gave him a chance to survive. This was the flying I'd always wanted to do. It wasn't herding bears, looking for fish in the ocean, taxiing businessmen to appointed rounds. This was important. *"The heart of a man can want no more than this..."*

In June 1983 I put Evansville in the rearview, and sped off to Iowa City, home to the University of Iowa Hospitals and Clinics. The Air Medical helicopter program at UIHC is called AirCare. My bouncing around for aviation work was done. I would leave Iowa City twenty years later with a logbook full of time, a bushel of memories, and the satisfaction of a career I'd wanted forever.

The Sky Behind Me

As I left Interstate 80 that scorching June day in '83, and drove south on Dubuque Street, past frat houses lining the grassy banks of the fabled Iowa River, the hair on my arms tingled. It was one of those welcome home to a place you've never been before feelings.

I'd been hired by Omniflight Helicopters, at that time based in Janesville, Wisconsin. Omniflight brokered the sale of the helicopter I flew in Evansville, so I got to know a few of their pilots and admin staff. Omni was the second biggest provider of Air Med helicopters in the U.S. at that time, with fifteen aircraft posted at twelve hospitals. In Jansesville I scribbled the right documents, filled in the columns and blocks and recorded my commercial flying credentials. Once the FAA was happy, my creds and the required paperwork done, I flew an orientation hop with Omniflight's director of operations, a fellow named Marshall. Once Marshall was happy with my performance I was cleared to fly air medical missions. I'd flown in a big airplane over Iowa a time or two—it is in the middle of flyover country, after all—but I'd never spent any time there. Iowa has a surplus of corn, more pigs than people and a lot of flat forced landing areas. It's greener than green in all directions, and has a relatively uncluttered sky. Was it heaven? No, but pretty close. I looked forward to getting started.

Air Medical flying is an ideal job for helicopter pilots, at least those with a family and looking for stability. The work is the definition of steady. There are more ways people can maim themselves than Carter has peanuts. The job requires overnight shifts, but they're close to home, at the base hospital. The schedule has a lot of flexibility with a seven shifts on, seven off arrangement being common. The pay is at least industry standard, or higher depending on the equipment flown. The work is interesting, different every shift, and extremely gratifying.

In a medical emergency or trauma, EMTs or a doctor determine if the helicopter is needed. If so, they call the base hospital to request the Air Med team. The pilot accepts or rejects the flight based on weather and other criteria, and the team goes flying, or not. When I started Air Med in 1983 the medical team consisted of a pilot and one flight nurse. We thought nothing of this bare-bones arrangement at the time. It was industry standard. I'd take off with one nurse, for the worst-mauled, most fragile, the sickest patients. Needless to say any nurse attracted to Air Medical has a large ego, and a lot of skill, or they wouldn't aspire to the position. In 1985 a second nurse was added to the crew.

When I arrived in Iowa City one of the two pilots at the program had just quit. There weren't many times in my career when my hiring doubled the staff, but that was one of them. Speaking of bare bones, an appropriate analogy in the medical arena, here's another one. The commercial Air Med business was eleven years old when I came into it, and the standard pilot staffing was two per program at that time. Two pilots shared the duty week after week, month after month. Hospitals demanded that a pilot be on duty in the hospital at all times, and protocols dictated that the helicopter should be airborne within five minutes of an emergency call. With 168 hours in a week, and pilot on call demand being 24/7, that meant Air Med pilots at the time were on duty 84 hours a week. Each pilot was required to relieve the duty pilot if he were to 'time out,' that is, to exceed his FAA-mandated crew rest requirement. In other words Air Med pilots were at work in one capacity or another all the time. Technically I couldn't sit at home sucking a beer, since I may have had to report back to work at the hospital, couldn't leave town, couldn't be sick or injured myself, lest the program go without a pilot.

Seems insane looking back on it, but pilots did sign up for the arrangement, and I was one of them. There were numerous reasons pilot staffing was that limited. For one, it was a simple case of supply and demand. Helicopter contracts are always bare bones for staffing, partly because helicopter flying is almost always single pilot. This says nothing about a pilot's marital status. It means one pilot is all that's needed in the cockpit. Another reason is that hospital Air Med programs procure services based on the lowest bid, with several operators competing against each other. The company that provides the service cheapest wins the bid. No surprise there. One of the few variables in the process is pilot salary, so the fewer pilots the better.

In 1983, because of the lax oversight and collective confusion about crew rest regulations, the FAA was indirectly complicit in that staffing arrangement. There was a gray area, the definition of 'duty' time, versus 'off-duty' time. Companies argued that the pilot was off duty if he wasn't flying; the FAA said he was on duty if he was *available* to fly. Thus, any time I was in the hospital, according to the Feds, I was on duty, therefore subject to the regs. By the company's interpretation, if I wasn't in the cockpit I was off duty.

The standoff got worse before it got better. The company claimed that a pilot could 'rest' inside the hospital. The FAA said 'rest' meant no potential for flying. Between the two entities, operators and the FAA, the nit-picking went on for years, as pilots wanted relief, the addition of a third—or fourth pilot FTE; operators and the hospitals waited to see who'd blink first, and cough up the necessary financing. Meanwhile, patients had to be flown, so pilots were caught in the middle. As goal oriented as pilots are, we didn't demand time off. We wanted to fly.

Another obstacle to more pilot staff came from pilots themselves. When I started flying Air Med it was common practice to pay a nominal per-hour bonus for every revenue flight logged at the contract. The money was pooled, then divided evenly, and disbursed at months end. It wasn't much, ten dollars per flight hour as I recall, but the bonus did supplement our salaries. So two pilots sharing the bonus received more net income than three pilots would have, creating resistance to a third position.

Suffice to say that, at least in 1983, two pilots per program was the norm. I found myself half the pilot staff in Iowa City with a fellow named Charles. The nursing staff didn't like Charles very much. I heard their antipathy to him, and sensed that very soon I might be the only pilot. I was right. Within 6 months of my arrival in Iowa, Charles was shown the door, and I was lead pilot, along with a new hire, a guy named Bob. Those proceedings taught me a lot about the politics and day-to-day administration in hospital flying. The fact that I was not a hospital employee but vendor personnel figured in my longevity. I understood that my role, especially as lead pilot, was to act as liaison between the company and the client, tend to routine operations, put out brush fires, make sure the aircraft was maintained properly and somewhere way down the list of duties to fly patients.

I make it sound onerous; it was anything but. I immersed myself in every aspect of the program, played nice with others, and enjoyed learning along the way.

In the hospital the first day, Marshall handed me a pager. He showed me the pilot quarters, the cafeteria, the refuel site. He gave me a tour of the helipad, dispatch office and maintenance shed. Before he left he gave me this advice: fly safe, stay away from the nurses, and call me if you crash so I can bring you a new aircraft. Then he left, and I was on my own.

My orientation flight at the hospital was with the company check pilot, Jack Cunningham, the fellow I'd met in Evansville. To make the insurance guy happy I had to fly five hours in the contract aircraft with Jack. It wasn't a hard transition, but it was my first experience in that particular aircraft, a French helicopter called an AStar. The AStar was just like any other single-engine helicopter I'd flown, with one important difference. The rotor blades turned the opposite way from what I was used to. This doesn't sound significant, and it's not, except that certain control inputs are opposite because of it.

The difference took some getting used to. Depending on which way the main blades turn, the foot pedals must be moved accordingly. In an American helicopter, a Huey for instance, the blades turn (looking down) counterclockwise. In the AStar they turn clockwise. In the Huey, the power pedal is on the left; in the French machine it's on the right. Once I flew the AStar for a few hours it became second nature. But having flown 3,000 hours in American equipment beforehand, I had to think about which pedal to push. (Imagine having to think about which way to turn the handlebars on a bicycle.) The puzzlement was compounded by the fact that any time the AStar was in the hangar for maintenance, our backup machine was a Bell product. Jack said, "just fly the nose." I did that, and it worked every time.

The AStar's French name is the Ecureuil, meaning squirrel. They named it right. The AStar has a mind of its own. It's far and away the hardest to maneuver helicopter I ever had the pleasure to fly. A pilot who claims he landed an AStar well the first time is lying. For the first few months the flight nurses referred to my arrivals as snowflake landings, meaning no two were alike. When I got within six inches of the ground, the AStar's so called ground cushion, a pillow of air built up under the rotor system, had sufficient mass that it affected control inputs. Like trying to squash a balloon, only to have the thing squirt away, landing the AStar required a bit of finesse. Wayne's advice years before to treat it like a woman didn't work; the AStar had the temperament of a mean (male) drunk.

But for all its aerodynamic quirks the AStar is an ideal single-engine Air Med helicopter. Its interior space is wide open for easy patient access, with lots of wall space to hang medical junk, and lots of glass for good visibility. Range is around 300 miles without refueling. The Iowa City aircraft had a few novel items, things I'd never seen on a helicopter, things that made me scratch my head till I understood what they were, and why they were there.

One of those features was a warning horn, a loudspeaker,

installed on the belly of the aircraft. I'd not seen such a thing before, so I asked Jack about it. He told me the horn had been ordered by the hospital. It was connected to the low rotor rpm warning system, Jack said. If the engine failed, when the rpm sagged, and the aircraft dropped from the sky, the horn would automatically blare. Like a car horn honking when the motor dies and the brakes fail, the horn would (allegedly) screech a warning to anyone beneath the plummeting aircraft.

The history of the horn was a bit unsettling. Before I came to Iowa City a pilot had experienced an engine failure in the hospital's AStar. He did a good job putting the machine on the ground, but, as might be imagined, the episode worried the staff. Hospital administrators were concerned for the safety of their people, of course. Beyond that, they saw a liability issue. If the aircraft toppled onto someone strolling by, the unfortunate person it clobbered could sue the hospital out of every bandage and bed pan they owned. The horn was installed to address that exposure. The assumption being that, if the aircraft engine failed, and the machine hurtled from the sky, the horn would chase anyone away. The theory was sound; the execution, I wasn't so sure about. Deer tend to freeze in headlights, even in Iowa.

From the presence of that horn I gained another valuable insight to Air Medical aviation. I flew critical patients. But every time I lifted off I also flew the hospital's reputation. This understanding came in handy many times in the twenty years I lifted from the roof of the hospital, and then landed on it again. In many ways I was a flying billboard for the institution. It was something I kept in mind, always.

Something that figured in the flying was how much leeway medical personnel had in aviation decisions. At this late date I'm certain the FAA would not have approved that horn attachment. In 1983 no one bothered to check. It reminded me of my frustrating efforts a few years prior in Toledo to acquire an operating permit.

I knew that if the subject of the horn was broached, the FAA would kill the idea. Easier to obtain forgiveness than permission. In simple terms, the company heard the client hospital's request, and they installed the horn. A small thing, perhaps. But it spoke to a larger issue. The overlap between medical and aviation was often too broad, and lines of authority often blurred. It never became a critical issue in Iowa City. Elsewhere in the country it did, sometimes with damaging results.

When I started, in the mid eighties, Air Medical aviation was in its adolescence. The first program took off from St. Anthony Hospital in Denver, in 1972. Iowa City's program launched in 1979, and was fifth in the nation. It was an exciting time in the Air Med industry. As with any pioneering endeavor we felt our way along, making up protocols and procedures as situations arose. It was also a time filled with peril, because the limitations were unexplored. That in itself would not have been problematic. But the combination of goal-oriented people, desperately ill patients and shiny-new technology screaming to be used conspired to hide certain realities. Weather is a primary danger, and weather doesn't give a flying flip if a badly-injured patient is eleven years old, what their injuries are, or their prognosis.

The Air Med business is just that, of course, a business, thus subject to all the competitive pressures of any other. Several helicopter operators vie for lucrative hospital contracts, to place as many aircraft as possible on hospital pads. Because of the exorbitant cost of operating a helicopter, and the relative similarity in overhead costs, operators look for efficiencies in every corner and closet. One place they trim costs is in aircraft equipment. The AStar I first flew in Iowa City had minimal equipment for communication and navigation, a cross between the Wright brothers and Professor Marvel. The front office had a crude GPS box, with just nine waypoints available, compared to more than

300 waypoints in current versions. The instrument panel had the standard 'T' configuration: altimeter, vertical speed, airspeed, gyro horizon and electronic compass, but little else. There was a wet compass, almost useless, since it danced and gyrated with the slightest control input. Besides engine and transmission gauges, and an odd blinking light or two, the cockpit was Spartan, not much different than the little Hughes I'd learned to fly at Fort Wolters.

Cost was one consideration. Weight was another. Any pilot worth a nickel is always mindful of the weight of his or her aircraft. Every body, heart monitor, oxygen tank, even IV kits and bandages weigh something, and it all adds up. And if it adds up to one ounce more than the aircraft can (legally) lift there's a problem. The AStar had a listed maximum weight of 4,300 pounds. At 4,301 pounds it would fly, but the pilot would be in violation of FAA regulations. The only variable is fuel weight. As soon as a helicopter pilot takes off he's looking for a gas station. So put on enough fuel to complete the mission? Or take a chance with the (legal) load I have on board? I'd leave the pad with the fuel gauge reading 70%, which was about 100-gallons, enough go juice for an hour and thirty minutes. Gas stations being few and far between in Iowa, the mental math was a constant.

I was ready to start flying Air Med. First I had some concerns, so during my orientation flight I asked Jack for answers. He addressed my questions one by one:

B: "What if a patient dies?"

J: "They're not authorized to die on the helicopter."

"Why not?"

"Flight nurses aren't allowed to pronounce people dead. But you know what?"

"What?"

"The Highway Patrol can."

"Can flight nurses write tickets?"

"Nope."

"That's not fair."

B: "What if the patient is too heavy?"

J: "Make two trips."

B: "What if the flight nurse tells me to hurry up?"

J: "Lean forward. It looks like you're going faster."

B: "What if I can't find a hospital in town?"

J: "Look for a crane. There's always a crane at a hospital."

B: "What if a caution light comes on with a patient on board?"

J: "Hit the dimmer switch so the nurse doesn't see it."

B: "What if the weather turns crummy, and I can't get home?"

J: "What do hospitals have lots of, besides lousy food, pissy doctors and sick people?"

B: "Beds?"

J: "You got it. And they're free to stranded pilots, or so I've heard."

My briefing done, Jack scribbled his signature in my logbook. I got the requisite five flight hours in the AStar so the insurance man was happy, and became an official Air Medical helicopter pilot. I knew enough to get in way over my head if things turned brackish. It was hard to know how much I'd absorbed. Jack left for Omniflight HQ in Janesville, and I was on my own. When the pager announced that first flight, I found out how little of his advice I'd absorbed.

20

Air Medical

July 7th 1983 was my 35th birthday, and my first day on duty at the hospital. Halfway through lunch at the cafeteria the pager bawled like a hungry newborn, its siren sound squawking on my belt loop. "AirCare Team this is a go to Ottumwa, multiple trauma." My arms prickled, and the hair on my neck stood up. My first Air Med mission. I left a half-eaten sub sandwich on the tray, and scrambled out of the lunchroom. It wouldn't be the last time I threw away a perfectly good meal.

I keyed the elevator, and hopped aboard for a quick trip to the roof of the hospital. As I aimed my special key at the elevator slot marked 'Helipad,' and twisted it my hand wobbled, and my heart raced. The door zipped shut, the elevator rumbled to the top of the hospital. The door swung wide and a bolus of heat greeted me. Glaring sunlight blasted the helipad, and the shiny black and white AStar gleamed in the summer sun. I untied the blades, walked around the aircraft checking that all was secure, and waited for the flight nurse. As I climbed into the cockpit one word danced in my head—Ottumwa. I'd seen it on the chart, and knew roughly where it was, but I'd never been there. I hoped I had no trouble finding it.

By that time I'd flown for fifteen years, and logged three thousand hours in the air, so the mission seemed pretty simple. Take off, aim for Ottumwa, land, grab the patient and reverse course to home base. What could be easier? But the gush of new information was almost overwhelming: navigation, fuel management, weather, radio calls, air traffic control, any one of dozens of potential mechanical failures, requests from the flight nurse, other aircraft, patient updates from the dispatcher, the list went on and on. I was glad my first mission occurred during the day, and a clear day at that.

Then the flight nurse shuffled across the pad and boarded the aircraft. LuAnn had been with the AirCare team for several years, and she had tons of experience. As she hopped in and buckled up I asked if she'd been to Ottumwa, and she assured me that she had, many times. As it turned out it was a silly question; Ottumwa wasn't just the boyhood home of Radar O'Reilly, it was also one of the AirCare program's bigger customers.

I punched the start button and brought the engine up to max enthusiasm. The blades lashed overhead, gauges in the green, radios blinking on with their maze of yellow lights. I called the dispatcher to announce my departure, and lifted the collective. The helicopter danced a bit, then hovered, kicking up a froth of dust. I checked the gauges once more, scanned ahead, and took off. My heart in my throat I angled southwest, next stop Ottumwa Iowa.

Leveling at two thousand feet, I scanned a sea of corn, beans, and plump little piggies. The view out the front window put me in mind of a painting I'd seen of a fellow with a pitchfork standing next to his daughter, a Gothic window behind them. But despite its board-flat reputation, Iowa is mostly rolling hills, and an expanse of rich, fertile farmland that was once covered in prairie grass. Ahead of my flight path small towns sprouted water towers, all splashed with graffiti and faded tributes to everlasting love: Jake hearts Brenda, KG/LA, Mary me (sic) Tracy. Head-high letters announced town names: Kalona, Keota, South English, Sigourney. I made an effort to orient myself, to learn every section line and silo of the landscape.

Nearing Ottumwa, I saw something that made me laugh. Jack was right; on the north side of town a crane pierced the cloudless sky. It was parked at the hospital, its angular frame a crude navigation device to home in on. I steered toward the crane, and landed on the Ottumwa hospital pad without further ado. If LuAnn was impressed she didn't make a fuss.

Twenty minutes later she and I climbed back into the aircraft with our patient. I fired up the Lycoming and launched into the steamy Iowa sky. Beside me on the cot lay the badly injured female accident victim. She'd been on her way to work, fell asleep, and crossed the centerline where she met an oncoming semi. Under a mass of bandages and splints, casts, braces and devices she was barely visible. She had an IV in each arm, and a breathing tube jammed in her gullet. LuAnn tended the IVs, mashed the ambu bag, a bag the size of a loaf of bread that forced air into the patient's lungs, watched the girl's heart rhythm, took vitals. She was busy every second. Like all the flight nurses she seemed to love it. With their credentials and training, the flight nurse staff was a close-knit group with almost no attrition in their ranks. Of the seven I first flew with in 1983, four were still flying when I left twenty years later.

On that flight to Ottumwa I saw how well the integration of aviation and medicine worked. In the front office I had plenty to do, with navigation, weather avoidance, communication and just moving the sticks around to keep the aircraft upright. Ideally, the patient could levitate off the cot and recite sonnet 29 and I wouldn't hear their bootless cries. In the cabin the flight nurses tended to the patient, doing whatever magic they did to keep them alive, sedate, and reasonably stable, with little regard for life outside in the open air. The sky could turn green and rain rat turds and the nurses wouldn't notice. In other words, once airborne with a job to do, between flying and a patient to tend, there was almost no overlap between roles. It was only on the ground that the two worlds intersected, sometimes to the detriment of both.

A case in point was the five-minute lift-off rule. Air Med programs advertised their ability to have a helicopter in the air toward an accident victim or medical emergency within five minutes. At least in theory the boast sounded great, even necessary, but it ignored certain aviation realities. For one thing a pilot is required by regulation to check weather prior to any flight. Depending on the time of day or night, and depending on the weather itself, that process could take several minutes.

The more important consideration was to make sure the machine is airworthy prior to takeoff. If it's bad on the ground it will only get worse in the air, and several helicopter accidents have proven that.

An Air Med ship in Reno Nevada crashed in '84, killing a pilot and mechanic, when someone left a cowl unlatched on a hurried takeoff and the cover flew up into the rotor system. In Billings Montana a pilot took off with a weather cover installed on a control surface. It ripped loose shortly after takeoff and fouled the tail rotor. The aircraft crashed a few blocks from the hospital. In Hartford Connecticut an aircraft crashed into wires at an accident scene, wires that had not been identified before he arrived. A Des Moines helicopter nearly had an accident when the pilot took off for a patient flight, only to discover that the mechanic had drained the tail rotor gearbox of oil. When the pilot landed thirty minutes later, the tail rotor, lacking lubrication, was within seconds of seizing up. All these incidents had a common theme; a rush to get airborne plus a degree of complacency, a deadly combination in aviation.

I sensed a counterintuitive need to slow down, take my time, make sure the aircraft was ready to fly, and that I was, too. But the pressure was always there to get moving, take off; in time I learned that a lot of that pressure was self-imposed.

~*~

My first Air Med mission was almost complete. The hospital in Iowa City appeared, (with two cranes,) and I landed on the home pad. After shutdown, the flight nurse and patient disappeared into the hospital. I scribbled paperwork to complete my first hospital mission. The next 3,199 were a variation on that theme.

Surely it wasn't the alarm clock already? I couldn't figure out what the hell the God-awful screech was. I sat up in my bunk, blinked sleep-goo out of my eyes and stared at the clock: 1:53 a.m. As I swam up through the cobwebs I realized the noise was coming from the pager in the pocket of my flight shirt. Then my brain connected, and I heard the dispatcher's voice. "...Go... scene flight near Iowa City airport. AirCare team, go..!"

My first on-scene mission as an Air Medical pilot, and it happened in the middle of the night. A scene flight was just that: a call from Paramedics at the scene of an accident or other medical emergency. No hospital crane this time, just an ambulance rig and, usually, a bloody mess for a patient. I was about to discover how simple it would be to cut my career short by having an accident of my own.

I leapt out of bed, and hobbled into my flying clothes. Then I yawned toward the elevator where I met Jan, the night flight nurse. Jan rubbed sleep from her eyes, and stared at me. "What do we have?" she said.

She's asking me? It was my first night at the hospital for Pete's sake. "Uh, an MVA," I said. "Motor vehicle accident," I added stupidly, realizing Jan likely knew what an MVA was. She'd been a flight nurse for three years; I could barely spell MVA.

The elevator whisked up nine floors and zipped open. We boarded the helicopter. I cranked the engine, flicked the radios on, called dispatch and lifted off at 2:05 a.m. The accident scene wasn't hard to find. Five miles away a huddle of flashing fireworks on the ground showed two emergency vehicles, and a sheriff's car. I steered toward the beehive of lights, and circled overhead, looking for a place to land. The accident vehicle was easy to spot as well; it was upside down on a bridge, the only finished section of highway under construction. The driver of the ill-fated vehicle had been zipping down the dirt road in the dark. Too late, he saw that the bridge structure stuck up a foot higher than the dirt path. The dune buggy hit the raised concrete and flipped over. The driver and his girlfriend launched like astronauts, their bodies scrabbling along the concrete. Reentry was tough. She was dead at the scene. He was all busted up, but still breathing.

I landed in a cloud of rotor-blown dust, and put the collective down. Jan jumped out and raced to the patient. I secured the blades, and prepared the cot. This'll be easy, I thought. My first scene flight out of the way, no glitches, close to home, simple. Then I saw it. A dark metal pole two feet from my tail rotor. One twitch of the left pedal on landing and I would have hit it. I'd almost become an accident statistic myself. My arms chilled, just like they had when the pager went off. Same feeling.

Circling above the crash sight, I'd focused on the accident, mesmerized by the flashing lights, and the hypnotizing mayhem at the scene. The landing spot was pitch dark, and the pulsing ambulance overheads had reduced my night vision. There was no way in hell to see that pole. It was three feet tall, jammed into the ground for no apparent reason other than to catch an unwary rookie pilot by the tail. The gray-black marker was hard to spot ten feet away. Small wonder I missed it from the cockpit with debris flying everywhere, and blinded by emergency flashers. If I'd hit that pole on landing I would have been calling Marshall in the morning, asking him to send a new helicopter. On my first shift. I took a deep breath, thanked the aviation god for giving me a pass, and took it as a teachable moment.

Then a curious thing happened: I got mad. My gut welled in hot anger. Anger because I hadn't anticipated the obstacle. Because no one at the scene had surveyed the landing site. Because I half expected them to do so, when it was my responsibility. I actually, believe it or don't, walked over in the dark with nobody watching and kicked the daylights out of that blasted pole. Guess what? It didn't budge.

But I did; I got the message. I knew there were dangers I couldn't anticipate, and the thought disturbed me. I looked for an upside to it, and it came right away. Call it air sense. Why did I think an extra ten seconds made a difference to that patient? Ten seconds might have shown me that pole. Also, it was a nice warm night, why not tell Jan to open the helicopter door and look out, like I'd expected my crew to do in Vietnam? I may have been the only pilot around, but I didn't own the only set of eyeballs. The solution was obvious; I'd take my time, refuse to get caught up in the hypnotizing charm of flashing lights, use whatever resources I could and do what I was trained to do, fly the damned helicopter.

My foot tingling from the kick, I stared at the pole once more, and planned my takeoff to avoid it. The flight home was uneventful. For me that is. The night offered another introduction. This one was to the other side of Air Med flying: patients die. When Jan scurried back to the helicopter with the battered victim, what I saw was a mass of bloody blankets with two mangled legs wrapped in pressure trousers. The man was barely alive. Every time the EMT pumped his chest his ears spouted blood. Every time the ambu bag squeezed air into his lungs, and then let go, speckles of blood tinged the tube. His pupils were one over two, a sign that his brain had been banged around like a cabbage in a bucket. He was only the second multiple trauma victim I'd seen since the war, but even I knew he was taking his next to last ride in a motor vehicle. His girlfriend lay under a sheet on the hard concrete in the middle of the bridge.

I landed on the home pad at 2:30. Jan whisked the patient to the ER. The staff worked on the fellow until four a.m. Then they gave up.

~*~

I'd been an Air Med pilot less than twenty-four hours, but it was obvious to me that Jack's snarky comments carried a lot of truth.

"What if you can't decide to go or not?" It was a legitimate question; weather can change pretty quickly in that part of the country.

"Here's the dirty little secret," Jack said. "Patients got to the hospital long before they had a helicopter; they'll get there long after it's gone, too."

As much as I liked to think we saved lives, swooping from the sky like the cavalry coming, air medical helicopters and crews can't be directly connected with saving lives. There's anecdotal evidence that they make a difference in the so-called Golden Hour post trauma. But the majority of our missions were routine transports, for stable patients. One reason programs have proliferated is that, as rural emergency rooms shut down, because they're broke or nearly so, patients needing emergency medical care have the helicopter take them to a bigger hospital. There are currently 74 air ambulance companies that operate approximately 850 helicopters in the United States. The NTSB estimates that 400,000 patients and transplant organs are transported by helicopter each year. For a number of reasons, the expansion of aircraft programs has had a deleterious affect on the accident rate, a concern since day one.

I'd been an Air Med pilot less than a month when I saw first hand one of the reasons too many helicopters can add to the accident rate. It's called competition.

Weather was marginal, so I told the dispatcher to call me before paging a flight. It was a routine request. Pilots had final authority to accept or reject any mission.

The call jangled my phone at nine p.m. In Burlington, 60 miles southeast of Iowa City, a heart attack victim needed the helicopter.

The sky was newly dark, and I'd been to Burlington only once. It was late July, and weather had been clear all month. That day and night, misting rain and low clouds persisted in central Iowa most of the day and into the evening.

I told the dispatcher I'd check weather, and call him back. What I heard from the weather guesser wasn't good. Rain and scud hung over Eastern Iowa, not forecast to clear until after midnight. The numbers for accepting the mission were marginal but legal. It was a maddening middle zone situation. When visibility is zero the decision is simple; we didn't fly. Marginal weather was the real dilemma.

I grabbed the phone, my fingers dancing on the redial as I debated with myself whether or not to fly to Burlington. Hesitant, I put the phone down. This, I thought, is the Air Medical dilemma; the weather's not good only because it's not bad. The numbers the weatherman gave me are flyable—ceiling and visibility both above accepted margins. If I had lots of experience at the hospital, and if I'd been to Burlington several times, and if I'd flown with that nurse, and if... There were a lot of ifs. Knowing the team awaited my decision I stewed about it for a few minutes, armpits heating up under the pressure.

Was it indecision? Or something else? Did I secretly fear going out there, being unsure of what to do if the weather went south? Did I not trust my own ability? That's absurd, I thought. I flew in a combat zone for Pete's sake. Surely I can fly 60 miles to Burlington Iowa and home again. Then something else came back to me, something Jack said in my orientation.

"What if the weather guesser's wrong, and it's worse than you thought?"

"They're the only guys that, if they're right 50 percent of the time they get a raise."

I called the dispatcher and declined the mission. He thanked me for checking, and hung up. I second guessed myself for another fifteen minutes. Then I went to bed where I stewed a bit longer. I tossed and twisted, trying to convince myself I'd made the right call. Until I flew Air Med I never realized how goal-oriented I really was.

A while later the other Air Med dilemma arose for the first time in my career, driving the tension up a notch. I was half asleep, still fretting, wondering about our heart attack victim in Burlington. But I didn't need to worry very much. As it turned out he was on his way to our hospital by way of a competing helicopter service. In the Air Med business it's called helicopter shopping. If one service declines a flight, a requestor often calls a competing service.

The dispatcher called. What he said made me angry, and I didn't even know why. "Just so you know," he said. "Lifeguard from Cedar Rapids accepted the mission to Burlington. They'll be landing here in ten minutes."

"No pressure there," I muttered. It was the first time I'd faced competition in the flying game. I'd felt the urgency of combat, the demand to go no matter what. But the Army couldn't fire me. In the commercial world I had a paycheck to protect. Getting killed in Vietnam would be a bad thing. In Iowa I had a family, bills and a reputation as a professional, not to mention the impulse to fly patients. I learned to deal with the pressure, but it was unsettling.

Looking back, I realized that flying in combat for a year, and escaping unscathed, I must have done something right. It was my commitment to safety. Another pilot's risk had no affect on my decision. Helicopter shopping was a down side of the job, one that would happen time and again. Safety is a strange goal. We know we're safe only when nothing happens. It felt bad to hear my competitor's aircraft clatter onto the helipad that night. But I knew there'd be plenty more opportunities to make the right call. And those chances weren't long in coming.

21

Missions

There are missions in every pilot's career that stand out either for a fond memory, or something we'd rather forget. My downwind landing in Vietnam was a forgettable event, except that it taught me a lot of caution. I'd come close to a midair collision that evening in the Camp Eagle traffic pattern. The grenade in my cabin could have had a much different outcome. It seems that in aviation more than any other activity the test comes first, then the lesson.

The sky was crystal clear that chilly November evening. Forecast was good. Weather appeared to be stable for the remainder of the night. So when the call came in I accepted the flight, and saddled up.

The patient had a heart attack. He was 68, a farmer whose house was twenty miles from the hospital. When I took off the temperature was forty degrees, dew point 35 and wind west at six knots. There were no clouds, and the sky was awash with stars. A beautiful winter night. I lifted the collective at ten-thirty, climbed to 1,500 feet and leveled the aircraft. The scene was close by, so I didn't need or want more altitude. As I lifted off the helipad the Cedar Rapids radar controller called me. He was closing up shop for the night, he said. He noticed my takeoff, and wished me a good flight.

I thanked him for the call, and the radio fell silent. It was always a comfort knowing the radar folks were handy in case weather turned ugly. When radar closed down for the night the feeling of solitude was almost palpable.

On the horizon, like a swath of glittering gems, lights of emergency vehicles marked my landing spot. I aimed for the lights, began a gradual descent and angled for the scene. I flew past a radio tower that loomed well above my altitude, its white strobes blinking every five seconds. Then I flew on for another three miles, circled over the scene, and landed. Dust and weeds gusted up, and the waiting paramedics shielded their eyes. Before I cut the engine the medical crew popped the doors open, then they hustled inside the farmhouse. Jan was flight nurse again that night, and an aide from the ER was with her. I watched the two of them disappear into the victim's house. I finished shutting things off in the cockpit. When I stepped outside and looked up, the sky was a mass of stars, visibility unlimited.

I walked into the farmhouse and saw the old man, our patient, on his back, his overalls cut away. A Paramedic pumped his chest. Another squeezed the ambu bag, forcing air into the old man's lungs. With every wheeze of the rubber bag our patient's chest rose and fell. The Paramedic leaned over the old man, and beads of sweat dripped from his forehead: he'd been there awhile, working hard to save the old guy's life. My limited experience with heart attack victims told me that the old man likely wouldn't make it. But the code for rescue personnel is simple: if they start CPR, they must continue until a physician says to stop.

The medical team gave the old fellow the gamut of life support protocols. High-powered drugs, more oxygen, IV meds and continued CPR. His wife stood in a corner, arms crossed, her face a mask. The kitchen was crowded, so I stepped outside to wait.

When I looked up this time my arms chilled. Fog. I'd been on the ground half an hour. In that time a mist had formed, its sticky wetness gathering on the helicopter's windscreen and control surfaces. The stars were now smudges in a white blanket, a pall of cloud that hadn't been there thirty minutes before. I drifted inside to see how much longer the team might be.

They'd begun another round of CPR and drugs, so it appeared I wouldn't be taking off soon. I whispered to Jan about what mister weather was up to, not wishing to add to her already full plate, but to keep her apprised of the situation. She thanked me for that, and returned to her patient. I went back outside, where the sky seemed to be closing down.

Another thirty minutes passed before the team appeared at the helicopter with the old farmer. We loaded him inside. I secured the doors, hopped in and soon had the engine purring, blades spinning. Prior to takeoff I looked once again into the misty sky. The horizon was gone; visibility was a mystery. I took a deep breath, and lifted the collective.

As soon as I cleared the trees I knew I'd made a mistake taking off. Why I didn't land again is still something I can't explain. Peer pressure, inertia, or the challenge to save the old man's life, something. I cleared the treetops, and surged ahead, thinking the fog might be local. The river wasn't far off, so perhaps that was causing the low visibility? I scanned forward, able to see less than half a mile. Visibility was near zero in places. I leveled off at four hundred feet, slowed to fifty knots, and then slowed to forty, groping my way ahead.

Beside me in the cabin the medical team worked on the dying man, pumping his chest, forcing air into his lungs, giving life-saving drugs. With every compression of his chest, the helicopter rocked back and forth. On the ceiling of the ship the IV bag swayed like a pendulum. I pressed ahead into the murk, one farm light after another slipping under the nose of the aircraft and then disappearing behind me. Each time I lost sight of one light, I strained ahead to see the next one. It was open farm country, and flat as a board, lucky for me. The down side was that the land being sectioned, farms were a mile or more apart, so lights were sparse. Almost hovering along I pressed on, hoping things cleared a bit, dreading the alternative. The visibility could go to zero at any time.

Then I remembered the tower. It stood directly between me and the hospital, and it was a lot higher than I was. It had stout guide wires angled four directions, splayed out like a giant spider web. I knew those lines were somewhere in front of me. I leaned forward peering into the darkness, scouring ahead for the tower's flashing strobes. I didn't see them. Not sure if that was a good or a bad thing, I pressed on.

Then things got worse. The windscreen fogged up. At first I couldn't figure out why. Then it hit me—the team was huffing and puffing, trying everything in their bag of tricks to save the old fellow, and in so doing they'd worked up a sweat. The added moisture in the cabin built up on the inside of the windows, decreasing my already limited view. No problem, I thought. I'll just turn on the defroster. Well, if it's bad on the ground...

I reached down and to my left, twisted the defroster knob, and...nothing. The knob wouldn't budge. Stuck harder than a rusted hinge. Try as I might, I couldn't get the defog valve open. Loading the patient we'd inadvertently jammed that knob till it was too tight to move.

All war stories begin with *there I was*. Well, there I was, four hundred feet off the ground, my windscreen fogged up, the outside fogged up worse, careening from farm light to farm light, not sure where the radio tower and its support wires were, but knowing they were somewhere close. The radar controller was gone for the night. I was on my own. It was entirely up to me, and whatever depths of experience I could draw on to get out of that pickle—or not. I found myself in the classic air medical dilemma: a dying patient on board; weather sour; an aircraft system malfunction; low altitude; and no outside assistance available. Unlike my Toledo aircraft, this one had no autopilot, and was not certified for instrument flight. I had to hand fly it every second. It wasn't just aviation, it was raw survival.

My mouth like cotton, I peered into the murk, and called on my past experience. I wasn't going to become a statistic. I was going to fly the damn helicopter like I knew how to do it, and somehow, some way, get back home safe.

I slewed the aircraft sideways into a skid, and opened the vent in my side window so I could look through the tiny porthole. Peering through the opening accomplished two things: it gave me marginally better visibility; and it brought in a stream of fresh air which splashed against my face, bracing me for the task at hand. It was similar to my decision in Vietnam to turn loose the left pedal for more power. It may not have been a good decision; but it was a decision, and it got things off dead center.

Then a new problem. The airspeed needle bounced on thirty knots, then lower, almost to twenty-five. If that needle reached twenty knots or lower the airspeed gauge would become unreliable. If that happened I wouldn't know if I was moving forward, sideways or backward. I had to keep moving forward or all was lost.

The medical team continued CPR on the old farmer, oblivious to the *real* life or death matter at hand. Visibility dropped to a quarter mile or less. The aircraft's navigation lights reflected off the wall of white outside, so I turned them off to avoid the distraction. I didn't need those lights. I was the only pilot crazy enough to be out that night anyway.

I scanned ahead again looking for the damned tower, but I didn't see it. After ten minutes that seemed like ten hours the visibility came up to perhaps half a mile. I still didn't know where the tower was, but I knew it had to be close. So I decided to climb till I reached clear sky and call for assistance. Just as I brought the collective up I saw a faint glow dead ahead. The glow gave way to outlines of houses, streetlights and cars on the freeway. It was Iowa City, five miles away. I breathed for the first time since takeoff, aimed for the rooftop pad, and settled onto it.

I took no more flights that night. Instead, I spent the time second guessing myself again, beating myself up over my poor judgment. Could'a, would'a, should'a. It was a tough realization that I'd almost shared the fate of some of my colleagues who'd crashed in similar situations. The difference was I'd survived. One thing experience teaches is humility. I was a lot more humble after that night.

Then I gained a different kind of experience. Upon arrival in the ER the old farmer was pronounced. I'd endangered myself and my crew for a dead man.

I had an ethical and contractual obligation to fly any patient who needed the helicopter, provided the flight could be made safely. I loved the flying, and my default was to accept rather than reject missions. But I couldn't get over the simple realization that instead of one assured fatality that night there could have been four.

Weather has nothing to do with patient condition, nor vice versa. Fog, nor sleet, nor ice nor dark of night care a whit that a patient is a child, or in misery, or eleven months pregnant or at death's door. Wind and weather are every pilot's best friend, and greatest adversary. There was anecdotal evidence in the early days of hospital helicopter rescue that pilots were routinely told patient status when making flight decisions. They may have overlooked poor weather, the thinking went, when the patient was a child, or related to someone, or in some way the patient's medical condition produced more sympathy in the crew. That concern led to a protocol at Air Med programs that pilots were not told patient information until after a weather decision was made. It was an entirely reasonable concept. It's also one of the places where overlapping roles between medical people and aviators appeared.

Sometimes none of the weather calculus, or medical infirmity, or contractual obligation matters much and you have a flight that turns out to be, well, amusing.

The dispatcher called at seven p.m. The Oskaloosa ER had a fellow with chest pain, shortness of breath, pain down his left arm and in his jaw, typical symptoms of a myocardial infarction, a heart attack. The doctor wanted AirCare to fly the fellow to Iowa City. I told the dispatcher I'd check weather and call him back.

It was mid-March, weather clear, temperature fifty degrees, dewpoint forty. With those values fog should not have been a factor. Typically, fog can form when temperature and dew point are within three or four degrees of each other, particularly with no wind. A ten point temp-dewpoint spread can be ignored—usually. I accepted the flight, and soon my crew and I were happily winging toward Oskaloosa sixty miles away.

I landed at seven-thirty, shut down the engine, secured the aircraft and wandered into the hospital with my medical team. We met our patient in the ER. He was a quiet fellow who said he was looking forward to flying with us on such a beautiful night. Plus, he was anxious to get to Iowa City to the big hospital, to see what was wrong with his ticker. We made him comfy on our cot, grabbed equipment and paperwork, and marched back to the helicopter. At ten after eight I lifted into a clear, chilly sky that was blanketed with stars. After leveling off at fifteen hundred feet I called the dispatcher with an ETA. "Back on the roof in twenty minutes," I said. Then I punched coordinates for home into the GPS, and watched the machine settle on its digital red numbers. IOW-44.7nm ETA 21 mins—ground speed 127.7 knots. Great, I thought, a healthy tailwind. I'll be on the pad by eight-thirty, refueled and back in business by nine. No sweat, no problem, no...visibility...wha?

Farm lights disappeared one by one, then two by two. Like a black curtain dropping, the world went dark. From clear sky to zero visibility in seconds. It was the fastest I'd ever seen weather change, and it was completely without warning. For a second I thought something had made the windscreen go dark, a chemical reaction, or something I'd flown into. I hadn't heard any noise, hadn't lost or gained altitude. I flipped on the landing light and it was like I'd walked from a dark room into the glare of floodlights. I killed the light, and slowed down.

The fog had formed a cocoon around me, the outside lights reflecting in a soft glow, red on the left, green on the right. I switched off. Remembering a previous flight in fog with another heart attack victim I dropped power, slowed to fifty knots and began a gentle turn back around from where I came.

Both nurses stopped tending the patient. Their heads snapped up, and they peered into the same murky mess outside.

"Where the hell did this come from?" Mike, a veteran said.

"Weather guesser blew it," I answered, the only alternative forming in my brain. As I began turning back to where visibility was better I saw scattered lights of a small town. Angling toward the ever-present water tower, I dropped down for a look. The tower had the usual hieroglyphics: DHS class of 84, JS♥'sKR. In the center of the structure, in eight-foot letters was the word DELTA. Never one to be fooled easily, I mentioned where we were. "This is Delta," I said.

Dazzled by my navigational skill, the flight nurses looked at each other, and marveled. "That's why you're the pilot, and I'm not," Mike said.

I aimed for the tower, while searching for a break in the fog, hoping the murk I'd encountered was a temporary phenomenon. No such luck. The weather had shifted. Fog had formed in earnest; I'd flown as far as I was going that night.

Adjacent to the water tower in Delta Iowa is a scrubby, ill-tended football field. I angled over a stand of trees by the forty-yard line, and landed at the ten. It may have been first and goal, but the clock had run out on my Oskaloosa flight. I radioed for a ground ambulance, advised the medical team of my plans—I had none, other than to spend the night on the gridiron in Delta—and shut off the engine. Than the amusing part.   As the blades wound to a stop our patient sat half upright, and he looked around. I leaned over, told him what had happened, and why I'd put down in this tiny, Godforsaken town. "Had to land," I said. "Foggy."

From the credulous look on his face I should have realized that he knew more about the situation than I did. "This is Delta," he said.

"Yes sir, it sure is."

He pointed over his left shoulder. "My house is right up the street."

It wasn't exactly the high point of my air medical career. I did manage to land safely, got the fellow alternate transport to the hospital, and secured the ship for the night. I had the foresight to transfer him onto the ground ambulance cot so I'd have a place to rack out, and shortly the team—with patient—was en-route by ground to Iowa City.

Another memorable weather event happened the first winter I flew in Iowa, and it had a less mirthful ending, though the sleeping arrangements were better. Not many pilots can claim that they've spent a night in a psych ward, but I can. There are a number of pilots who likely ought to spend a few nights there, but that's a story for another day.

It was a chilly, but reasonably clear New Year's Eve in 1983. My destination that night was Dubuque. At the hospital there, an eleven-year-old girl lay in a coma awaiting a flight to Iowa City. The child needed an operation to save her life. The flight nurse that night, Katie, was another veteran of the airborne scar wars. Katie and I took off at 7:30. I leveled at 2,500 feet to catch a tailwind, and bent the nose over. The GPS showed groundspeed at a respectable 146 knots. Not bad, except that it told me I'd fight a headwind going home. But all was well in the cockpit as Katie and I sped toward the Mississippi River town, and our young patient.

Halfway to Dubuque I noticed a dim halo encircling farm lights below. The aura was faint, but it caught my attention. I mentioned the ominous haze to Katie, telling her that we'd need to hurry with our young patient, put her aboard and head for home.

Katie had flown a lot of missions. She knew exactly what I was saying; we had to land, hurry inside, grab our patient and head home before Mr. Fog came a-courtin.' With any luck we could land at Dubuque, package up the child, and be back in the air by 9 p.m., with any luck at all. I landed at Dubuque at exactly eight o'clock. So far so good.

The first indication that my plan was flawed came right away. When we entered the ER, the child was still in x-ray, and not able to fly for at least fifteen minutes. No problem, I thought. I could still have her in the air by 8:30, and maybe—even with a headwind—land on our home pad by 9:15. I slipped outside to check the sky. A bit dank, but not bad. Back inside I went.

Then the next glitch: the girl's x-rays were unreadable. Back she went for more films, and back outside I went to check the weather which was, by now, equally unreadable.

Two hours after I landed the child was finally stable enough to fly. As I walked beside her on the way to the helicopter I looked up, and saw...white. I didn't say a word, just secretly hoped for the best. As I climbed into the cockpit I had a sense that I was about to make a very short, very disappointing flight, and I was right.

With the girl inside the cabin, Katie buckled up for the return flight. I climbed aboard, the engine whined, blades spun up, radios blinked on. Then I lifted the collective, launched, and headed southwest into the murky sky.

The city of Dubuque sits in a bowl hard by the Mississippi River, surrounded by rising terrain. The airport is on a bluff south of town, at the high point, which makes sense. The upshot is that in order to fly home past the airport I had to climb. I looked for the beacon at the Dubuque airport but I didn't see it. To clear the bluff I continued climbing, but still no airport light. I called Dubuque tower to see if perhaps the light was out of service. The tower fellow informed me that no, the light was not burned out, and yes, the airport was below VFR minimums. In other words, weather had closed the airport to all visual aircraft.

I told the tower operator that I was a lifeguard flight, with a patient aboard, requesting clearance through his airspace.

He issued the clearance, and told me to call clear of his airspace to the southwest. I said I would, and pressed on. When I reached cruise altitude I ran into a wall of fog, like flying into a grocery sack. I was at four hundred feet, in Dubuque tower's airspace, with near zero visibility, and a really sick kid on the cot beside me.

I did what I had to do; I banked toward the airport, since I knew it was flat there, and called the tower for clearance back to the north. As I crossed over the airport property the runway lights appeared, so I let down, regained visual reference, and pointed the helicopter toward the lights of beautiful downtown Dubuque. Katie didn't need to be told what was happening; she already knew what the verdict was. Two minutes later I landed back at the hospital, and shut down the engine, finished flying for the night.

A ground ambulance took the girl to Iowa City. I called my dispatcher, told him I was grounded, and secured the aircraft for the night. Then I wandered into the hospital prepared to sleep on a couch in the waiting room. A kindly staff nurse tracked down an empty bed on the seventh floor, and took me there. I did kinda wonder why the door to the ward was locked, but a nurse soon opened it, and allowed me in. It was the psych ward. No tie-in-the-back jammies for me, but it was a lockdown, nonetheless—not that I was going anywhere. The next morning, New Year's Day 1984, I took off at ten a.m., and was home by eleven.

The girl never went home. She lingered in ICU for several days before she died. Could we have saved her? Who knows. It is what it is. Patients die. Even at age eleven.

22

View from the cockpit

I could have found another job in the corporate world, a Monday to Friday position flying double-breasted MBAs and CEOs hither and thither to attend to their busy-ness. I could have taken a job in the Gulf of Mexico flying roughnecks to oil rigs, or helicoptered around an American metropolis reporting traffic and local news, the cops and robbers and gruesome wreck stuff that inquiring minds want to know about. I did that kind of flying later on, and saw first hand why I'd avoided it. I could have gone anywhere in the world on any number of adventures. But once I discovered Air Medical aviation I stuck with it, because it felt so good and I was so good at it.

There are people who are attracted to such things as altruism and what for lack of a better word I'll call empathy. Nurses, Paramedics, EMTs, and yes pilots who gravitate to pre-hospital emergency medicine do so because they want to help people in crisis. Oh, there are a few of the so called adrenaline junkies, people who gravitate to trauma and chaos for the thrill, or the physiological rush of diving into a wreck, but those folks are rare. Like most of my pre-hospital emergency medical colleagues, I did it because it felt good doing it.

It certainly wasn't the money. I was a salaried pilot. There were days in wintertime Iowa with fog was so thick I couldn't see the end of the helipad. Sometimes for a week or more the helicopter sat, blades tied down, weather covers installed because of snow, or fog, or visibility numbers so low there was no chance to fly. The numbers on my paycheck never changed. My check came in the mail whether I flew or not. When weather canceled the flying I'd stay in my quarters at the hospital, hour after hour, watching TV, scribbling memos, posting company notices. I'd wander the halls visiting patients, chatting with the dispatchers, hanging around the ER. I developed a crossword addiction. I suffered and died with the Chicago Cubs on WGN. I took long afternoon naps. It all paid the same.

But the calls kept coming nonetheless. Despite the crummy weather, hospitals and EMTs continued asking for the helicopter. I'd field those calls, check weather, accept the flight and take off, or decline the mission and go back to my crossword. But even after twenty years, turning a flight down was hard. From flight number one to number 3,000, my instinct was to go, not stay behind. A quick rundown of some memorable missions is in order. These show just how much I loved the job, and how experience helped me do it for so long. They're in no particular order. Fair warning: Some of them border on the fantastic, some on the gruesome. In observance of patient propriety I've changed names and locations to preserve patient confidentiality.

One February night I flew an old man who'd fallen through ice on the Mississippi River. He was underwater for thirty minutes. The Fort Madison ER called asking for the helicopter. I launched at 9 p.m., landed at Fort Madison at 9:30, and then flew the old fellow back to Iowa City. Why? He wasn't warm enough to pronounce dead. Before physicians could legally say the old guy was dead, they first had to warm him up. It was a simple liability issue. Could he have revived from the so-called diving reflex, the body's ability to preserve life underwater? Hard to know. That phenomenon usually saves five year olds who fall into cold, backyard pools and stay underwater less than fifteen minutes. A seventy-eight year old? It could be that the man's family wanted everything done, and that included an evacuation to a trauma center. That flight was many years ago. But it contains all the items present in today's health care controversy. There's potential dignity in any death. Extending life's official end the way we did that night in Fort Madison didn't seem all that dignified to me. It still doesn't. But I was a pilot; I just flew.

Another opportunity for showing human dignity in crisis is how well (or how poorly) people react to pain and suffering. The spectrum is wide. I saw patients with minor scars thrash and scream and cry. Others with searing, life-threatening trauma, burns, eviscerations, fractures and lacerations often stayed calm and serene.

A fellow in Leon Iowa fell out of his boat, and the prop caught him across his belly. His lower abdomen looked like ground hamburger. The tiny hospital in Southern Iowa called at 2 p.m. on a summer day. It was a thirty-minute flight. I landed at Leon at two-forty-five. As I circled the helipad in Leon, sunlight sparkled like gems off nearby Lake Rathbun where the patient had been boating. An assumption I always made about trauma patients in recreational settings was that there was alcohol involved, and that victims were, therefore, a bit belligerent, even to those of us who tried to help them. I was pleasantly surprised to learn that the fellow in Leon fulfilled neither assumption.

When I walked into the small ER the guy was on a cot, hands behind his head, laughing and joking with the doctor about what a mess his guts were, and how clumsy he'd been to allow it to happen. He did have a dose of morphine on board, so that explained some of his laid-back 'tude. But the dude was right about the hamburger part; his abdomen looked like fresh road kill. We covered him up, put him on the cot and flew him to Iowa

City where surgeons put his insides back where they belonged.

The accident scene was five miles from the hospital, a single vehicle rollover. I landed on the road, the medical team jumped out, and I shut off the engine. Walking to the bunged up car, on its lid fifty yards away, I sidestepped a mass of what appeared to be cottage cheese. Then another gob, a small ball of wet, white, pulpy stuff. I almost stepped in the second one. When I saw the patient I realized what it was. The boy's head was broken open like a cracked egg. His brain matter had spilled out, littering the roadway. It was a revelation to me in many ways. It took me back to my own feckless youth, and the cavalier attitude I'd had while operating a motor vehicle. From the position of the car, the gouges in the roadway it had made on its way into the ditch, and the fresh imprint of black skid marks it was clear that the boy had been driving much too fast. I thought of the numerous times I'd dodged a bullet in a car of my own, convinced I was bullet proof, that I'd never lose control. It was sobering.

The other revelation was that the boy's brain matter drying on the road in the summer sun didn't faze me physically. Despite almost stepping in it, I'd had no repulsive reaction to it, just simple curiosity. I suppose I gained my objectivity to seeing human trauma in the war. In Vietnam I'd seen so much death and bodily mayhem that it didn't bother me any more. I'd seen men shot, burned, with limbs missing and stumps exposed. One afternoon I was called out to evacuate two bodies. One was a dead American; one was North Vietnamese. Both were in body bags, but they'd been in the heat of the jungle for several days. Once you've been exposed to the cloying sweet smell of dead human flesh nothing else comes close. So the blood and gore in Air Med didn't bother me.

One of the attractions of Air Medical flying was that every shift was different. In 3,200 patient flights over twenty years I never flew the same mission twice, and never knew what a shift would bring.

I flew to the hospital in Mount Pleasant Iowa one balmy summer evening. The patient was a motorcyclist, bare from the waist up, who'd lost control of his machine and gone flying without benefit of an aircraft. When he left the bike and went sailing through the air he hit the top row of a barbed wire fence. The wire sliced through his arm, severing it at the shoulder. The amputation was nearly surgical.

My team entered the ER, where the one-armed patient was sedated, and chatting with the staff. We put him on our cot, preparing him for the twenty-minute flight to Iowa City, where a team of surgeons would try to reattach the severed arm.

I was awarded the task of carrying the amputated arm to the helicopter. A nurse wrapped the limb in a towel with an ice bag. I picked the package up, surprised at its heft. It felt like carrying a load of firewood. Walking toward the aircraft, another man's arm in my arms, I handled it with great care. At one point the towel slipped, and a bloody hand stuck out. The fingers curled spider-like, and a bloody wedding ring glimmered in the evening light. As I studied the soiled, waxy limb covered with dirt and flecks of straw I had a vision of the hapless EMT scouring a field for the arm, knowing it was in the weeds somewhere. I never did think EMTs and Paramedics are paid enough. That evening I was quite certain of it. I covered the arm with the towel, and laid it, like a bundled newborn, alongside its owner on his cot.

In twenty years there was only one time my immunity to the emotive power of gut-wrenching gore was challenged. It was the worst trauma I ever witnessed, and it was completely bloodless. The crash occurred five miles from the hospital on Interstate 80. It was so close I saw the accident site, the pulsing emergency lights from the rooftop pad, and I wondered why the EMTs had called for the helicopter? When I landed in the median at midnight, and saw the shattered vehicle, I understood why. Tire tracks angled left off the westbound lane, cut down through the grass in the median and climbed the berm into the opposing lane of traffic. The driver of the westbound Honda Civic had crossed the median into the eastbound lane, where a semi hit her head on. Then the massive truck rolled over the tiny car. The Civic looked like it had passed through a press at a salvage yard. I landed, shut off the engine, stopped the blades and snapped off the battery. The team grabbed equipment, and raced to the ambulance where our patient had been taken. I thought I was immune to the effects of blood and gore, the nauseating response that trauma can produce. I was right; I was mistaken.

Our brains play tricks on us. They take information from our senses, interpret those impulses, and conjure reactions we never expect. Often those brain tricks reveal a worst fear, or a long suppressed anxiety. When I was ten years old, on a hike with my brother at a state park in Ohio, I sat on a ground hornet's nest. In an instant I was covered with bees, my left arm a mass of yellow-black moiling, swarming creatures. Those hornets stung me in about a dozen places. To this day, out of pure brain reflex, I overreact when a bee lurches into view. Our brains hide those slivers of sensitivity, those subtle fears, allowing them to appear at the most unexpected times.

I left the cockpit and wandered toward the ambulance, approaching it from the front. The rear doors were open, and light from inside spilled out. When I reached the back of the rig I turned, peered inside and saw the patient supine on the cot. Two IV lines draped from bags on the roof of the ambulance, one line in each of her arms. I stared at the broken body, bruised and welted, amazed that there was no blood to speak of.

Then my brain took over. Something was terribly wrong with the picture in front of me. Something in the image was awry, completely off, but what?

Then the awful incongruity of the picture emerged, like a bee entering my vision, forcing my reaction. The woman stared at the ceiling. Her feet pointed straight down at the floor.

My stomach gurgled. Sweet, hot saliva gushed into my mouth. My hand came up to hold back the sour surge rising in my throat. My eyes teared up, my arms were a mass of swarming gooseflesh. I tore away from the sight like I'd been stung.

I walked around in the median, cool airdrying the sweat on my arms and chest. I'd managed not to throw up, but it was touch and go for a time. The reaction puzzled me. It was the first time I'd had such a thing happen, and I'd flown so many trauma patients and so many bloody, gory, eviscerated bodies I'd lost count.

I still see that woman's contorted body, her hips and legs twisted fully backward. The amazing part of her story is that she lasted almost twenty-four hours in ICU before she died. It was a testament to the human body's ability to withstand abuse. My reaction was testimony to the human brain's ability to protect us from witnessing that abuse.

By sounding timely alarms our brain protects us from other things, too. Call it experience demanding to be heard, or a little voice buzzing away like an alarm clock, warning us of danger.

I landed on the dark, rural road, an ambulance close by, flashing lights, a crumpled car. My landing spot was a two-lane blacktop way out in farm country. Such scene flights were a common occurrence. In the middle of nowhere, sometimes an hour or more from a hospital, ambulance crews with a bad trauma patient call for the helicopter. It may be the best use of air ambulance assets there is. When I landed that night I expected the usual hallmarks of a MVA, shattered glass, plastic car parts, fresh skid marks. The wha-wha-wha, and the stench of two-cycle smoke from the Jaws of Life™ pulsed in the night. EMTs angled the hydraulic tool's twin-ripping jaws to chew up the mangled car, and extricate the victim.

I traced the vehicle's wayward path: the start of fresh rubber where the driver jammed the brakes, the fishtailing marks of desperation. The fellow had clearly been speeding, realized too late he couldn't make the curve. Skid marks essed left of center, creased the gravel, and then flattened the shoulder grass as the car grabbled into the ditch. A fairly typical mark; the vehicle had sheared off a road sign. The splintered pole was snapped away a foot off the ground, the sign lay crumpled in the weeds: SLOW-CURVE. Another all too common factor, the vehicle's trapped occupant reeked of alcohol.

The car was halfway in the ditch, its roof peeled back like a sardine can. I crunched through broken headlight glass, and red and yellow plastic pieces scattered on the road. The victim, a young white male was alone in the car. In minutes, the EMTs removed him from behind the twisted steering wheel. They lifted the unconscious fellow onto our cot, and we took him to the helicopter. I glanced at the sky, climbed into the cockpit and snapped the battery on. The scenario was entirely routine...until I took off.

With the patient aboard, medical team ready, engine revved, rotor rpm 100% I lifted off and raced forward, skimming the asphalt. Then something, my brain's little voice...my inner dumbshit alarm...something told me to flip the landing light up to illuminate my flight path. And there they were, fifty feet ahead, a triple strand of wires sagged across the road.

My reaction was likely the same one our victim had when he saw the curve dead ahead. I yanked the cyclic back and the aircraft shot up like a ride at Six Flags, clearing the wires by ten feet. If you don't think a flight nurse can yelp like a schoolgirl, think again. Pilots can, too.

Air Medical aviation was a heartbreaking job at times. I lifted off from Ames Iowa one summer afternoon with a youngster who'd been climbing a tree and was electrocuted. He thought the dark thing was just another limb, so he grabbed hold of it. It was a power line running through the tree. The current jolted the boy so hard he fell twenty feet to the ground. He was awake and alert, and not in bad shape, considering, with bumps and bruises.

Every kid climbs trees. Or they used to, before childhood interests branched off to computer games, and kids became grounded in electronic distractions. If I had a nickel for every tree I climbed when I was a kid I could have retired a lot earlier.

When I took off with the boy I wondered why we were flying him at all? He looked fine to me. Awake, alert, smiling. He seemed to be just another active kid who fell out of a tree. The nurses explained to me that, because of the high voltage through his arm, the bone would die, and he'd lose the limb. I felt awful for the youngster, for what awaited him, partly because he was unaware of his fate. It was tempting to revert to metaphor, the child grabbing onto an electric source and reaping the whirlwind, but not till later.

When I took off he stared out the cockpit window, watching the world sink away. "This is really cool!" he said.

While flying Air Medical I learned a fair amount about medical jargon, procedures, drugs and the basic stabilization tool kit. Pre-hospital emergency medicine is all about basic life-support: airway, blood flow and perfusion, and the stabilization of the patient until they reach an emergency room or OR. During my tenure as an Air Med pilot I performed CPR once. I make no claim to competence in that procedure. But with one flight nurse, and no other trained personnel on scene when we landed, I was recruited to pump a man's chest. Full disclosure, considering his major trauma and advanced age he had no chance anyway. My feeble compressions weren't helping him. They weren't hurting, either, and they relieved the nurse, so he could tend to something that might help. No, I did not give him flying lessons on the trip home.

One of the strangest missions I ever had was a winter flight in 1996 for a fellow named Daniel. Daniel's heart attack had put him in the Burlington Medical Center, and then put me in the air that night to go get him. What started as a routine transfer for a stable, ho-hum cardiac patient turned out to be one of the more memorable flights of my career. With all the technological advances of so called modern medicine, our sophisticated machines, diagnostic tools and interventional capabilities there's still something out there beyond it, some ethereal therapy available, if only we understood how to tap into it.

I landed atop BMC's rooftop pad at nine-thirty. Off to the ER I went with my crew, helicopter cot, orange trauma bag, the monitor and all the fancy modern medical stuff that would, hopefully, make Daniel all better. We walked into the ER at nine-forty p.m. Our patient was in a room surrounded by doctors and techs who were busy trying to stabilize him.

But Daniel's ticker wouldn't cooperate. Every time he was moved his heart lost its rhythm, and he needed CPR again. Daniel lay on his back, mostly conscious, aware of his predicament. If we couldn't fly him to Iowa City he'd die right there in that tiny room. Empty medical packaging littered the floor. The suction canister was half full of fluid. Two IV lines snaked from clear bags, then wound around and around over Daniel's sheet and into his arms. White-coated orderlies raced back and forth. The graph-like rhythm strip showing Daniel's erratic heart action spit out of the monitor like so much ticker tape, and curled up on the floor.

Try as they might, with all their equipment and expertise, the medical staff couldn't transfer Daniel to the helicopter cot. Another attempt to move him interrupted his heart's useful rhythm. Defib brought it back. Move him again, more CPR, then another defibrillation. We tried to move him, his heart gave out. Try again, same result. This went on for more than an hour. At eleven p.m. the physician told Daniel's wife to say her goodbyes, because her husband wasn't going to make it. She wouldn't hear of it.

The woman sailed into the room like a wraith. She was thin as a young girl. Her black, ankle length coat swept around her like a vestment. Equally black hair hid most of her face. With her hands tucked away she looked like a penitent nun. No one spoke; no one moved. Like a ghostly presence, she stopped next to Daniel's bed. He turned and stared at his wife, waiting.

She laid her hand on his chest. Husband and wife locked eyes. Their silence sent a message we knew not to interrupt. The room was a dark nave filled with reverent subjects awaiting a spirit visit, or Wiccan announcement. And then it came.

"You're going to live, Daniel," she said. Then she turned and left.

In that instant Daniel's heart rhythm stabilized. After several seconds, we lifted him onto our cot, took him to the helipad, and put him aboard the helicopter. On the flight back to Iowa City that night no one said a word.

The most heartbreaking flight I had in twenty years involved an equal dose of sadness and anger. There must be a word for the combination of those two emotions, but I'm hard pressed to know what it is. I do know how it feels.

When I landed beside the freeway that frigid night the victim's pickup truck was on its side in the median. He was in the back of an ambulance, his injuries bad but not life threatening. He was conscious, alert, with mostly fractures and lacerations. As inappropriate as it seemed at the time he kept asking about his truck, and whether it might still be drivable. "How's my truck?" he said, over and over. The beat up Chevy seemed to be his most precious asset, for work, getting around, getting by, whatever. In all the mayhem, the disruption in his life, the fellow wanted a bit of truth, something he could hang onto.

After twenty years of flying Air Medical patients I knew one of its attractions quite well. Especially considering my own stolen dreams of early childhood, I wanted, like most people, to find a truth, no matter how harsh. Flying people and their families at the worst possible time of their lives often revealed a truth about them. Often it was hard to see, hard to comprehend. But it was the truth as they saw it nonetheless. So his concern made a lot of sense.

Until the Paramedic showed me a small white bundle in the frozen grass next to the truck. It was a sheet, the kind EMT's use to cover the deceased. Under the sheet the man's ten-year-old son lay dead. The fellow never asked about the boy. Only the truck. I hoped he was in shock, or denial, or both. "How's my truck," he said again, and again.

After seeing that white sheet it was hard to listen to. The harsh truth had another edge as well. Flying him to the hospital that night I had to suppress my feelings about his priorities. Slowly, as the helipad loomed ahead, I allowed the possibility of another truth. Maybe he knew about the dead boy? Maybe he couldn't allow himself the awful truth that he was responsible for that small white sheet lying in the median? Maybe that was too much truth?

America is not the classless culture we like to believe it is. There are indeed levels of society based on income, background, sophistication, political and religious affiliations and simple yet undefinable characteristics. There's a geographic component to these levels as well, territorial markers consisting of language, values, religious sensibilities and other intangibles. In certain parts of America, rural and agricultural areas for example, people are just more rooted in the common and the vulgar. A terrible generalization, but it has a grain of truth to it.

Ottumwa Iowa is a few miles above the Missouri state line in a rural, bucolic setting. It's a beautiful town, a calendar perfect vision of Americana, and the mythic home of Corporal Radar O'Reilly of M*A*S*H fame. It's also a nexus of NASCAR fans.

I landed at the Ottumwa hospital one July afternoon to transport a fellow who'd busted up his car and himself. He was in bad shape, internal injuries, lots of broken bones, a punctured lung, head injury, the works. His prognosis wasn't good. His family, several of whom were gathered outside there, had been told he likely wouldn't survive. I loitered outside the ER, while my medical team tended the patient.

Fireworks went off in a nearby waiting room, incredulous shouts and outraged venting coming from the victim's wife. She was incensed about something the doctor had done. I heard bits and pieces of her hyperbolic rant, but my brain couldn't process it right away. Then, for my benefit or not I don't know, the woman screamed it again. "...can't believe those sons'a bitches ripped it off 'im! That was his Dale Earnhardt T-shirt, and they just cut it right off!"

I peered into the ER. Sure enough, on the floor lay a tattered #3 T-shirt, a family heirloom it appeared, wadded up in a glitzy black and multi-colored ball on the floor. Ironic, I thought at the time, that the shirt hadn't worked any magic for Mr. Earnhardt, either. I don't know this, but I'd guess the Ottumwa hospital got sued over that ruined #3 'T' shirt.

Somewhere near Grinnell Iowa lives the luckiest woman in the whole wide world. When I landed that evening, Lucky Woman's compact car was in the freeway ditch. It took me a while to find the car, not because it was so small, but because the tractor part of a semi sat, mostly on top of it. Lucky Woman hit an icy patch and slid off the concrete. Directly behind LW, the semi driver saw her fishtail and slammed on his brakes. It was no use. LW's car grabbled off the road, and skittered into the ditch. The semi skidded next, following her down, down, down. Seventy thousand pounds of metal and rubber and Omaha-bound auto parts plunged down the embankment. The massive truck hit the compact, its front bumper chewing up the tiny car, from trunk to rear window to back seat, to front seat...and then stopped. Lucky for LW. When the dust settled, the back of her head rested against the truck's cold, shiny bumper.

An addendum to the tale is the trucker's reaction. We hear stories of how tough, how crude long-haul truckers are: Their aggressive driving, reckless speed, their insistent honking at smaller vehicles. That night I witnessed the other side of a trucker. When the Paramedics pulled the woman from her car, alive and relatively unscathed, the trucker cried like a baby. It was indeed a heartwarming sight.

The real heroism I witnessed in Air Med didn't come from my crew and me. It came from loved ones of patients we took away. We flew people into an unknown the family couldn't imagine. Countless new mothers, dads, long time husbands and wives stood by, as I lifted into a sky filled with uncertainty. They couldn't know, as the helicopter got smaller and smaller in the swallowing sky what the outcome would be. Family members knew that if the helicopter came the situation was dire. I tried always to be attentive to them, to allow them one last moment of contact, a kiss, a hug, or a lingering look before I closed the doors of the aircraft and lifted off. We couldn't fly the family; there simply wasn't room inside the aircraft. So I attempted to include them in the process, even asking for their assistance in loading the patient. Sometimes a parent's reaction at seeing a child flown away was both unexpected, and deeply gratifying.

~*~

The mission was to Monmouth Illinois. The small hospital there had called for the helicopter. An eleven-year old boy was in their ER with a gunshot wound to the head. My flight nurse and I landed at Monmouth at 2 p.m. The boy had been shot, accidentally, by a child his own age, while the two boys played with the gun. His injury was critical; his prognosis dire. Doctors told his mother that her son wouldn't survive, that she ought to consider donating his organs.

The woman wouldn't discuss it. Her boy was going to live, she claimed, and he was going to keep his organs for a very long time. She stood by the helicopter as we put the boy inside. Shortly, I blasted off toward Iowa City, assuming the worst.

Assumptions rarely take the shape we expect. The short version of the story is that the boy survived. The longer version is that he survived quite nicely. Years later he returned with his mom to the hospital, to thank me for helping save his life that day. The visit included an invitation to the lad's pending graduation from a technical school in Galesburg. Despite his traumatic brain injury he'd finished a course in computer repair. (!) He'd grappled back from all that and is now repairing the brains of injured computer systems.

That was a wonderful outcome all by itself, but it got better. After her son was shot, the boy's mother focused her rage and feelings of helplessness at people who leave guns lying around where children can find them. She turned that energy into a campaign to change the law and won her battle in the Illinois legislature. Now, in the state of Illinois, an adult can be held not only civilly, but criminally liable if a child is injured by a weapon that adult owns. Illinois State Law 720 ILCS 5/24-9 Sec. 24-9 Firearms; Child Protection is the result of one mother's battle to keep kids safe.

When I loaded the boy on my helicopter that day I didn't see a grieving mother, a parent resigned to the worst, the death of her eleven-year old son. I saw a woman with grit and determination in her eyes, that her son would live, and that she'd see to it that no other mother's child ever again was shot with a poorly tended gun.

Flights for newborns were some of the most gratifying, and most challenging of all my missions. Years ago an infant born before twenty-four weeks gestation simply died, its lungs and other organs too immature to support its young life. This is no longer the case. Twenty-four weekers commonly survive, and even thrive these days, partly through massive interventions, new drugs and new technical knowledge of their special needs. The intervention includes helicopters flying those babies to hospitals with a level of technical skill and equipment unavailable just a generation ago. Of course there's a cost to all of this. The longevity added on the front end of life, the neonatal side, creates interesting new family dynamics and problems. And it seems the generational issue becomes more visible the younger the infant.

I flew to Dubuque one afternoon to transport a newborn, a premature infant of only twenty-five weeks. On neonatal flights I carried a large isolette aboard, like an incubator, for the tiny patient. The device was similar to those found in nurseries or hospital labor & delivery wards, with a clear plastic canopy, sled-like design and massive battery and oxygen assembly. The incubator was essentially a four-foot long, three-foot high, 150 pound mechanical womb.

I was on the ground for a couple of hours in Dubuque, while the team prepared the newborn for flight. As I waited, I struck up a conversation with a family member, a woman about my age. I was then forty-six, so she and I had something in common, high school times, favorite music, the Beatles, Stones, Peter, Paul & Mary, the tenor of the sixties. Then a jarring difference. I took a chance, and asked if she might be the child's grandmother. "No, " she answered, a forgiving smile on her face, "I'm great-grandma."

I was astonished, as much at her ease with that reality as with the idea that I could be that old myself. It made me realize that we're seeing generational patterns made possible only by modern medicine.

There were times I questioned the wisdom of transporting certain patients, but of course my job was to fly, not question the medical efficacy of the mission. Life is precious, and despite assurances from some, mostly those who are convinced of an afterlife, the alternative is unknown. But there are always social costs involved in medical care as well. There's a financial burden shared by all of us when medical decisions are made about people who may be better off without them. Irresponsible talk of 'death panels' notwithstanding there are times society would be better served allowing patients to overrule physicians concerning interventions and low-benefit procedures. I flew the old fellow from Fort Madison who'd drowned, just to warm him sufficiently to be pronounced dead. Another time I flew a ninety-year old man who'd been approved for a costly heart procedure. There were several cardiac patients with a long history of alcohol and tobacco abuse, and no regard for their own health. Depending on one's viewpoint and judgment, those were patients who received multi-thousand dollar medical interventions to address self-inflicted deficiencies, with a very poor long-term prognosis. I flew many, many patients who rode with me only because they refused to wear a seat belt, making their injuries far out of proportion to the energy of their accidents.

Beyond the monetary considerations, there are familial, mindful considerations, spiritual factors if you will. Many times I flew away from a rural hospital with a badly injured or medically doubtful patient aboard, leaving a family behind to wonder what would happen to their loved ones. Many times my team and I knew it was the last time that family would see mom, or dad, or son or daughter alive. So instead of a death surrounded by loving, caring family, the victim would die far away, among strangers, albeit caring and professional ones, but strangers nonetheless, not people who loved them, and wished to be with them at the end of their life.

How much medical intervention is too much? When do we accept that death truly is a part of life, and allow the dying a bit of dignity? Also, when do we begin to understand that there are indeed ways to find honor, even a kind of joy in death after a life well lived? I was no authority; I was a commercial pilot. But I've seen death up close many times, and it seems to me that, since it's inevitable, we have an obligation to make death as dignified and natural as we can. It sounds like heresy among the intervention-minded, but the concept of letting go, in my opinion, has been dismissed and denied for far too long. And more heretical is the proposal that such massive interventions as medical helicopters, monumental end of life procedures and the mentality that drives us to do everything possible to extend life, regardless of how diminished it is, seems somehow misguided. It's not about economic factors, but the humaneness of it all. Prolonging lives in such ways seems to me to be more about those remaining than the patient who is about to take the longest flight of all.

23

Follow up

I flew in Iowa City for twenty years. In that time I carried 3,200 patients aboard my helicopter. All day, sometimes all night, one mission after another in my travels across the Iowa sky I saw all manner of weathers, and winds and different experiences. There may be nothing more beautiful than a midnight flight over frozen fields, total snow cover, under a full moon. No more stirring sight than the sun coming up after a night of back-to-back missions, knowing I've made a difference in people's lives. Nothing more gratifying than knowing that many people left the hospital to return home, partly because of my skill and dedication in the cockpit. There are flights that made a clear, positive difference in a life. Those flights justified a lot of those that either failed, or seemed needless for whatever reason. The mission to Elkader that night in 1984 was one of those.

I lifted off the pad at nine p.m. that February night, and raced toward Iowa City. Touching down at nine-thirty, I helped the off-load crew take our young patient inside. Then I refueled, checked the ship, and turned in for the night, wondering about the boy's chances. The doctors weren't optimistic. The next morning I checked on him. He'd made it through surgery, but was still critical.

Three weeks passed. One morning I got a call in the pilot's

quarters from the boy's parents. They were in the hospital lobby, they said, and they wanted to thank me for my efforts with their son that night. They were about to take him home, they said. I met them in the lobby, and what a reunion that was! Across the crowd I saw three sunny smiles. Mom and dad pumped my hand, thanking me again and again. The boy grinned, and thanked me, even though he remembered none of the flight. The adulation was embarrassing. I assured them that any other pilot would have done exactly as I had. Dad wouldn't hear about that. He mentioned something I'd told them when LuAnn and I put their boy in the helicopter that awful night. "You said you had a child the same age," the fellow said. "That meant an awful lot to his mother and me."

Watching those parents wheel their son outside to take him home was a powerful and rewarding feeling. Just knowing I'd been part of that success was so gratifying I can't explain it. It was like Stu Roberts saying he'd delivered the youngster in Vietnam, the one I'd rescued from another kind of storm.

Air Med flying was far and away the most rewarding part of my aviation career. But after twenty years it was time to move on. I was thirty-five when I started flying at the hospital. Nearing fifty, I was finding it increasingly difficult to roll out of bed on below zero winter nights to navigate the frozen Iowa tundra. Plus, I was beginning to see neonatal patients, babies born of parents who'd been neonatal patients themselves when I started flying! It was time. I started looking for something else. In a roundabout fashion something else found me.

I left Iowa City in the spring of 1998 for a brief move to St. Louis. I found a job there with varied and interesting flying assignments. Some were an adventure. Some were routine to the point of tedium. But after flying for twenty-five years, I knew that every takeoff promises something new.

Within a month of moving to St. Louis I landed a job with a company called Helicopters Incorporated. Heli-Inc. fielded helicopters for whatever aviation needs a prospective client had short of a prison break, and even then...

Most of Heli-Inc's business was news and traffic, so called ENG work, Electronic News Gathering. My introduction to this kind of flying was rather auspicious for a couple of reasons. One was that the fellow who took me up the first time, to check my flying skills in one of the company JetRangers, mentioned that I could do the work he was doing. He even asked if I'd be interested in filling in for him, with the intention of taking over his position sometime in the near future. It was a bit puzzling. The query came on my first flight, my first day with the company. I'd lived in St. Louis for a month at the time.

The fellow's name was Allen Barklage, and he was something of a celebrity in St. Louis. Allen's morning and evening airborne traffic and news reports had a wide following. Because of his local celebrity Allen was often asked to inaugurate new city parks, to help kick off carnivals, visit schools for career day, kiss babies and other PR functions. I wasn't in St. Louis long before I realized that Allen Barklage was a local celebrity, almost a hero of sorts.

So imagine my surprise when Allen took me flying the first day at Heli-Inc., signed off on my competence in the cockpit, and then asked if I'd like to have his job? It was a bit like Mike Bloomberg showing me Rockefeller Center, making sure I knew how to skate, then asking if I'd like to take over as Mayor of New York. I humored Allen, wondering if he was serious, and went about the day-to-day flying as Heli-Inc's new journeyman pilot.

I mentioned the various venues and charter options Heli-Inc. pursued, with a reference to prison breaks. Well...

The Allen Barklage adventure is legendary in helicopter circles. Barklage was flying a Heli-Inc. JetRanger when he became the only helicopter pilot on record to be hijacked. In May 1978 a woman chartered Allen's aircraft. She wished to fly with him, she claimed, to 'check out some real estate.' Her real purpose was to snatch her boyfriend from prison using the helicopter.

Cut to the chase. Barklage managed to thwart the woman's plans by wrestling a pistol away from her, almost losing control of the aircraft in the process. He then shot the would-be hijacker dead in his cockpit. Two ironies attach to the story: one is that the imprisoned boyfriend was in the big house for, what else, an aircraft hijacking! For those who don't believe criminality is genetic, think again: Later the same year the dead woman's seventeen-year-old daughter hijacked a TWA flight in an attempt to spring the very same bird from his perch in the Marion (Illinois) Federal Pen. Whatever that family's predilection for crime, it always seemed to involve aviation.

I'd lived only a short time in St. Louis. I knew where the Arch was. Hell, people in China know where the Arch is. But I could not have done Allen's job reporting news and traffic. I would have detoured every commuter in St. Louis into Kansas, and made them late for work.

Then, a month after I started flying at Heli-Inc, Allen Barklage was killed in the crash of his home-built helicopter. It happened on a Saturday morning. I didn't learn of the accident until I grabbed the Post Dispatch the following Monday, and saw the headline—'Pilot Barklage Critical After Crash.' In disbelief I hurried in to work, and got the details.

Allen had built the one-seat experimental aircraft from a kit. He flew it to the inaugurals and festivals that he attended on his days off from Heli-Inc. That Saturday morning he was scheduled to visit a PR function in a suburb of St. Louis. He buckled in to the experimental machine, fired it up, and took off from the Heli-Inc. hangar. When he'd reached only 200 feet of altitude the engine coughed and quit. Barklage didn't have time or altitude to recover. He crashed in a field adjacent to the company office.

When I arrived at work that Monday morning Allen was in

critical condition at Barnes Hospital. That afternoon his spouse ordered life support stopped, and Allen died. He was fifty.

Helicopters are not forgiving machines. They're sophisticated, touchy and maintenance intense. I'm proof that a pilot can fly helicopters for an entire career without personal injury, but it takes attention to detail, and a kind of wary attitude about those temperamental aircraft.

Harry Reasoner was right about helicopters. For some reason the crusty old newscaster had a soft spot for pilots of rotary wing aircraft. In an essay, Reasoner once wrote: *"This is why being a helicopter pilot is so different from being an airplane pilot, and why in generality, airplane pilots are open, clear-eyed, buoyant extroverts and helicopter pilots are brooding introspective anticipators of trouble. They know if something bad has not happened it is about to."* Harry Reasoner was a fine judge of human behavior. After flying for forty years I've known a lot of pilots, fixed-wing and rotary-wing. Those of us so called sling-wing pilots, for the most part, are indeed anticipators of trouble.

And one of the biggest troubles helicopter pilots anticipate is an engine failure. In a single-engine aircraft, when the motor spits up, there's no better way to prove that gravity exists. Harry said it best; *"...there's no such thing as a gliding helicopter."*

But Harry Reasoner wasn't a pilot, so his treatise needs a bit of interpretation. Helicopters feature a mechanical/aerodynamic capability called autorotation. Simply put, autorotation allows a helicopter pilot to make an engine-off landing. If the engine fails, a pilot enters autorotation by taking all the pitch out of the main rotor blades. This is done by putting the collective to its lowest position. It must be done fairly quickly, or rotor rpm will dissipate. Time is of the essence.

Time is what Allen Barklage didn't have. In the flying business altitude equals time. One of the oldest adages in flying is this: you can't use sky above you. What that means is that altitude provides enough time, in most cases, to figure out what malfunction or emergency has happened, then take necessary measures to address it. When Allen took off that day he'd reached about 200 feet of altitude. By the time he realized the engine had stopped he had too little time to diagnose the problem, get the pitch down, and enter autorotation. Another three or four hundred feet of altitude and Allen might still be alive.

My own experience with engine failure happened years before. I was flying a Huey for the Ohio Guard that August night. My crew and I left Lunken Airport in Cincinnati after refueling at 7 p.m., on a return flight to Columbus after annual training. I leveled off, cleaned up the cockpit, settling in at three thousand feet. I set the power for cruise, checked rpm, engine gas producer, exhaust temperature, torque setting, engine and transmission oil pressures and temps. I scanned the flight instruments: altimeter set, vertical speed indicator on zero, heading zero-four-zero for Columbus. Radios were set to air traffic control and company frequencies. I was number four ship, with four other Hueys behind me, all with about a mile separation. At eight o'clock the sky was just dark on a hazy, seventy-degree summer evening. The ship cruised along, blades bumping their standard one-to-one vertical vibration, the hallmark of every Huey. I wop-wop-wopped through the dimming sky, fat, dumb and happy. Home was sixty miles ahead. Norm, my right seater, crossed his arms, and disappeared in thought. Three troopers behind me in the cabin snoozed after a hectic two-week summer camp. On my ship all was well.

The red flashing light lit up the cockpit, a scarlet flare in the dim space. Then the *whoop-whoop-whoop* of the warning horn buzzed in my headset. Low rotor rpm! A sinking feeling lifted my ass off the seat, and my mind formed the words—engine failure!

Rotor rpm dropped like a backward clock. Torque went to

zero. Oil pressure, exhaust temp, gas producer, all fell toward the bottom of the gauges. Vertical speed sagged to two-thousand feet-per-minute, and headed lower. The Huey fell out of the sky.

I slammed the collective down, and jerked the cyclic aft to set the aircraft at a lower speed. Norm's hands flew, a radio call, harness locked, a yell to the crew to brace. Fifteen hundred feet. I saw an open field, angled the Huey toward it, and rechecked gauges. Rotor rpm was stable at 320, VSI stopped at twenty-four hundred feet per minute down. The altimeter passed through a thousand feet. Nine hundred. Eight hundred. Ground elevation was 650 feet. I had one chance to make the landing. The autorotation looked good, gauges good, angle good. The ground rushed up. At fifty feet I eased back the cyclic, and the Huey flared like a reined horse. Twenty feet, forward motion almost stopped. Ten feet, I leveled the aircraft. The Huey dropped straight down. I jerked the collective to arrest the descent, and the skids plowed into soft dirt. I pulled the last inch of collective. The ship rocked forward on its nose, blades whipping toward the ground, missing the soil in front by a foot. Then it rocked back, settled down. I dropped the collective again and watched the rotor blades drift by whop—-whop—-whop, lazy, and lift-less.

I breathed again, checked on my crew, shook it off. Norm radioed the ship behind us. They'd watched us fall from the sky, and followed us down. A minute later the other Huey landed behind me. I shut things down in the cockpit. Troops in the cabin unbuckled, and started gathering personal stuff, duffel bags and field gear. We secured my disabled ship, and climbed aboard the other one. An hour later we were at home plate.

Flying home in the back of the other Huey I went over the event, and realized that I didn't remember the descent, the screaming drop from three thousand feet to the surface. All I remembered was seeing the red light flash, then hearing the warning horn, then performing as I'd been trained by rote. I remember yanking the collective at the bottom, then sitting in the cockpit as the blades slowed to a stop.

Traffic congestion happens for all kinds of reasons: wrecks ahead, emergency vehicles coming through, disabled cars, big trucks bullying their way along and too many cars. Like every big city St. Louis has all those traffic challenges. I took off every morning in Sky 5 at 6:30, flew up and down the freeway system, and then landed at 8 o'clock. I lifted again at 4:30 p.m., same routine, same pattern, landing at 6 p.m. I'd board the JetRanger, climb to eight hundred feet, cruise west past the Arch. Then I'd angle southwest over I-44, turn right on 270 and fly toward the Northwest corner of the city. I'd hover at a designated spot, call Lambert control tower and zip through their landing and departing traffic. When I reached the Chain of Rocks Bridge I'd circle west, and do it all over again. It was ho-hum stuff, entirely routine, just boring holes in the sky twice a day. Traffic patterns and bottlenecks were always in the same place, at the same times, every morning every afternoon. I could have phoned in the report. Once or twice when weather was crummy I considered it.

Living in St. Louis was an adjustment for a lot of reasons. For one, I'd moved there from a town of 60,000. A murder in Iowa City is major news. In St. Louis, it's on page eight, under the fold, if it's listed at all. There were sections of St. Louis proper where it wasn't safe to walk at night, regardless of ethnicity. In Iowa City a locked door meant someone forgot and locked it by mistake. Reporting traffic showed me another aspect of big city life, something I never anticipated learning at six hundred feet. It was the ubiquity of drugs. There were a lot of car fires in and around St. Louis. In a month of flying traffic reports it wasn't uncommon along a busy freeway to see half a dozen cars on fire. Hoods yawned open, angry flames and black smoke boiling from the vehicle's interior. Firefighting teams aimed hoses at the moldering wrecks, their tires flat, as commuters shot past six feet away. It seemed odd to have that many cars on fire, and on such a regular basis. Was it the quality of gasoline in Missouri? The maintenance of those vehicles? What was going on?

I didn't want to look like the hick arrived from Iowa in the big city but one day curiosity got the better of me. I quizzed the reporter in my cockpit about it. He told me that my observation was correct; there were a large number of car fires around St. Louis. It was the meth trade. Methamphetamine cookers in rural Missouri smuggled the hot, crystalline stuff to St. Louis to sell. The raw product was unstable, and as the mixture jostled around in the car it sometimes erupted. By the time firefighters arrived on the scene the dealer/drivers were long gone, the vehicle abandoned. Cost of doing business, the reporter said. Life in the big city, I thought.

Once I hovered outside the window of the O'Hare International airport control tower, at peak traffic time, with heavy iron taking off and landing all around me. Boeings, and Airbuses, 747s, MD-80s, the occasional DC-10 flew past my tiny JetRanger on the way into and out of O'Hare. I hovered by the tower cab, watching through the windows. As controllers pushed all that heavy tin on and off Chicago's runways, I waited for them to send me on my way. I wasn't begging the FAA to grab my flying license; I was following procedures. And as I flew the procedure I once earned a scolding from a fellow pilot.

Flying news and traffic in Chicago was an adventure. O'Hare is one of the busiest and biggest airports in the world. I maneuvered through its airspace in one of the world's tiniest helicopters.

I went to Chicago in January of '99 to fly relief for the regular news and traffic guy. Every morning I lifted from Midway airport, headed west along the Stevenson, then banked north along the Tri-State expressway. In my left seat, a reporter droned on about backups, and bottlenecks, and bumper-to-bumper traffic snarls in all the usual spots. He reported nasty wrecks, sunshine slowdown on the eastbound Stevenson. He offered alternate routes to commuters coming in from the western 'burbs. As the winter sun stretched across Chicagoland I'd reach the Eisenhower, then turn northwest to I-290. On occasion, depending on the needs of the TV station, the reporter asked me to cruise up the Tri-State as it winds past the east boundary of O'Hare International.

The procedure to get through O'Hare airspace had no room for error, no latitude for misjudgment. I stopped at the east boundary of the airport, at five hundred feet, and then turned left to face the tower. Then I crept forward until I was stopped at a hover, 100 feet from the tower window. Needless to say, I was on the radio with ATC all the time. When a gap in traffic opened up, which didn't happen often at O'Hare, the tower guy told me to proceed along the northwest runway, and to depart O'Hare airspace at I-90, the Northwest boundary.

I took off one bitter morning, headed west out of Midway, and flew along the Stevenson. At the Tri-State I angled north. The reporter wanted to check things around O'Hare, so I banked that way, went over the transition procedure in my head, and radioed O'Hare tower. The controller cleared me into his airspace, so I crossed over the Eisenhower, prepared for the O'Hare transition. It was a beautiful if frigid January morning. Bright sunshine warmed my cockpit. When I departed O'Hare I got a frigid greeting from a fellow pilot, his odd, yet funny comment on my flying skill colder than the air outside.

I stopped at O'Hare's east boundary, turned as the procedure dictated, and moved west inside the airport property. Then I hovered next to the tower, waiting for the signal to depart. Three hundred feet below, at the circular terminal entrance, where yellow cabs ejected travelers. Buses wheeled away in a cloud of diesel fumes. Red Caps competed for most-mangled-bag award. I hovered, watching the tower guys earn their keep, waiting for the signal.

A minute later the call came. "Sky 7 proceed Northwest."

"Roger, Sky 7, departing O'Hare, thanks." I did a right pedal turn, nosed the little JetRanger forward, and tracked at 400 feet, parallel to the northwest runway. Big airplanes lumbered past on and off runway Ten, Nine, Four, and One-Four. O'Hare is no place for a Bozo pilot. As I flew parallel to runway one four, I looked ahead and saw a daisy chain of planes angling toward me, sequenced onto that runway. When I reached the approach end of runway one four, a landing American Airlines MD-80 passed beside me less than a quarter mile away. I was on the approved track, talking to the tower, doing what I was told.

My presence that close must have made the big airplane's fish finder go off, because the pilot snapped the radio open, and went ballistic. His radio call whined in my headset: "Tower get that damned helicopter out'a here, that guy's a Bozo!"

Amused at my fellow pilot's outburst, I watched the big plane pass behind me, and head for landing. Seconds later the tower operator called. Ignoring the other pilot's rant, he released me to the northwest, and wished me a good day. I keyed the mike, hoping the airline pilot was still on the frequency. "Roger, O'Hare, Bozo-seven, clear northwest." The reporter laughed so hard he required a tissue.

The advent of GPS (Global Positioning System) changed everything in aviation navigation. Before GPS the standard cockpit nav devices consisted of radios that captured signals a pilot used for orientation information. Satellites are replacing those ground-based navigation aids. Before a new assignment starting in New Orleans the company had installed a newfangled GPS on the LongRanger. One of the company techs taught me how to use it. I'd learned how to put waypoints into the device, and how to dial them back up to help me navigate. I'd punch in latitude and longitude for various places.

From the ramp in St. Louis I read the results: Kansas City-230 NM-hdg-273, Cedar Rapids-191 NM-hdg-348. Then I flipped through other features of the shiny new GPS. I scrolled the knob to find airspeed. Turned the knob one direction for an altitude warning, then another for distance to station, time en route, location of nearest fuel. I flipped to find airports, tower frequencies, maintenance centers and information on landing fees etc. It was a great device all in all, but on my latest assignment I didn't use it. Instead, I relied on an even simpler navigation device. Call it a system of low-tech grain elevators.

I met the clients at New Orleans airport, six men from the St. Louis headquarters of a major grain buyer. The company operated several grain elevators along the Mississippi and White Rivers. Every year they visited each elevator to inspect it, and to chat with the personnel working there. I loaded the executives on board, and took off for the first elevator site thirty miles west of New Orleans.

I landed at the first site, shut off the engine, and waited while the clients did their inspection. Then back in the air we went, toward site number two. That one was forty miles upriver along the Mississippi. When I leveled off at two thousand feet en route to the second site, the fellow in the left front seat pointed forward. "There it is," he said.

Straight ahead, stabbing the morning sky, a white grain elevator loomed. It was the tallest thing around for many miles. I aimed toward it, and landed.

All I had to do was take off, climb a few thousand feet, and the next elevator appeared on the horizon. Most of the towers were only forty or fifty miles apart. With all the expensive apparatus on board, I used the old fashioned mark-one eyeballs, and completed the mission.

The high point of that job was spending the night at Natchez Mississippi. I landed on the lawn of the Holiday Inn, parked the LongRanger outside the door to my room, and tied it down for the night. The next morning, after a proper breakfast, I gathered the clients, fired up the helicopter and took off on the hard work of finding more grain elevators. The job took ten days. I landed at towers in Louisiana, Mississippi, three on the White River in Arkansas, a few in western Tennessee and the rest in southern Missouri. With the job done I landed the clients at Lambert Field, and returned to the office. The next assignment was somewhat less straightforward.

Another kind of navigation involves flying from one electric power pole to the next, one after another, at minimum airspeed, while two passengers play Marco Polo without benefit of a swimming pool.

The contract required me to fly over electric power poles, while a technician marked them with GPS and a camera. To do the job, I had to fly at double the height of each pole, in other words fifty feet above a fifty-foot pole etc. There were three of us on board, a front seat spotter, back seat marker, and me front right seat in the JetRanger.

From a fifty-foot hover I looked straight down at the day's starting point, a sub-station near Wheeling West Virginia. A web of high voltage lines painted an ominous grey crisscrossed under the helicopter like a labyrinth. Yellow ceramic conductors gleamed in the morning sun. Like buzzing robots, arms extended and ready to grab anything within reach, eight black transformers squatted row on row. A sign on the ten-foot high chain link fence read 'High Voltage—Keep Out.' I studied the gauges, praying that the engine didn't spit up. If it had quit right then one of those menacing robots would snatch my little JetRanger and fry me for lunch. I hovered. Hovered a bit longer. The technician fumbled with his laptop device. A tweak here, a twist there, trying to locate the GPS signature. "Ready to go." Finally, we were off.

I nosed the helicopter forward, headed down the line of poles, and the count began.

Behind me in the cabin another tech with the marking equipment responded. "All set back here." The first pole passed under the nose of the JetRanger. When it did the left-seater opened his intercom, and said, simply: "pole."

Huddled over the camera/GPS device in the rear, the other tech waited. When he captured the pole in his camera lens, he sang out: "mark pole." Then he punched a button to record the GPS coordinates of the structure, and to take its picture. "Pole, then "mark pole." On it went, back and forth, a litany all day long: pole—a beat, then, mark pole, pole, a beat, mark pole—pole, mark pole, on and on, all day, from first light till it was too dark to mark or see the poles. "Pole—mark pole."

I had to fly at thirty knots, 35 miles per hour, just above a hover in other words. If I flew faster the equipment couldn't keep up. Small birds passed me. Children ran alongside waving, then zipped ahead. The airspeed needle sometimes bounced on zero. I sauntered along, fifty feet high, at thirty knots, the refrain pinging in my headset, "pole—mark pole, pole—mark pole," all day long. I started hearing "pole-mark pole" in my sleep. It was one of the most dangerous flying assignments I ever had. Why? Because it was a recipe for complacency. The monotonous chant, and the stultifying routine almost caused my demise.

I took off at seven on a hazy morning in July. The poles were in Eastern Ohio, not far from the town of Coshocton. It's hilly country, undulating terrain peppered with the typical woodsiness of deciduous trees thick as hair. The line of poles that day ran east, threaded through the lowest level of a valley. I found the substation outside town, and hovered there while the technician oriented his equipment. "Ready to go."

I headed down the line at thirty knots. The chant started, "pole—mark-pole—pole—mark-pole," and so on, as I cruised through the swales and gulleys, heading east, tracking the power line. Each pole was about 100 feet from the next.

At a low point in the valley the line took a heading that put the morning sun dead ahead. I tried shielding my eyes, but it was no use; the glare was nearly blinding. Left hand cupped to my forehead, right hand on the cyclic, I guided the ship along into the glare. Every minute or so I slowed the helicopter, scanning for obstacles ahead, taller trees, an outcropping, or a set of wires hidden in the blinding sun.

After thirty odd years in the cockpit I'd developed a sixth sense. The feel of the aircraft, weather changes, external threats that rattled my inner alarm. Call it experience. As I crossed a small stream I noticed a lone structure, like a flagpole, atop an adjacent hill. It seemed to have no purpose, no reason to exist all by itself way up there. But the little voice in my pilot brain snapped at me. It shouted stop. So I did. I yanked the cyclic back, ballooned about a hundred feet up, and stopped at high hover.

The techs stopped their "pole—mark-pole" and looked up. I stared at the lone pole atop the hill. Then a touch of left pedal, and I looked opposite, across the valley to the other side. Sure enough a matching pole stood there, apparently by itself...connected to the other pole by a strand of wires draped across the valley. I turned the aircraft sideways to lessen the sun's glare, and still had to squint to see them. The wires hid in ambush less than a hundred feet ahead, perpendicular to my flight path. Had I run into them, instead of pole—mark pole, it would have been mark one for the poles.

I dropped back onto the track, flying higher than necessary just in case. The clients didn't seem to mind.

Flying for Heli Inc. gave me a chance to do things with a helicopter I never would have done otherwise. After flying Air Medical for twenty years it was a refreshing change for a number of reasons. Every day provided a different challenge, a different client needing the helicopter, sometimes for the oddest reason.

I took off in a JetRanger one night to find an artifact from the 1904 St. Louis World's fair. The client was looking for the axle of what was, a hundred years before, the world's largest Ferris Wheel. The ride had been erected at the west end of Forest Park in St. Louis, and it was a feature attraction of the fair. The Ferris Wheel itself has an interesting history. First built for the Chicago World's Fair in 1893, it arrived in St. Louis for the Louisiana Purchase Exposition, the St. Louis World's Fair, in January 1904. The wheel's axle was solid steel. The piece was forty feet long, three feet in diameter, and weighed seventy tons. With those dimensions it should have been impossible to hide, but the axle had disappeared, and my client wanted to find it.

I helped install a highly sensitive metal detector on the underside of the helicopter. The black box with a single eye clipped onto the skids. Wires sprouting from its sides snaked through a side window, then attached to another magic box in the cabin. We installed a small TV camera in the cockpit, with a screen that measured ten inches. The device recorded infrared images. It would, hopefully, show a ghostly outline of the axle below ground. Temperature differences would help me orient the aircraft above all that hidden metal in the dead of night. With the equipment in place, I left the ground at 1 a.m.

As I cruised past the Arch and downtown St. Louis the client recited the history of the mysterious hidden axle. When the Exposition disbanded in '04, the Ferris Wheel came down. But the axle was too heavy to move, so, allegedly, it was buried and left behind. He was convinced that the massive piece of iron was still buried beneath the grass and elms of Forest Park. He hoped to find it, dig it up, and either broker a sale to the Missouri Historical Society, or, failing that, melt it down and sell it for scrap. Before the city would issue him a digging permit he had to know the exact spot. I felt like one of those old men on the beach with their metal detectors and shovels.

We arrived over Forest Park at 1:30. Then the fun started. I had to hover at two thousand feet, the optimum altitude for the equipment to work. My client found a hot spot right away, and he told me to stay over it. It sounded easy. It wasn't. I'd flown helicopters for thirty years. Hovering was like brushing my teeth, only easier. But hovering at two grand, in the dark, with no reference to back, forward, sideways, up or down wasn't easy. Plus, a stiff northerly breeze that night yanked at my tail. It gusted, bumped, pushed me forward, let me go. On the tiny TV screen the blobbed image darted up and down, right and left. I wrestled the cyclic to recapture it, then it shot off again. I found it, settled down, held it dead center for a second or three, then the image zinged off the screen. It felt like learning to hover all over again with Wayne Alexander in the Texas heat.

The fellow marked the spot where he thought the axle was, (and to my relief he didn't say "mark pole"), so I headed back to the hangar, and landed at two-thirty. I was drenched with sweat from some of the toughest flying I ever did. All for nothing, it appeared.

Later on I did a bit research on that axle. There's been an ongoing debate as to its whereabouts. The final word comes from the Missouri History Museum. After the Exposition ended, in December 1904, the Ferris Wheel was destroyed with dynamite. The axle wasn't buried in Forest Park after all. According to folks at the museum it was shipped by rail back to Chicago in 1906, cut up, and sold for scrap.

Flying news and traffic around Cincinnati one afternoon I won a smart-guy award. The talent in the left seat conducted a daily quiz of sorts for his listeners. Just as he gave his traffic report, I cruised past the 74-75 split north of the Queen City. With his report done, the fellow announced the question of the day, a bit of schtick he offered faithful listeners. The day's query concerned an Ohioan who'd been heavily involved in libraries. It was, the reporter said, someone who invented stuff. He then opened the discussion to his audience. Who might this historical figure be?

I opened the intercom and asked if the pilot was eligible for the contest? He nodded yes, and I told him my guess was Thomas Edison. A light bulb went off in his head. Astonished that his very own pilot knew such trivia, he pronounced me the day's winner, and told all of Cincinnati Ohio, or at least those people listening, that I'd won. Andy Warhol was right about those fifteen minutes of fame.

I could have stayed at Heli-Inc. for a long while, taking whatever exotic flying jobs that came along. But I missed Air Medical, and the satisfactions it offered. After so many years of doing the job it had branded my soul. In many ways Air Med was where I cut my teeth in commercial aviation. When I started flying for the hospital my logbook showed 3,000 hours of flight time. When I left after eighteen years it showed 9,000. There's something about the comforts of stability in a job, plus the recognition of one's peers that's truly satisfying. I enjoyed the diverse flying options in St. Louis, but there was no satisfaction in the work beyond its successful outcome. That should have been enough. The clients were happy; the boss was happy; the jobs got done.

But I needed more than the same traffic jams every weekday morning, finding buried metal objects and grain elevators, and marking electric power poles. I needed personal gratification from my job, every day. I guess was spoiled. I missed Air Med flying.

24

Back to Iowa City

There's another reason I left St. Louis. I was in love. And when the heart knows what it wants, the heart prevails. This most ancient of human axioms pertains to pilots as it does for other mortals. She was (and is) simply the love of my life, the woman I cannot live without. The challenge was simple, and exquisitely complex. I lived in St. Louis; she lived in Iowa. The advent of e-mail, and cell phones, and such electronic luxuries that evolve into necessities are wonderful. But they don't come close to satisfying the human desire for personal contact.

I'd met her at the hospital when I flew there, and we'd been best friends. Then, in Hollywood fashion, or that's what acquaintances claimed anyway, after I departed she and I realized that what we had was much more than friendship, and the drive-time started. I know the route between St. Louis and Iowa City better than I know the inside of a cockpit. Before long the distance, not to mention the gasoline bills became intolerable.

Then a serendipitous event. The pilot who'd replaced me in Iowa City moved on, leaving a hole in the staffing. I applied for the position, got my old job back and resigned my St. Louis posting. Heli-Inc. gave me a rousing sendoff, and I left that fine company with regrets. I'd been the go-to guy, a journeyman pilot doing all manner of flying jobs. I'd loved the adventure and complexity of it.

But I was in love, and that trumped all else. The heart wants what it wants. So in the spring of '99 I said goodbye to the folks at Heli-Inc. and headed north on state route 218 again, the road I could then drive in my sleep, and sometimes did, I think. Back in Iowa City I fell into the job as if I hadn't left, and into the arms of the sweetest, most wonderful woman a man could ever hope to have as his best friend. We married in March 2000, and I still pinch myself at my good fortune.

Life is filled with convergences, some predictable, some routine, some almost eerie. I started flying in Iowa City once again on May 18th 1999. My first patient flight was to Ottumwa, just as my first Air Med flight had been in 1983. Like the first time, the patient was a female multiple trauma victim. It was like being in a time warp. Same flight path; same hospital, patient condition; roughly the same time of day and weather. The difference was the aircraft, medical crew, and upgraded equipment. Plus, I was a different man then, not the same one who'd left Iowa City less than two years before.

I'd aged beyond the simple calendar passage of those two years. My divorce and its stresses and strains were responsible for most of that aging. The end of a long-term marriage is like a death for many reasons. Expectations are shattered, lives disrupted, friends disillusioned and somehow wary that the scourge of the 'D' word will happen to them. People wondered aloud if any of what went before was real, or true, or of value. Long-term friends took sides. They avoided me, ignored my overtures for simple things like lunch, or a cup of coffee. It saddened me. Their avoidance forced me to look at who I was at a time when I felt the most intense yearning to shield myself and hide from reality. Divorce hurts, a lot, but it showed me who my friends were.

Life goes on, and death does, too. The Air Medical flying business is pretty much depression proof. Even though I'd changed in fundamental ways, I reported back to work full of enthusiasm, matched by the energy of new love and commitment.

Something besides my status among friends and my address had changed, too. It was my priorities. For the first time I chafed at extended night shifts at the hospital. Before, I looked forward to reporting to work, now I wished to be home instead. I never refused a patient flight that might make me late leaving for home. But when the pager pinged near quitting time I sensed a kind of resentment. I responded to those late calls with some dread, and did whatever I could to expedite the flight. But my impatience with patients showed a time or two.

Before, I looked forward to flying, the exhilaration of an emergency call, the chattering pager. I'd race to the helipad like a giddy kid, start the engine, greet my crew. I loved the physical rush at takeoff, the ground falling away, as a patient waited somewhere for the helicopter to arrive. Now I looked harder at weather conditions and forecasts, parsed the numbers longer. I teased out possible reasons not to take off. Before, I never questioned medical rationales for using the aircraft. Now I wondered why I flew certain patients, when a ground ambulance could bring them in? Flight nurses talked about burnout; for the first time I truly understood the term. I'd given Air Med work the best years of my aviation career. I began to think that it was time to move on.

I knew what the genesis of those feelings was. It makes me sad to acknowledge it now, but it's true. Before, I looked forward to time at the hospital because my marriage was unfulfilling. It was a burden I no longer wished to carry. The hospital was a respite, and a damn convenient one, with night shifts that kept me from my marriage bed. She was a fine woman, a terrific mother to our daughter, and an accomplished person who finished a rigorous college engineering program in midlife. But the romance had left our relationship like a pinned balloon, and there was no re-inflating it. Work provided the comfort, the focus of my attention instead. I worked every shift I could back then, even volunteering for extra duty to fill holes in the schedule. I flew all night to rescue strangers, but I couldn't save my relationship at home. It wasn't fair or considerate to my former mate, but there it is.

In my new life my attention was where it should have been, on my spouse and her needs. Instead of working for a living, I'd been living to work. No more. I worked when necessary, volunteered for nothing, and hurried home.

Speaking of changes, and the redirection of priorities, just watching the towers fall on that otherwise sublime Tuesday morning of September 11th 2001 I understood in my bones that the world was changing in front of me.

I reported to work that morning at the usual time, walking into the pilot's quarters on the hospital's top floor at 6:30 a.m. Central time. My colleague, Mike, had flown only once during the night shift, and that mission had been early. Mike gathered his belongings, slipped into his light jacket and left for home. I looked over the previous night's activity sheet, aircraft hours before maintenance, outstanding glitches and general status. Then I walked to the helipad and looked over the ship. The rotor blades were tied down against a steady breeze, and the engine intake cover was installed. I took that off, and left the tie-downs on the blades. Then I checked the cockpit, plugged in my helmet, and hung it on its ring over the pilot's seat. I punched the battery master on and checked the gauges, fuel, power calculator and medical oxygen level. Then I flipped off the battery, signed off the preflight checks in the logbook and shut the cockpit door. The helicopter was ready to fly.

The elevator rumbled down to the first floor. I got off, went to the cafeteria and picked up a few items to take back to my room. By the time I entered the elevator again it was 8 o'clock in the morning in Iowa. Riding up to the roof that morning I was unaware that, as I'd stood in the checkout line paying for breakfast, at 7:45 Central time, American Airlines flight #11 had hit the north tower of the World Trade Center in lower Manhattan. I stepped off the elevator, walked into the pilot's room and switched channels on the TV. As in New York, the weather in Iowa City was chilly but clear, a pristine early fall day. The television in my room at the hospital was almost always tuned to the Weather Channel. That allowed me to get an early idea of what weather was developing, to save a few minutes before launching on a patient flight. The morning of 9/11 there was no need. Weather wasn't a factor, so I switched over to CNN.

The image is indelible in our minds: the devilish vision of those stricken buildings; bodies of actual human beings tumbling down beside striated columns; the awed timbre of newscasters unsure of what to say, or if to say anything; cascades of smoke billowing, fuel-fed flames boiling. It was a vision no one had ever seen before, a vision of hell itself.

I stared, mouth agape at the hideous sight on the TV screen, one word flashing in my head: unbelievable. As I watched, it became twice so. If it had been impossible for something to be twice as unbelievable before, it wasn't for long as United flight #175 crashed into the south tower. The clock by the TV read 8:03 a.m. Central time.

The flight nurses walked into the room, arms crossed, riveted on the spectacle. We knew something fundamental had changed that morning, but none of us could know the depth and breadth of it. Then the inevitable happened when such a massive pillar of steel and glass loses its physical integrity, and gravity takes over: the south tower collapsed like a fragile cake in a gush of smoke. Ten minutes later the north tower fell.

The first taste of how my world changed that day was a phone call from the company office in Utah. My chief pilot called. Jim was contacting all the company contract sites, passing on the FAA order to stay on the ground. "No flights until further notice," Jim said. "Keep 'em on the ground."

I hung up, redialed the phone to the administrator's office and told him we were grounded. Then I called the dispatcher to tell him the same. Together he and I came up with a script to use when emergency calls came in requesting the helicopter. There's no option, we said; the FAA will not allow us to fly.

I went back to the TV and watched the news from Manhattan. The towers were, inexplicably, gone. In their place was a moldering heap of smoke and ash and steel and glass, the burial mound of almost 3,000 human beings. Unbelievable. For some reason the shocking event took me back to November 1963 when I was fifteen.

I'm a sophomore in a High School seminary, sitting in study hall that afternoon at 1:30 p.m. Dallas time. A priest rushes into the room, ordering us all into the chapel. I see Father Sala standing by the altar. He tells the last boy to close the chapel door behind him. Then Sala's announcement, shocking, unbelievable. "...President Kennedy...shot and killed in Dallas." My world changed that day as well. The feeling was the same.

I went to the helipad, put the engine cover on the helicopter, called my relief pilot for that night to tell him not to come in and left the hospital. The FAA grounding was indefinite. I'd been told that, even after I was released to fly again, there'd be restrictions and protocols I'd never needed before.

Wednesday September 12th 2001. I reported back to work, where my first task was to figure out our flying status, so I called the FAA in Cedar Rapids. The fellow said I still couldn't fly, but to check back later that morning. There might be exceptions, he said, such as those for emergency medical aircraft like mine. I told him I'd continue checking.

At 1 p.m. the dispatcher called with a request for the helicopter, a scene flight for a motor vehicle accident. I called the FAA and asked if there'd been any change. They said I could fly as long as I called off from the hospital, and again landing at the scene. I had to use the transponder code assigned to the ship, the code we used as a 'LifeGuard' flight, and I had to call right away after liftoff. He stressed that part: anomalous targets popping up on radar were considered hostile, until positive ID was established. "Make sure you call airborne as soon as possible," the fellow said. I assured him I would.

I called the dispatcher back and said we could fly. In minutes I was ready for liftoff, on one of the strangest flights of my career. As soon as I took off I sensed the change that had taken place, the difference wrought by the evil actions of those nineteen men in New York, Washington and Pennsylvania. Instead of the usual chatter of aircraft radios, routine exchanges between pilots and each other, pilots and air traffic control the radios were quiet.

Ordinarily, any time I went flying, even in the most rural parts of Iowa, my headset was filled with chatter from other aircraft, air traffic control entities and the general litany of flight as pilots talked back and forth. It would have been unusual for the frequency to stay quiet for longer than thirty seconds. On this flight, at 1:30 in the afternoon, September 12th 2001, the sky was utterly silent.

At first I didn't know what to make of it. I turned the volume up on the radio, thinking perhaps I just wasn't hearing other pilots, or the ATC people. It wasn't that; there was nothing to hear. In the silent sky no aircraft crossed in front of me, to the side, in the distance. The sky wasn't only silent, it was empty. No vapor trails of high altitude commercial jets; no arrival and departure traffic calling into and out of Cedar Rapids. On the apron at Iowa City airport nothing moved. The airfield was deserted, as if everyone, line crews, instructors, charter pilots all had gone home.

I did as I was told, called Cedar Rapids approach control on takeoff, announced my landing at the scene, and then called off again right away when I lifted, headed back to the hospital. Before 9/11 that procedure was a courtesy call; after 9/11 it was mandatory. On the way back with the patient aboard I considered the eerie quiet again, like my radio had failed. Leveling off, I called the ATC fellow. "Kinda spooky, isn't it?"

"Never anything like it."

"Back to normal soon, I hope."

"Whatever that is."

I landed on the rooftop pad and shut off the engine. Whatever normal is, he'd said. There was a new normal, and I think we all knew it. The change was bigger than any of us could imagine.

Something else had changed in my second Air Medical life. I'd lost the stamina necessary to do the job well. As I passed my fiftieth birthday, working shifts that didn't tax me before exhausted me now. After an all-night shift of flying I drove home shaky with fatigue. There are people who can work night shifts, then sleep all day, then do another all-nighter. I am not one of those people. An all-nighter for me now means I don't have to get up to pee. And interrupted sleep costs more than the daytime recovery nap can pay back, so my sleep bank was always overdrawn. Night shifts kicked my tail, even those without a flight, or two or four, a not uncommon scenario. My attention wasn't fully on the job, either. I responded to radio calls late, my altitudes and airspeeds wandered. I always took pride in my pilotage. Watching it erode bothered me. Helicopters are not forgiving machines. They're sophisticated, touchy, with a lot of moving parts, and a lot of opportunities to grab a complacent pilot and shake him really hard. Helicopters do not fly themselves.

The Iowa City program is a busy Air Med operation, with more than seven-hundred patient flights per year. In a typical year half those flights occur after ten p.m. So the usual night shift wasn't an easy turn-in to bed at ten o'clock, with the expectation of sleeping till morning. It was routine to be interrupted during the night at least once by a patient mission. As much as I loved the job, I knew I had to find something else.

A night shift mid-January of 2002 hardened my resolve. The phone startled me awake at eleven for the first patient request of the night. Weather was no factor. At ten degrees below zero Fahrenheit, wind-chill hovered at twenty below. The mission was to the little hospital in Vinton Iowa, a twenty-minute trip. I'd fly the mission, finish in an hour or so, crawl back in bed by 12:30 and maybe sleep the rest of the night. I walked around the helicopter dressed like an Everest climber, shivering, breath fogging. I removed covers, took the space heater out. I took off the rotor tie-downs and the blades creaked with cold. I clambered into the cockpit, mashed the battery switch and cranked the engine. The sound was more grinding than the smooth, easy turbine whine heard in temperate weather. With the blades spinning, rocking the cold airframe, I tapped the OAT gauge in the windscreen to see if it was stuck. It wasn't. The needle registered twelve below zero. The medical team joined me, and we took off at eleven-fifteen.

As planned, I finished the mission at midnight, and was back in bed by one a.m. Chilled to the bone, I crawled under the covers, and snuggled in the fetal position trying to rewarm myself. The electric blanket had almost removed the cold when the phone trilled again. The mission was to Fairfield, a thirty-minute flight. Again, weather was clear. Off I went, back into the ten-below Iowa winter sky. The mission finished at three-thirty.

At four a.m. the phone rang yet again for a flight to Dubuque. I looked for a reason to reject it, but weather was perfect, and the ship had no maintenance issues. The crew waited on the helipad. Duty called. Alone in the pilot's room, zipping my coat closed to meet the frigid night I said it aloud, the admission I never thought I'd make: "I can't do this anymore."

A wave of raw emotion washed over me. It was a feeling I never anticipated having about hospital flying. But it was the truth; I couldn't continue that way. I was beyond bone tired, and half frozen from three flights during the night. I was no longer safe to fly, and I knew it. I took the flight to Dubuque. But I knew that, had something happened, a mechanical failure, an emergency of some kind, a close call with another aircraft, anything requiring focused attention and I may not respond to it well, if at all. I felt it in my bones, along with the cold that I'd been drenched with all night. It was a lousy feeling. Frightening. And sad. The upshot was that for a long time I'd relied on experience to get me through events that I should have handled with ease, and without thought. I knew I had to find another job. That winter ended, another started, and I kept my options open. Then another serendipitous event came along out of the blue, by way of a simple e-mail.

It was from Connie Shelton, author of the Charlie Parker and Samantha Sweet mystery series. I'd been taking a writing correspondence course with Connie for several months. As fate would have it, her husband Dan was a helicopter pilot. Connie and I had exchanged a number of stories about flying. She and Dan met on Kauai when he took her for a tour of the island.

I'd shared with Connie some of my feelings about Air Med work, and had mentioned to her that I was starting to look for something else. In the return e-mail, Connie asked if I'd consider flying in Hawaii? Dan no longer flew there, but he knew helicopter operators on Kauai were looking for pilots. At almost the same time, out of the blue, my sister asked why I was flying in Iowa when I could be in Hawaii? She and her husband had traveled to Kauai, and they'd taken a helicopter tour there, thus her question to me.

Connie's message came in late August of 2003. Another winter in Iowa loomed. It would make number forty-two for my wife, and twenty for me. I loved Iowa, its rich, foundational beauty, its fecund geography, its people, who are an interesting mix of hard core conservative and nonjudgmental progressive. But Iowa winters are brutal, and long. Many times in mid-winter Iowa we'd go for weeks with temperatures in negative numbers. And the wind! Lordy Magordy the wind. Windchills of forty and fifty below zero are not uncommon in Iowa.

The upshot of the tale is that Hawaii sounded pretty good. I printed off a copy of Connie's e-mail, and showed it to my wife. To her great credit, and one of the many reasons I love her so, she took one look at Connie's e-mailed question about moving halfway around the world and she said..."why not?"

Things are a blur after that. We bought two round trips on United to Kauai, took time off work and visited the island in early October. I interviewed with Air Kauai Helicopters; she talked to Wilcox Hospital. Both companies offered us positions. We got back on the plane, flew to Iowa, and started planning and packing for a move to the middle of the Pacific Ocean. Within a month we'd packed or given away everything we owned. We found a ready buyer for the house, and made arrangements with an attorney to handle the closing. We put in notices at work, closed accounts, sold one car and arranged to ship the other one to Hawaii. We said aloha to family and friends, and bought two tickets to Kauai, this time one-way.

25

Flying in Paradise

I never imagined finishing my flying career as a tour pilot. But there I was looping around Kauai seven times a day, surrounded by six happy, camera-snappy tourists. It was a tough job, but someone had to do it.

The differences between tour flying and Air Medical are mostly obvious: tourists tend to be conscious, and they (mostly) choose to be on board. There's no third-party *tourism* insurance that pays for their cruise. They leave the aircraft alive and well, though on occasion passengers doubted that outcome for themselves prior to takeoff.

Also, the difference between Kauai and Iowa is more than just having three vowels. I don't need to mention the weather, although Kauai has its own unique patterns that offer a challenge to pilots. Simply put, if there's such a thing as ideal weather, it's possible that Kauai has it. Temps on the island vary between 65 and 85 degrees year round. A constant trade wind cools the island day and night. Rain is a daily event, for five minutes, about six times a day in 'winter,' and less so in summer. Imagine a place where homes are built without a furnace or air conditioner and you have Kauai. If either appliance fails in Iowa the situation is dire, if not life threatening.

The day after my arrival on island I checked in with company owner/president/chief Kahuna and benevolent dictator of Air Kauai, a fellow named Chuck. He may be the only helicopter operator I ever worked for whose company enjoyed continuous positive cash flow. Chuck knew how many paper clips were floating around the office at any given time. If a few turned up missing he knew about it, and he expected their return. This is not a derogatory comment; such fanatical attention to detail isn't just a good idea in aviation, it's a necessity, especially in the middle of the ocean with aircraft parts deliveries days away.

In the interview, Chuck asked about my past flying experience, so I handed him my logbook. He riffled the pages, and frowned. I studied his sour expression, my pits turning tropically hot, wondering if I'd made a mistake applying for a flying job in the middle of the ocean. "What's the longest day of flying you ever had?"

"You mean logged hours?"

"Yeah, I see here you fly one hour, then one point three, then one-point five..."

Chuck was concerned about two things. My age, and my stamina. I'd heard from other pilots that the tour business was grueling. It meant full days in the cockpit, blades turning all day, with a break only for a quick lunch. Air Kauai's schedule booked seven flights per day, on each of two aircraft.

"The hardest part of Air Med, for me, was sitting around waiting to fly," I said.

Chuck scowled. "Man, I don't know. It's tough out there. One trip after another, no breaks, and the goddam FAA snooping around all the fucking time."

I decided to speak Chuck's lingo. "The Feds crawled up our ass in Air Medical. Man we couldn't do a thing right."

"Goddam weasels don't know a fuckin' thing about safety, just paperwork."

"The FAA's motto is "We're not happy till you're not happy.""

He snorted. "Think you can handle it?"

"I can fly the box it came in."

"The schedule, I mean. Some guys can't hack it."

"I love to fly, does that help?"

"So do I." He stood and shook my hand. "I'll put you on, partly because you showed up."

I signed on the dotted line, and joined Air Kauai. It was a great company, run like an airline only better. Chuck knew the business to a gnat's ass, including marketing, aircraft and maintenance, personnel, financials and the most important item, how to please tour customers. One thing Air Kauai did different than other operators was shut off the engine after each tour. Other companies on the flight line kept engines burning, blades turning. Flight line personnel herded customers aboard the helicopters like frightened sheep, under spinning blades, amid the noise and confusion of the running aircraft. Air Kauai machines shut down after every tour. It gave the pilot a chance to get out and stretch. But it also allowed him to meet each tour group in a personalized way, greet them face-to-face and learn their names.

My first tour of the island was as a passenger with a fellow named Brandt, the company chief pilot. Brandt took my wife and me for a lap around the island on one of his tours. Palm trees dripped after a short cloudburst that morning. The same rainfall pumped waterfalls full, their shuddering splash exploding over mountain crags. WaiMea Canyon yawned, its red dirt rusty and bleak, cliffs and razor ridges jutting up through green jungle. The flight lasted almost an hour. The last site Brandt showed us was the inner recess of the volcano that created Kauai. It was as if we'd finished up at the beginning, where the island itself started. With the cascades of falling water inside the volcano's crater, ferns and vines a thousand shades of green inside the gloomy nave, I had to fly my own tours of Kauai. I was hooked.

~*~

Hawaiians call it Mana'. Translation: spirit, or energy, or soul, or Aloha or all those combined. Mana' is one of those believe it or don't kind of concepts, and it took me a while to get on board with it. I'd left behind a job that exposed me to the cold, harsh realities of human suffering and death every time I flew. The idea of some spiritual, touchy-feely, wind in the willows energy sounded like so much tribal lore, or another way to tap tourist's wallets. When I first heard of Mana' it sounded like another way the haoles (How-Lees) kept the local people under their thumb. It isn't, and it doesn't, but that's what it seemed like. By the way, haole is the Hawaiian word for foreigner. Any non-Hawaiian is a haole. It is not complimentary.

To explain Mana' further I should detail a (very) short history of Hawaii, and specifically Kauai. I gathered books from the local library about Hawaiian geology, geography, culture, history, even some documents detailing the religious beliefs of the local people. I did this because the tours demanded it. Tourists asked questions about all the topics listed. Some of my pilot colleagues made up answers, off the cuff explanations. I could have done that, but I chose not to. I wanted to know, if only for my own edification, not just to be able to respond to my passengers with some authority.

The story of Hawaii, its geologic formation, discovery, habitation, culture, conquest and religions is astounding. For more than a hundred million years a volcanic vent has been forming Hawaiian Islands. The so called Hawaiian Emperor vent is still active, still making new land. Once the islands form they migrate northwest, one by one, via the Mid-Pacific tectonic plate. As the plate moves northwest the wind and sea and erosive rain claims each island, and they disappear beneath the ocean from whence they came.

The oldest island is called Kure. (Koo-Ray) One hundred million years old, Kure is 1,200 miles northwest of the big island of Hawaii, and it is nearly submerged. The newest island is called Lo Ihi (Low-EE-Hee) and it's fifty miles offshore from the southeast tip of the big island of Hawaii, thousands of feet below the waterline, blooming upward in its fiery ascent to become a new island. Geologists predict that LoIhi will break the surface in about 10,000 years.

Hawaii's first inhabitants paddled 2,000 miles in open boats, arriving from the Marquesas Islands and Tahiti fifteen hundred years ago. No one knows why they left their homes to cross all that water. It may have been religious intolerance, or dwindling food supplies at home. No one knows how they navigated, either. Some speculate that they followed the birds.

The Hawaiian people first met white men when HMS Discovery, with Englishman Captain James Cook in command, anchored off WaiMea Kauai on January 21 1778. Results of the encounter between two cultures were similar to others between white and dark-skinned people almost everywhere throughout history. The Hawaiians suffered and died from exposure to diseases the English carried, illnesses for which they had no immunity. Hawaiian women discovered that their freely given favors with Englishmen gave them more than pregnancies; it gave them venereal diseases they'd never known. The English crews discovered a native people obsessed with the iron fittings on their ship, people willing to strip those fittings bare despite repeated warnings. And the English stripped treasure from the Hawaiians in equal measure. Over the course of several years, the natives lost land, access to the sea, their religion, and their language for the most part, although there are a few Hawaiians, many living on Kauai, who keep the Hawaiian language alive.

As for Mana' and its presence, it has a lot to do with the deep desire of the Hawaiian people to reclaim their land and heritage. A kind of ethereal belief that eventually all will be well, the Hawaiian equivalent of 'it is what it is.' And the Hawaiians' hope of regaining their ancient heritage is not an outrageous idea. The islands once belonged only to the Hawaiians; other people wrested the Aina away from them, often illegally.

Since I didn't arrive on island as a tourist but a potential inhabitant, I felt the presence of Mana' right away. People told us how to save money on food. They pointed out farmer's markets which moved between local towns. We frequented those markets not only as a place to purchase fresh produce, but as a social event, a true movable feast. They warned us about tourist traps, and told us that, since we lived on Kauai, we were now KamaAina (Komma-Eye-Na) which meant we were not tourists but residents. The advantage was, that if we told local vendors and retailers we were KamaAina the price of goods and services dropped dramatically.

Despite (or because of) this and certain local customs, I sensed that Kauai would stay with me regardless of how long I lived there. Part of it was the outrageous beauty of the place, a landscape littered with color, warmth, richness and plant life that Rousseau himself couldn't have imagined. It may have been the lethargic pace of island life, a slowness and ease that's difficult to get used to. People on Kauai pay no attention to the speed limit. They drive below it. They stall checkout lines to catch up on relatives, hammer out picnic schedules, discuss kids' school performance. Standing behind them in line I had to force myself to remain patient, to stay calm and go with the flow of island life. It wasn't easy, but it was necessary. It was Mana'. Let it go. I once told a passenger, a physician considering a move to the island, that Kauai made Iowa seem frantic. I think he reconsidered his plans to relocate. As for so called island fever? I never felt it, never caught it.

Mana' is the connection the locals still feel to the Aina, the land, the sea and to each other. Mana' is on the trade wind, in the rustling of palm fronds, the musky smell of breadfruit trees and plumeria and hibiscus. It's in the fireworks colors of the bird of paradise plants that litter the islands. It's in the fantasia of foods that Hawaiians prepare from their beloved poi, a product of the taro plant, to seafoods, breadfruit and bananas, mango and macadamia, papaya and pomegranate. To this day, when I can find them, the thickly sweet, luscious taste and texture of fresh papaya melting on my tongue brings tears to my eyes. And sweet memories of the island. My wife can't watch videos of whales breaching in a spray of turquoise water without choking up. It's all Mana.'

It's also in the other element of Hawaiian culture, the spirit of Aloha. That spirit is both the local people's great virtue, and their downfall. As much ill fortune as has befallen the Hawaiians since HMS Discovery anchored at WaiMea in 1778, they should resent us haoles more than they do. The fact that they share their islands with us is also Mana.' But the only way to truly explain it is to go flying.

Everyone remembers a first kiss. First sight of a lover's smile, first trip to Disneyland. I'll always remember my first trip around Kauai with passengers: liftoff, the music, the tropic sun bathing my cockpit as I cruised toward the interior of the island.

I was the second schedule pilot that day, takeoff set for 8:45. My radio call sign was Air Kauai 3. The aircraft was identical to the one I'd been flying in Iowa, with some differences in equipment. Instead of three back seats and a patient cot, the aircraft had six seats for tourists, plus one for me. Instead of a crude intercom system for intra-cabin chats about patients, weather, hospital politics and personnel gossip, the Air Kauai ship had an expensive Bose music system. Noise-canceling headsets allowed passengers to relax to music that I tailored to match sights on the ground. Instead of the standard fuselage configuration, the Air Kauai ship had custom designed doors, with Plexiglas throughout. Instead of doors, they looked like windows with a latch, all designed to maximize visibility.

In Iowa, I'd flown from the right seat, the standard pilot-in-command seat in a helicopter. On Kauai I flew from the left side. The difference had important implications for tour flying. Tours of the island were flown clockwise, in other words by (mostly) turning right. Thus, a pilot in the left seat stayed on the outside of the turn, away from passengers' line of sight. The arrangement gave customers a better view. It was all about visibility, and all about the product, which was the best possible tour of the island.

As for on board equipment, the Air Kauai ship had plush leather seats, and extra insulation to dampen aircraft noise. It carried three separate microphones in the cabin, to allow passengers to communicate with me, and each other. One thing the medical and the tour helicopter had in common: both had a sufficient supply of what tour pilots call 'aloha bags.' To limit their use, I carried sacks of ginger candy. It was not for snacks.

"LiHué tower, Air Kauai 3, pad five with information Hotel, I'm off to the harbor."

"Roger, Air Kauai 3, cleared for a harbor departure."

I check the rpm, engine gauges, temperatures, fuel gauge, lights on the panel. All in the green. I click off the collective lock, ease the stick upward and the landing gear skitters on the concrete. Another touch of collective and the AStar lifts to a hover. I back off the pad, swivel left, and ease toward the takeoff circle thirty yards away.

The first liftoff and departure on any new job is a moment of anticipation. Though my passengers had no idea it was my first solo tour with the company, I wanted it to be perfect. I'd cruised the island with the boss on my orientation, but that was a bare-bones inspection of various sites, a check of how I moved the sticks around, and a way to demonstrate various protocols while flying the island. On that trip Chuck had a set of controls, too, and he did a lot of the flying. Now I was on my own.

I reached the departure pad, scanned the traffic pattern, and punched the play button on the music machine. The snappy rhythm of slack key guitar music filled the headsets. With a touch more power I eased forward. The helicopter leapt off the ground, and raced forward. As the ground fell away, my passengers and I rose into the Hawaiian morning. "Just another routine day in paradise," I said, as we crossed over the airport, banked south and headed toward Nawiliwili Harbor where the cruise ships dock.

Across the Pacific, rippling crests glittered like gemstones in the morning sun. This wasn't a midnight flight at ten below zero, crossing a desolate Iowa landscape to rescue a dying patient a hundred miles away. This was wafting into the Hawaiian sunlight, seventy-degrees, a gentle trade wind jiggling the aircraft, surrounded by six happy, fully conscious, smiling passengers.

As I cruised past the HaUpu ridge the first time, headed west, I had a rather sobering thought. In some ways my new tour-flying gig carried more responsibility than Air Medical. In Iowa my passengers were often at death's front door. Their prognosis was poor or they wouldn't have been flying with me. If my medical passengers died, after all was said and done, it was not an unexpected outcome. Also, health insurance carriers picked up the tab for my life or death flights, a trip for those patients they'd not planned or anticipated. On Kauai, no third-party payer wrote the check. Tour passengers paid quite a bit, and their expectations were to live life to the fullest in the hour they spent aloft.

I sensed the weight of it on my first trip. The six people in my cabin had anticipated the tour for a long time, planned for it, shopped for the best value. They paid a lot of money for their hour trip around Kauai, upwards of $200 per seat. For a few of them it was real bucket list item. My job was to give the finest tour they could have. To do that I'd learn what makes a good tour, what tourists want. I'd learn what they really didn't want. The answer surprised me; they mostly wanted for me to shut up and fly, so I did.

I learned how to tailor each tour to the group on board, and to the weather existing at takeoff time. What music people wanted to hear as they cruised over paradise. Perhaps the most important lesson I learned as a tour pilot was addressing peoples' fear of flying. The ideal situation is for them to forget they're airborne, so they can relax and enjoy the passing scenery. I wanted them to imagine themselves on a magic carpet of sorts, suspended over each tour site as if floating, safe, gliding by, while music played and they soaked in the magical scene below. To make that happen I avoided unnecessary jerks, or wide variations in the controls. I never used 'cowboy' maneuvers, never dove toward ridgelines, or yanked the cyclic back to pull up hard or tear down in a roller coaster move. I sensed that people disliked that kind of adventurous flying, the daredevil banking and angular turns that some pilots used. I saw those tactics performed on the island by colleagues, and I always wondered if their passengers truly enjoyed them, or just put up with them hoping the flight was over soon? I chose a gentle, predictable style instead, always looking for ways to reduce the fear factor. When I saw the results, it was gratifying.

One evening, as I put the aircraft to bed and started for home, the boss brought a woman, a potential customer, out to the helipad. "I want to see if I can do this," she said.

As Chuck stood by, I helped the woman into the front seat of the helicopter. I buckled her in, put her headset on to give her a sense that she was flying. She looked around the cockpit, out the windows, into the cabin. Then she unbuckled and climbed out. "Can I fly with you?"

"Uh, well, it depends on what time your tour is..."

"I'll go if I can fly with you."

I looked at Chuck; he nodded, and that was that. The next

morning she arrived for my second tour. I put her in the same seat, buckled her in, even put the headset on for her. I lifted into the morning sky, and headed out for the tour. Before I left the airport traffic pattern the woman was snapping pictures, laughing, her face alight like a child's. She said later it was the hardest thing she ever did, but she knew she had to do it. I told her I was proud of her, and thanked her for flying with me.

Why are people afraid to fly? A lack of control? Fear of heights? Maybe the real question is why are some people *not* afraid to fly? Why did I always look forward to climbing into the sky, leaving the ground far below? I believe their fear had something to do with helicopter itself, the whirling, intermeshing, edge-of-control sound and image those machines convey with their frantic, deafening arrivals and departures. Even today not many people have flown in a helicopter. People think they're dangerous, unstable. It's a perception I noticed before I climbed into a cockpit the first time. When I told my folks I'd signed up for helicopter flight school, my mother's immediate reaction were these exact words: "You're going to fall out of that thing." Her fear was irrational. I didn't know how to respond to it then, and I didn't even after I quit flying, never having fallen out of 'that thing.' I wanted to remind her that Van Johnson hadn't fallen out all those years ago when she and I watched him land near our backyard. But I figured she wouldn't remember the helicopter back then, and didn't pursue it.

But answering the fear question on Kauai was paramount to delivering a great tour, so I focused on it. In my previous flying job my passengers' fear of flying was the least of their problems, or of mine. But flying tours meant taking people aloft who were not only conscious, they were conscious of every spatter of rain, every drifting cloud, every shift in wind direction and/or velocity. Some of them were quite vocal about it. On Kauai some of my passengers were fearful enough that I wondered if it was advisable to take off with them aboard.

I adopted standard responses, dialogue that bordered on the dismissive, yet held a reassuring message:

Q: What about the rain? A: No rain; no rainbows.

Q: Isn't it too windy? A: Wind helps us fly.

Q: Will I get airsick? A: People tend not to get airsick on my tours.

Q: What if I change my mind? A: Now's the time to do that.

There were variations on these questions, but not many. In summary: some people were fearful, they just didn't always express it very well.

So I learned to read body language. Legs and arms crossed meant, *"I'm scared to death but my husband wants me to go, so here I am."* Legs splayed, over-the-top gestures and too-loud laughter meant, *"My wife wants me to go and I'm damned if I'll let her know I'm scared spitless."* Holding hands, nuzzling, shiny new rings meant newlyweds. Plus, newlyweds always yawned, a lot.

I joked with my passengers, if I thought they were up to it. "About the noise? Only time I worry is when it gets quiet." They'd laugh, most of them. It was a fine line; some passengers didn't appreciate my brand of aviation humor. "You've already done the dangerous part of your trip today," I'd say. "You drove to the airport. Driving on this island is a lot more dangerous than flying with me."

I engaged the most anxious ones with polite, yet firm answers. "You know the highest roller coaster at the amusement park? The one that makes your arms tingle, and your stomach do flip flops?"

They'd stare, mouths agape, nodding silently as the chaotic image played in their minds, chilling their arms, making their stomachs do those same flip flops.

"It's nothing like that," I said. Then I'd continue the briefing.

I wanted to give people the best tour they could have, and in some ways that meant the most boring tour. If that sounds disingenuous it probably is. The bottom line was that I wanted them to forget they were in a helicopter. To imagine they were floating above the stunning natural beauty that is Kauai, with no thought of danger or unease. I believe I succeeded in that, most of the time.

Throughout my flying career my philosophy had always been to deliver an uneventful flight. A flight with no surprises, no sudden changes, no alarming events. On Kauai I saw the opportunity numerous times to tease out peoples' fears and deal with them, and it became a matter of pride. After a while I welcomed fearful passengers, because it was so gratifying to see them relax and enjoy the ride.

On one tour, a woman asked all the standard worry questions: what about the rain? Is it too windy? How long is the flight? She was borderline ready to bail. I assured her the best I could, and she and her husband boarded. We had a delightful tour, saw the most beautiful parts of the island, including a rainbow on the NaPali coast. On the way into home base, as I often did with my passengers, I asked the woman to choose the music for our final leg. The choice was between Rod Stewart's *'Rhythm of my Heart,'* and Louis Armstrong's rendition of *'Wonderful World.'* She opted for Louis Armstrong, and soon Satchmo was crooning about skies of blue and leaves of green, babies crying and people saying I-love-you. The ballad piped through the headsets as I steered into the traffic pattern, and prepared to land.

The last words of the song stretched out: *"...what a wonderful...world...Oh yeah!"* On the final note the landing gear touched the pad, and I put the pitch down, the tour officially done.

When my borderline passenger keyed her mike I heard a sniffle. I peeked over my shoulder, and saw tears tracing her cheeks. "What do you think?" I said.

She wiped her eyes and smiled. "Can I go again?"

As with every flying job I held, the tour business taught me something new every time I took off. I learned right away that it's a highly competitive, almost a cutthroat grapple for customers and cash. This, too, was the opposite of my previous experience where passengers called looking for my services, money wasn't discussed, Doctors, EMTs, Paramedics kept me in business and the supply of customers was guaranteed with no advertising.

Every year a million tourists visit Kauai. One fourth of them take a helicopter tour. With seven operators on the island, that's 36,000 tourists apiece per year to pick from. So the opportunity exists to fly about 100 tourists per day per operator. Every company fights for as many of those paying passengers as it's possible to fly. Helicopters are expensive machines to operate, and to show a profit they must be kept in the air as much of the time as possible. Seven tours per day per helicopter was standard. All tours ended at sunset. Darkness limits the view of course. And because of noise and aesthetic reasons, FAA rules require a sunset shutdown for helicopter tour operators. With all those tourists flying around, Kauai has more helicopter movements per day than anywhere else on earth.

Tour flying was my first job without a salary. I was paid per tour, so if I didn't fly I didn't get paid. The obvious default in that plan is to fly if at all possible. It's reasonably stressful flying, partly because the hours are so demanding, though a tour pilot on Kauai likely wouldn't get a lot of sympathy from other pilots.

One stressor is weather. In the middle of the Pacific Ocean, and one of the wettest places on the planet, Kauai has weather patterns that challenge the most experienced aviator. It isn't particularly hard flying per se, but the restrictions to visibility, turbulence, and the speed of weather changes requires all the experience a pilot has gathered in a lifetime of flying. In addition, FAA regulations of the tour business require arcane terrain and ridge line clearances, ground and obstruction avoidance and radio protocols unlike anywhere I ever flew. It may be easier to be cited with a flight violation on Kauai than anywhere else.

But weather is a constant factor. Despite the canard I used to calm my nervous passengers, 'no rain; no rainbows,' tropical rain does hamper visibility on Kauai, and it happens a lot. The heaviest rain on the island often shuts down forward visibility completely. The good news was that the restriction lasted a few seconds, a minute or two at most. Still, an opaque windscreen was unsettling for already nervous passengers.

Then there is wind. Wind is weather on Kauai. Northeast trade winds blow almost all the time, at a steady fifteen to twenty knots. Trade winds cool the island, keeping daytime temperatures between about 65 and 85 degrees year round. Trade winds bring the rain, and they make it dissipate quickly. Winds also diffuse the scent of plumeria, and hibiscus and the salty-sweet aroma of the vast Pacific across the island like a tester at a perfume shop.

Sometimes the wind changes direction, blowing from the southwest. When it blows this way, a so called Kona wind, then flying on Kauai is truly challenging because of the turbulence the Southwest wind creates. Kona wind turbulence was stronger than any I'd ever experienced. It blasted the aircraft upward sometimes 500 feet per minute, then slammed it back down every bit as fast. It jerked the ship sideways, banged it halfway over, making me wrestle the controls. It raised passengers in their seats, then banged them down. They'd yelp, and grab onto handles and each other, their eyes like saucers. More than once I turned back to the airfield and cancelled a tour during Kona wind days because it just wasn't any fun.

Along with all the bumps and jerks, Kona winds also produced some of the greyest, nastiest weather on the island. During Kona wind days streaky, flat cloud layers surround the mountains, and rain slants against the windows in a steady soaking. The good news about Kona winds is that they seldom last more than a few days before the sunny Northeast trades return. But with a Kona wind, flights over WaiMea Canyon, or along the NaPali Coast were gut-wrenching, toss-around affairs. On those bumpy flights aloha bags became a coveted item.

When I first flew tours it was a consensus that some passengers would become ill during a tour. It was inevitable; no one questioned it. A fellow pilot had even incorporated this 'fact' into his briefing. He demonstrated the use of the white bag in rather blatant fashion. I watched him do it once. He scanned his waiting passengers, opened the white bag and held it against his mouth. Then he faked retching into it, "A-Lo-Ha!" thereby planting the idea in his passengers' minds that they'd use that very bag at some point during his tour. I used a different approach. In my briefing I steered clear of the fake retching business, and the histrionics. I never mentioned needing an aloha bag. Instead, I gave my passengers another 'fact.' On my tour no one needed one of those bags. I simply didn't consider that they would, and they seldom did. To reinforce my conviction, I showed them instead the bags of ginger candy I carried. I told them, should they need it, to help themselves. There was no doubt in my delivery, no drama or subliminal message, just fact. In three years I flew more than 15,000 passengers around Kauai. Three of them used the aloha bag. One was a young fellow who claimed he'd never gotten airsick in his life. Another was a ten-year-old boy who pitched his lunch after I landed. The third was a young woman in the throes of morning sickness.

I belabor the airsickness theme for a reason. As a tour pilot I had to be a flying psychologist. I had to read body language, hear peoples' unspoken fears, even read their minds on occasion. Once the tour was underway, there was no turning back. I carried six passengers, so if one person demanded that I quit early and land, it had a direct impact on five other people. I did turn around once, when a woman simply couldn't relax and enjoy the tour, and demanded that I take her back. It caused her husband and four other people to lose their tour, and their money.

High emotion often reveals a lot about people. Another woman demanded, halfway along, that I end the tour. She wasn't frightened. She was bored! The picture of self-absorption, the young newlywed woman couldn't fathom why I refused her request. "Take me home!" she shouted. I'd just made the turn over Ke'e Beach, the halfway point of the tour.

Her new husband tried to quiet her. "Won't be long," he said. "We're halfway."

"I don't care. Take me back, right now!" The fellow couldn't convince her that he and four other people wanted to finish *their* tour. It didn't matter. She was bored, she said, and she wanted to land. Fear, or just selfish behavior? I couldn't tell. The only concern I had was that she was seated next to me, within reach of the flight controls, and she seemed to be getting more agitated as the tour progressed. She finally settled down, pouting the remainder of the tour. I felt sorry for her young husband.

Most people were simply delightful. I helped a family board one afternoon for their tour. Mom, dad and two daughters climbed in, ready to take a trip around the island with me. I put the girls in the front seats. One was nine, the other eight. Happy, fun sisters, if a bit peevish with each other, I looked forward to flying with them. I could tell that the two sisters shared a sibling tension. They competed for simple things, window seat versus interior, which one got to use the camera, that sort of thing. The nine-year old mocked her eight-year old sister, making no effort to hide her disdain. It was kind of the mom, she started it—did not—did too—kind of thing often on display during so called family vacations, a phrase that may be oxymoronic.

I stood outside the cockpit next to the nine-year old, who was looking for a way to get in the last word in the on-going sisterly contest. As I gave the safety briefing, I talked about the first aid kit, fire extinguisher, seat belts and the other safety items stowed on board. When I came to the part about emergency exits I addressed the nine-year old. 'Lindsey' was seated closest to the right front door. Eight-year old sister 'Laura' was next to her, in the middle seat. "Lindsey," I said, getting her full attention. "See this orange thing?" I tapped the door's emergency release handle with my fingers.

"Uh, yes," Lindsey said, as sister Laura gazed at her, wondering what came next.

"If you pull up on that orange handle, the door will fall off."

Lindsey stared at me like I'd pulled a frog from my pocket.

In the opposite seat, Laura stared at her big sister, wide eyed. Her announcement summed up everything she felt about Lindsey. "Oh, Lord!" she said.

One emotion I never anticipated dealing with on a tour was claustrophobia. The fellow insisted on taking the right front seat, because he was 'terrified of tight spaces,' he claimed. I helped him board, made sure he was all right and cranked up the engine. He seemed fine, even appeared to be enjoying himself. Until I aimed for the opening to the Hanapu Valley on the NaPali coast. The opening is a thousand feet across. But flying into it seems a bit confining, with greenery and sheer cliffs surrounding the aircraft. Plus, the valley tapers in on itself, like a large green magnet. Halfway into Hanapu, the valley walls now 500 feet across, the man squirmed in his seat. His forehead dripping sweat, he grabbed the intercom. "You gotta turn back," he said.

I did as he asked, and the other passengers seemed okay with it. It made me wonder how people live with such anxiety all their lives? I was glad I'd never acquired such a phobia. It must restrict people from living fully.

Another passenger showed me courage that I envied, the ability to look at life as it is, without blinders or self-deception. She arrived for her tour wearing a headscarf, several leis, and a smile like the Buddha's. Her name was Wendy, and she had her own reason for taking a helicopter tour of Kauai.

She got my attention right away, during the initial briefing. "We gonna see any rainbows?"

"We almost always do," I said.

Rainbows result from the separation of light into its various wavelengths. As sunlight enters a water droplet, it bends. Light then contacts the opposite surface of each drop, reflects back as if from a mirror, and then glimmers out the other side, separating into the colors we see. For a double rainbow to form the light bounces around yet again, creating a second bow. One detail of a double rainbow is that the secondary bow's colors are a mirror image of the primary's. Red, yellow, green, blue doubles back as blue, green, yellow, red. I'd become an expert at predicting where rainbows would form. A column of rain marched along, the sun at just the right angle to it. I'd add power, race to where the bow would appear, and slow the helicopter. The brilliant arc formed, my passengers made adorable noises, then they'd deplete film and pixels of the bow to take home to Des Moines or Toledo or Fort Worth.

Wendy was adamant. "If I don't see a rainbow today I want my money back!"

Her fellow passengers laughed. So did I. It'll be a fun tour, I thought, despite this woman's frail appearance and demanding style. Wendy was the picture of ill-health. Ash white, head bald, her arms were so thin the bones showed.

But Wendy was as chipper and chatty as a ten-year-old, and a delight to have on board. She acted like she didn't have a care in the world. With Wendy beside me in the cockpit, I eased the collective up and took off. The ground fell away, and our tour began. Shortly, we crossed to the interior of the island, which surrounded us in its lush, tropical splendor.

I launched into my tour talk. "Who saw the movie Jurassic Park?" Half the hands went up, the passengers who'd seen the Spielberg dinosaur classic. "Remember when the helicopter landed in front of a waterfall?" Crossing a ridge, I pointed to my right. "There's that waterfall." Cameras came up, shutters snapping pictures of MaunaWai Puna falls. I crossed in front of the waterfall so everyone could see its 250-foot cascade. Wendy had no camera. She smiled, and patted my knee. "Beautiful," she said. "Just beautiful." She pointed at places for me to take her, joked with other passengers, demanded that I return to spots so she could see them again.

I steered onto the NaPali coast, and entered its velvet green valleys, Hanapu, Kalalau, Hanakapiai. Valley walls were drenched with water, draped with foliage of every Hu□. Beyond the Hanapu Valley I saw the rainbow. Increasing speed, I raced toward it before it disappeared. On Kauai just blink, and rainbows are gone. I nudged Wendy and pointed. "No refund for you."

She stared at the shimmering arc, and a tear slid down her cheek. Eyes swimming, she looked at me, and she smiled. "Done."

"There might be more of them."

"Done," she insisted, staring ahead. "I can go now."

I made a face, wondering what she meant. At that moment I thought about Wendy's odd outfit, her upbeat attitude, her nonchalance. All those leis. Their perfume filled the cockpit. What was I missing about Wendy? If I was so good at reading people, why had I not solved her mystery? Maybe I wasn't such an expert at body language after all.

Wendy rose in her seat, and pecked me on the cheek. "Thank you. I can go now," she said again.

"We're only halfway through..."

"It's okay," she said, and she patted my arm. I finished the tour, Louis Armstrong singing *Wonderful World* as we landed.

As she walked toward the shuttle, Wendy stopped and looked

back. She flipped me a kiss, her leis tossing in the breeze.

A month after I'd flown Wendy around the island I got a letter from a friend of hers. The letter explained that a tour of the island was the last item on her bucket list. Wendy died a few weeks after our trip around Kauai.

26

A Tour of Kauai

I wander to the briefing tent, where six new passengers wait for me to take them flying. It's trip number four of the day, and just after noon. I have a full slate of tours, seven total, and this is my final lap of the island before lunch.

A mischievous tradewind rattles the flaps of the tent. Palm fronds grab at me as I walk by. A United 757 lumbers onto the runway at Lihu□, tires squeaking, engines in reverse thrust as more tourists arrive on island. I stroll under the quivering canvas with its embossed Air Kauai logo. "Aloha, everyone!" I greet my eager customers seated in a horseshoe. They wave, and smile. A brave few sing out "aloha!" I scan them one by one, sensing their enthusiasm, their mood, their physical and mental state. They're all wearing the standard Hawaiian tourist garb, shorts, sandals, bright prints and flowered shirts. Every one of them has a small yellow inflatable life-vest strapped to their waist. The vest is an FAA mandate, since part of the tour is over water.

"Who wants to go fly with me?" Hands go up, some slower than others, my first clue to who is reluctant to fly, who is eager. I ask about them, when they arrived on island, if they've been in a helicopter before? I ask where they're from, because I'll use that information during the tour. I match names against the manifest, and try always to memorize them. Once we're airborne, I'll single people out on the intercom by name, ask them a question, or point to something of interest. When people hear their name it enhances their tour.

I finish the preliminaries, escort the six passengers to the helicopter, and assign seats. After a short briefing about safety stuff—first aid kits, smoking, exit strategy and the infamous aloha bags, I close the passenger doors, and climb into the cockpit. I tell everyone to don their headsets, and they do. Then I punch the battery master on, and the panel lights up with red, yellow and green lights. I check the instruments once more, and then mash the start button. The engine whines and churns, gauges spin up. The smell of burned jet fuel wafts through the cockpit. The rpm climbs quickly, the blades lumbering forward overhead, turning faster, faster, and then whipping along invisible. With the engine and rotors idling, the aircraft rocks like a hand on a cradle.

Once everything is up and running I flip on the radios, mash the mike button, call tower and ask for clearance. "Lihué tower, Air Kauai three off to the harbor." The tower operator says I'm clear to go, so I ease the collective up. The ship breaks ground, hovers. I turn to my left, and ease away from the pad. Over the departure point I check gauges once more, and see that all is well on the panel. So I tip the cyclic forward, and the helicopter wobbles toward takeoff. I punch a button to start the music, and tour number four begins.

The ground falls away, and the ship accelerates, climbing away from the airport. Hawaiian music croons in the headsets, the trade wind bumps the ship around, bright sun warms the cabin. We head west and south across Nawiliwili harbor, where a cruise ship is docked, wisps of smoke curling from its stack. People mill around the pier, and in nearby shops. In the harbor, two outrigger canoes cut through the glittering water, their six-man crews in perfect synch, paddles jabbing at the silven sea. Palm trees sway their own version of a gentle hula.

I fly close to the ocean, because it's mid-February, and the Humpbacks are here. Then I see one. A spout of water gushes, and a whale breaches. Off the jagged point of the harbor, a half mile at sea, three of the magnificent animals wallow in the waves, spouting, breaching, flukes breaking the water. Massive backs slide under the water, and sun glitters off blue-black bodies. More spouts appear, and another whale breaches, its glistening body arcing high, then crashing back with an explosion of silvery-spray. I bank that direction, and point the whales out to my passengers. Cameras come up for the first photo op of the tour.

Ahead, a mountain range looms. I fly parallel to it. Running east to west, the HaUpu ridge juts up and down with the outline of Queen Victoria, or so the natives say. HaUpu (Hah-oo-poo) means 'Hoary Ridge' in Hawaiian. Years ago someone claimed that the crag atop HaUpu was the profile of Queen Victoria, the monarch who ruled England when Hawaii had a British presence. Cruising by so-called Victoria's Profile, I ask my passengers if they see the resemblance to the long-serving queen? Few of them ever do, not even the Brits.

I give a short spiel on what people might expect to see: waterfalls, of course; lush jungle scenes; the red crags of WaiMea Canyon; rainbows arced across the island. I recall the home city of a particular passenger, and compare the island's scenery to it. Martha and husband Tom are from Chesterfield Missouri, a few miles west of the Arch where I recently flew. I call them on the intercom. "Martha, Tom, you're going to see things today that are even prettier than...East St. Louis!" Laughter brings people fully on board, and helps them relax.

Passengers for my tours come from all over the world. Some don't speak English, so I have to improvise. It was another skill I had to master on Kauai, communicating without English. To show where I was taking them, I'd point at the map. When I saw wild critters below, I'd make crude animal noises. To advise of photo ops I'd do the universal square-fingers as camera sign. Mostly I allowed the island to speak for itself.

Once I flew a Chinese fellow who was traveling alone. He spoke very little English. To optimize our hand gestures to each other I seated him in front. I'd point to landmarks, then jab at the map to show him where we were. When I saw a mountain goat below I did my best imitation. My odd half circled hand gesture meant rainbow, but I'm not sure he got it. The other passengers reacted to my pantomime with a mix of amusement, and a certain amount of anxiety that they were perhaps in the hands of a madman. But the Chinese fellow ate it up. He laughed, and chattered at me, his grin as wide as the sky. Unable to communicate with the fellow, I made sure he got a good tour anyway, like everyone else.

At the end of the day, I went to the office to close out my paperwork. My in-box contained an envelope. It was from my Chinese traveler. I sliced it open, expecting a note, or a card of some kind. Instead, there was a five-dollar bill, and two singles. It was my tip, and likely all the cash the fellow had. The bills added up to the number seven. I smiled. I didn't speak any Chinese, but I understood that seven is a sign of good fortune in the Orient. It was the smallest tip I ever got, and by far the best. It made my day.

Cruising past HaUpu I'd discuss some of the island's geologic history, which is evident from that vantage point. North and West of LiHu□ a broad, grassy plain rises slowly to about a hundred feet above sea level. Five miles across, this bowl is the largest caldera in Hawaii. There were several hotspots on Kauai during the island's volcanic birth and adolescence, and more than a dozen different volcanic cones dot the island. The last eruption took place 2.8 million years ago near what is now Poipu Beach on Kauai's south shore. The cone of that eruption is one of the smallest in Hawaii, its circumference roughly 300 feet, height about fifty.

Ensconced in the middle of a field near Pe'e Road in Poipu, and crowned with weeds, the tiny, dead volcano could be mistaken for a haystack.

We move past Ha Upu ridge, and fly over the tree tunnel, a corridor of eucalyptus trees hiding Maluhia Road, which runs through the shady arbor. This is the route to Poipu, and the southern beaches of Kauai. Three miles later we leave the populated part of the island behind, and cross a ridge into the trackless, wild interior. This is the part of Kauai that people can see only by helicopter.

First we'll drop in for a visit to a waterfall called Mauna Wai Puna (Monna-Why-Poona). Mauna means mountain, Wai means water, and Puna is the district on Kauai, so the name means mountain water in Puna Falls. This waterfall was featured in the Speilberg movie, Jurassic Park. Scientists flew into the park aboard a helicopter, then landed at the base of these falls. Mauna Wai Puna's 250-foot cascade is on private property, land that belongs to the Robinson family, a big name in the Hawaiian sugar business.

The Robinsons' presence on Kauai goes back to the mid-nineteenth century, when the widow Robinson brought her four sons to the island. Shortly after arrival, the British family Robinson started growing sugar cane. Then the world discovered cheap candy, and the simple pleasures of sweetening other things, and the Robinsons' grew even more sugar. Then the world discovered rum, and the price of cane became intoxicating for those who grew it.

The Robinsons owned some of the world's finest land for growing cane, and in little time they became wealthy beyond measure. They still own several thousand acres of land on Kauai's south shore, a district called Makaweli. (Mah-Kuh-Way-Lee) They also own the island of Niihau seven miles offshore from Kauai. They bought Niihau (Knee-ee-how) in 1864 from King Kamehameha V for $10,000 in gold. It's the only private island in Hawaii, although recent rumor has it that billionaire Oracle owner Larry Ellison has purchased most of the island of Lanai.

Leaving Mauna Wai Puna, we cross the Makaweli cane fields, and halfway up a ridge we see the Robinson homestead. The sprawling, ranch-style home, with its commanding view of Makaweli and the Pacific Ocean is still occupied by members of that family.

WaiMea canyon is next. Wai = water, Mea = red. The red water canyon is named for the river of the same name, which cuts through it. Because of the volcanic origin of Kauai the land is mostly iron oxide, essentially rust. Red dirt turns the river red, and is also used as a dye for T-shirts sold to tourists. The ubiquitous rust-colored dirt is also why Hawaiian people take off their shoes when entering a home, a fine idea when you think about it.

WaiMea Canyon stretches ten miles wide and a mile deep. Like a jagged washboard, its crags and crevices rise and fall in a splash of contrasting red and green. I cruise through the crevices, red ground rising on left and right. I bank over, aim for a ridge and zip across it. The ground plunges away on the other side of the ridge, and passengers gasp in delight. Climbing a bit, I aim for the west end of the canyon, where another waterfall shimmers. WaiPo'o (Why-Poe-Oh) drops in two sections, about 500 feet total. Constant wind in the canyon blows the waters sideways and back, and WaiPo'o's spray dances down, dissipating as it drops, becoming a mist as it meets the river.

Veteran pilots told me that tourists often 'leave their brain on the Mainland.' A passenger once proved that derogative assessment for me. The fellow was in the back of my helicopter with his wife. The tour was going well. Cruising west from MaunaWaiPuna, I muted the music to give a short spiel about WaiMea Canyon. I spoke of its formation, various features, what to expect. Reaching the canyon, I lowered the collective, and the aircraft dropped between the red cliffs. In back, the fellow in question leaned forward, staring into the crevasse.

I finished up my spiel with a comment on the island's wildlife. "Look into the canyon, folks," I said. "...you might see wild pigs, deer, wild horses, maybe even a mountain goat."

Three seconds later, the fellow keyed his mike. "Ever see any animals down there?"

His wife whipped her head around, and stared. Then she leaned away like she'd never seen him before. The fellow looked at her. At me. Back at her. "What?" Finally, he realized what he'd said, and shared in the laughter.

WaiMea Canyon has a rich geologic history. Seen from the air, it appears to be almost a separate section of Kauai. And it nearly became so once. An ancient earthquake caused the great rift we see from the air, a quake that almost broke Kauai in two. A local myth claims that Mark Twain, during his visit to Kauai in 1880, called WaiMea the Grand Canyon of the Pacific. The misperception persists because it sounds good. But, like a lot of Hawaiian lore, it isn't true. The Canyon in Arizona wasn't called Grand until after Twain's death in 1910. Sam Clemens was a clever fellow, but it's not likely he predicted the appellation of one canyon, and its similarity to another.

There are a lot of myths on Kauai, and tourists seemed to love hearing them. One concerns the Hawaiian version of Leprechauns, the infamous Menehune people. The Menehune (men-a-hoony) were, allegedly, very tiny people with gigantic and quite magical engineering skills. On Kauai they supposedly built the Menehune fishpond near Lihué, and the Menehune ditch, an irrigation channel for taro fields near the town of Waimea. The fantastic part of the myth is that they built these projects in just one night. The reality is quite different, and a bit sobering. Those projects were indeed built by 'little people,' slaves of the Alii, the high priests of the island. The Alii worked those people savagely, often to death, to finish projects on the royal schedule.

Another Hawaiian myth refers to Glass Beach near the town of Hanapepe on the south shore. Local people say the glass-colored sands of this beach are a gift from the gods. Maybe so, but much of the actual glass, bead-like sand found lying there, is refuse that washes over from the public dump at Port Allen. If it seems that myths such as that one serve to hide unsavory things on Kauai it may be true. The local people put a positive spin on everything, and why not? No rain; no rainbows. I add power, and the helicopter surges out of the Canyon. It's time to visit NaPali.

The rugged battlement called NaPali along Kauai's northwest shore is a high point of the tour. NaPali, (Nah-Polly) which means 'the cliffs,' offers possibly the most beautiful natural view in the world. Volcanic cliffs drop a thousand feet into the Pacific. Sea birds wheel through sudden showers. Double rainbows burst into view, then dissipate, and then shimmer again. Monstrous waves rush toward NaPali's jagged rocks, exploding in a riot of salt spray. Wintertime swells along NaPali can grow to fifty feet, slamming the coast, sending fountains of spray gushing hundreds of feet upward. Valleys along NaPali nurture dozens of species of plant life, tropical flowers in massive arrangements, and waterfalls that stream into pools dotting valley floors. NaPali is a ten mile long tropical garden.

Halfway along NaPali, the Kalalau Valley is the largest recess on the coast. For more energetic tourists, the 11-mile Kalalau trail ends at the beach here. A number of people live 'off the grid' in Kalalau. I'd see them sometimes on tours as I cruised the valley. They keep to themselves, evading arrest for trespassing and living on public land. They beg for food and cigarettes from hikers on the Kalalau trail, grow what they need to subsist, including stands of marijuana, and tend to their own business. Many of them wear clothes, but by various accounts those individuals seem to be in the minority.

The Sky Behind Me

~*~

I turn the corner over Ke'e (Kay-A) Beach, where the highway ends on Kauai's north shore. It's the halfway point in the tour, and a good place to talk about Hawaiian history and culture. "Look west across the Pacific, folks," I say. "We're now at the farthest inhabited point of the United States. Below us, Ke'e Beach has great swimming and snorkeling, and it's the start of the Kalalau trail."

I do one last circle. "On Ke'e beach, in ancient times, young people learned the ancient art of hula. Only men were allowed to perform the hula. Back then it was kapu, or forbidden to women by the Alii." (Ah-Lee-ee) were the ancient elite class, Hawaiian priests who held total power over common people. "If you or I looked directly at an Alii," I said. "...or ate a royal fish, or spoke in their presence, we'd be put to death."

Ancient Hawaiian culture was violent and paternalistic. The Alii were all powerful, and often cruel. Shadows of this history remain in the way hula dancers invoke the warrior mentality, and in the reverence Hawaiians feel for their bellicose past, though now women do the hula. Arguments for the return of ancient Hawaiian culture appear in local newspaper op eds, and in daily conversation on the island. Political initiatives for the return of native lands are prevalent, especially on Kauai. It's common to see ads demanding that Hawaiian land be returned to its people, and for the end of statehood. Much of the political tension comes from cultural differences.

A common bumper sticker sums up local disgust with hard driving, over-eager tourists: *"Slow down, this ain't the Mainland."* Another sticker is a bit more aggressive, but truthful when and wherever encountered on roadways: *"The closer you get, the slower I go."* I once drove too close behind a young local boy who peered in his mirror at me, and then slammed on his brakes. I swerved left around him, missing his bumper by a palm frond.

I understood the anger the locals felt, their sense of alienation from ancient ways. Local people on Kauai are caught in a terrible vise. To survive, they depend almost completely on tourists and their dollars. But they long for the day the haoles go away, and leave them alone on their island paradise. They also sense that it will never happen.

I increase airspeed, and climb over the jagged ridge above Haena. To the right we see the Honokapiai Valley. In the farthest recess of Honokapiai (Hon-A-Kop-EE-eye) a single waterfall drapes the cliff, falling in one strand more than five hundred feet. I cross the ridge and the helicopter bumps around, turbulence ushering us away from NaPali.

Ahead we see a mountain crest jutting toward the ocean overlooking Hanalei. This is Mount Namolokama. (Nom-Oh-Lo-Komma) I aim for Namo's midsection at three thousand feet, and slow the aircraft. To the left, as we cross a saddle ridge, we see the little town of Hanalei with its postcard semi-circle beach. *Hana* means bay, so Hana-Lei means bay shaped like a lei. Another Hawaiian myth thrives around Hanalei. It's the persistent rumor that Peter Yarrow of Peter, Paul & Mary referred to the idyllic spot in the 1963 hit song *Puff the Magic Dragon*. Puff, the gentle beast that befriends Jackie Paper, lives in 'A land called Hon-A-Lee.' Mister Yarrow claims it isn't so. In 1959 a Cornell classmate of Yarrow's, Leonard Lipton, wrote the poem that led to the song. Lipton had never been to Kauai, never heard of Hanalei. But, like a lot of myths on Kauai, the story makes a tour more colorful, so a lot of pilots pass it along as fact.

Trying to debunk those tales was an interesting endeavor, partly because there are so many of them, partly because they sometimes contain a speck of truth. The Menehune myth is one example. Passengers asked about the names of canyons, spirits that visit on tropical nights, and the acceptability of taking home rocks and natural artifacts, only to suffer the Goddess Pele's wrath because of it. I told them it was myth, and most people accepted that, especially when I related the truth behind it. But many refused to let go of the native narrative, choosing to believe the myths instead.

Four thousand foot Mount Namolokama has the highest waterfall in Hawaii, and the highest continuous falls in the world. Namo runs all the time, fed by a high-altitude swamp on the roof of Kauai. The Alakai (Ah-Luh-kye) swamp originates a mile above sea level atop Mount Waialeale, the primary volcano of Kauai.

I steer the helicopter toward the high falls, and slow down. Namolokama's shimmering cascade is awe-inspiring in its own right. But Namo and its water show have cultural value as well. Namo's last segment of falls forms a pool a hundred feet across. In ancient times the Alii performed marriage ceremonies in that pool. The burbling water was a communal gathering spot. Its vine-covered bank was a meeting place for war councils, its waters a funerary pool for the Alii. Using the ancient holy water gushing from Namolokama's heights, Hawaiian Kahunas anointed their new priests.

Namolokama also marks the spot where I was stripped of *my* anointed status as a pilot.

Once everyone has enough pictures of Namo, I angle east, and cross a small saddle. Wind gusting up the ridge bumps the aircraft around. I drop into the Hanalei Valley, a north south chasm filled with waterfalls and foliage with more shades of green than an artist's palette. At the end of the valley I slow down, cross another small ridge and prepare my passengers for the high point of the tour. We'll soon fly inside the crater of Mount WaiAleAle. (Why-Alee-Alee).

"Folks, on the Big Island you can fly above a volcano. Here on

Kauai you can fly *inside* one." I see the usual looks of curiosity. "In front of us is the crater of the volcano that formed Kauai seven million years ago."

At times I had to qualify my remarks, or tone them down a bit. Once I flew a family of four with a young son. When I mentioned flying *inside a volcano* the boy stared at his mother in concern. I quickly assured the lad that the volcano's fire had gone out a long time ago. Another passenger, a fundamentalist fellow, once took me to task about the timeline of the island, and its geologic formation. After the tour, he pulled me aside and explained that my reference to 'seven million years' was not in keeping with Biblical precepts, that the island could be no more than 10,000 years old. I must 'refrain from telling people such mistaken ideas,' he said. He mentioned a website that would back up his assertions. "Pull it up on line," he said. "It's right there on the internet."

WaiAleAle is Kauai's mother volcano. The name means 'Rippling Water' because of the constant wind ruffling the pool at the mountain's peak. The five thousand foot crest is what's left of the shield volcano that formed the island of Kauai. WaiAleAle is the do not miss part of a helicopter tour of Kauai, the only volcano on earth where helicopters enter its inner sanctum.

Three million years ago the volcano's creative power ended in a sudden, earth-rending blast, when its east wall exploded. Like Mount St. Helens in Washington State, WaiAleAle ruptured, spewing rock, fire and ash outward for several miles. The explosion had several effects on the still young island that would be called Kauai. It silenced the mighty volcano, it caused the island to stop growing and it blasted a gap a thousand feet wide on the mountain's east face. I slow the aircraft and prepare to fly toward the monumental rupture.

At the north wall of the volcano I turn right, and slow to thirty knots. I start the music, a somber chant in a low register, like organ music in a cathedral. Almost hovering, I slip inside the dim, eerie recess of the dead volcano. Like it's time for a drama to start, the light dims. The temperature chills, and passengers hug themselves. Mist envelops the aircraft, and water streams down the windows. The crater's blackened walls and striated surfaces resemble a jagged washboard. Vertical scratch marks are the ancient scouring and scalding of sizzling lava forced upward with unimaginable power. Gashed and blackened corrugations are evidence of the ancient fire that once bubbled up from the sea floor. From thousands of miles below, a river of molten rock gushed from the bowels of the earth, funneled through this crater, then vomited from the volcano's white-hot top. During its 3.5 million-year lifespan, WaiAleAle spilled 14 million tons of liquid iron and basalt. For more than three million years lava spewed in thousands of separate eruptions, one layer atop the other, forming the 525 square mile island that is Kauai.

I pressure the cyclic and make a gentle right turn, easing forward, hovering now. We're four hundred feet above the crater floor. Five hundred feet from its charred walls, though they seem close enough to touch. As I hover, beads of mist streak the windscreen. Ropes of rain whip off the rotors creating a showery glow. Chanting fills the headsets.

On the south crater wall, a sheen of streaming water coats the charred black surface. This liquid flow collects in a small pond, which brims full, then overflows. The resulting stream courses through the crater, turns east out of the rupture and forms the WaiLua River, the only navigable river in Hawaii.

Pressing the right pedal I ease into the center of the crater. Directly below is an emerald, meadow-like pillow of grass a hundred feet across called Jack's spot. The tiny green landing pad was named for Jack Harter, an early aviation pioneer on Kauai. Before the FAA put a stop to the practice, Jack would land there and let his passengers get out and walk around.

Like a convex bowl, the vaulting sides of the crater are awash with waterfalls, and thick with foliage as high as we can see. Looking up, the vegetation and black volcanic rock disappear in a veil of rain. Flying inside the crater we're surrounded by the lush, exotic beauty of nature in all its ruggedness, its creative energies, its awesome power. A reverent hymn hums in the headsets, rain mists the windscreen, and the serenity of ferns, grasses, vines and variegated flowers thriving in the inner sanctum makes the crater of WaiAleAle a spiritual experience. Five thousand feet above, hidden in mist, is the rim of the ancient volcano.

At the crater's lip, a mile above sea level is a flat mass of sodden land stretching west for ten miles. This is the Alakai Swamp. Though it's one of the wettest places on earth, the land at the rim of the crater is barren. There's simply too much rainfall there for plants to thrive. Northeast trade winds blow, unobstructed, across four thousand miles of open Pacific. That moving mass of air entrains a lot of moisture. When the air mass reaches Kauai, it's forced upward by orographic lifting. This lifting causes the moisture to condense out, and it rains. Lordy, does it rain. The north shore of Kauai receives an average of 100 inches of rain per year. Because the lifting process is so sudden, so effective, the moisture is wrung out of the air mass quickly, leaving dry air. The southwest shore of Kauai, the downwind side of the island, averages 10 inches of rain per year.

Because of this same weather pattern on Kauai the high spot on the island, Mount WaiAleAle averages yearly rainfall of more than 450 inches. Five hundred inches is not uncommon. The current record atop WaiAleAle was set in 1982 when 680 inches of rain fell. That's 57 *feet* of rain in one year.

Atop the volcano sits an ancient Heiau, (Hey-Ow) or altar. Hundreds of years ago the Alii used the site in religious ceremonies. WaiAleAle was thought to be the home of the gods, such deities as Kane (Kah-Nay) the male god, and Ono, the god of fire, or light. Because these gods lived on the mountaintop, only the Alii were allowed to visit there. The area was kapu to common people. As I cruised over the collection of rocks that marked the altar, I wondered what the Alii would think of my helicopter profaning such a site. After the dizzy spell that ended my career, I thought about the kapu aspects of flying on Kauai. I wondered if perhaps the ancient priests had conspired to ground me? If so, the irony would be rich. Religious royalty had taken away my first dream, my desire to enter their ranks. Could they have intervened again?

But believing that flying over sacred ground had cursed me would grant the Alii too much power. Like a lot of the myths I heard on Kauai, I dismissed the possibility. Unlike the simple Hawaiian people I recognized no law of kapu; I'd come a long way from my seminary days, and my beliefs had evolved on with the journey. Just as the ancient Alii had done to the commoners on Kauai, I believe modern priests have disrupted and destroyed people's lives. I have no wish to defend any of them, ancient or modern. Instead, I pity those people who've been terrorized by self-appointed keepers of the moral high ground.

I hadn't angered the gods, and neither had anyone else. I may have been behind the controls, surrounded by passengers, but flying over paradise I knew this: unless unduly restrained, we can all fly; none of us have lost access to the mountaintop; no one can keep us from it, unless we allow them to.

With some reluctance I exit the crater. The airport is straight ahead, the tour nearly done. I call the tower for clearance, and then circle over one last attraction. Wailua Falls is the so-called twin falls of Kauai. The WaiLua River wends its way out of the volcano crater, runs east about five miles and arrives at a cliff. Boulders at the cliff's edge split the river's flow in two. Twin veils plunge a hundred feet into a pool half an acre wide, where swimmers bask beneath the billowing falls. Six miles Northeast of Lihué on route 583, Wailua Falls was featured in the opening sequence of a TV show in the late seventies. As I circle overhead I ask passengers where they might have seen the waterfall? If no one knew, I'd jog their memory. "De plane, boss—de plane!"

With the tour of Fantasy Island nearly over, I ask a passenger to choose the music that will take us to the airport. Either Rod Stewart or Louis Armstrong entertain people into the traffic pattern, and onto the pad. I land, thank everyone for flying with me, help them off the helicopter and watch them board the shuttle. After refueling I greet the next group, and do it all over again.

Seven times a day, twenty days a month, I'd take off, show Kauai's magical beauty, play flying psychologist, tour guide, Hawaiian cultural, religious, geology and history expert. I'd relieve people's fear of flying. I'd answer questions, and help make memories. Once in a while I'd help someone complete a bucket list item. It was the best flying job ever, and I was damned good at it.

Then it ended, like a dissipating rainbow.

27

A Final Tour

December 14th 2005 was a perfect day for tours. Winds from the northeast, gentle at ten or fifteen knots. Showers came and went all morning. Scattered cumulus clouds hung like lazy cotton stuffing. I flew three trips, and then took a break for lunch. My fourth tour started at twelve-forty-five, and, once airborne, everything seemed perfectly normal. I felt good, the ship was humming along, and my passengers laughed and joked, taking pictures of everything but the ashtrays.

On days like that I pinched myself at the opportunity I'd been given, not just on Kauai but in my working life. I'd take off on a morning tour, tropical sunshine streaming into my cockpit and think why me? What did I ever do to have this fall in my lap?

Squinting at me, arms crossed, a woman once said: "You actually live here?"

"Yep, right over there."

"And you do this for a living?"

"Tough job, but someone's gotta do it."

She shook her head, and brought her camera back up.

Flying tours on Kauai felt like recompense of some kind, reward for years of flying in harsh, cold conditions dealing with the cruelest and worst of human crises. I'd worked hard to keep my record clean. I'd flown for thirty-eight years at that point, avoiding the fate of a lot of colleagues. I'd never scratched the paint on a helicopter, never damaged the machine or injured anyone on board. I understood the woman's question. Yes, I flew for a living, in the most beautiful place on earth. And in some ways I felt I'd earned the privilege. It was almost like the flying god smiled and said, here's what you wanted when you were a kid. Too bad what happened to you back then, but this makes up for it.

My posting on Kauai seemed to be a convergence of sorts, reward for what happened when I was young, and the perfect way to close out my logbook. It all fit together. My interview with the boss at Air Kauai seemed to start the last chapter of my career. Chuck was like Wayne Alexander in many respects. Gruff, vulgar, no nonsense. Neither man had an ounce of sentiment. But they made up for that lack with a passion for what they did. Both of them relished their reputation as a hard ass, members of a special breed of humans who ignore what others think of them, and seem to seek out confrontation. Both men pushed me to be a better, more conscientious pilot. Wayne and Chuck were like the bookends of my flying career.

The fraternity of pilots on Kauai reminded me of my assignments in the active Army, and in three different National Guard units. The camaraderie I felt with all those military aviators was similar. Tour pilots share stories about passengers, employers, weather, and the crews who keep them flying. During weather delays on Kauai I'd mingle with my colleagues, while rain drowned the island, dropping visibility to zero and canceling tours. Just so, military pilots crowd ready rooms on weather days swapping war stories, sharing anecdotes and information. Something all pilots share is an understanding of how fortunate we are to be doing what we do. Both clubs, military and commercial pilots, are staffed with veterans of a lot of time in the sky. On Kauai, my 10,000 logged hours were a comparatively low figure. Some of my colleagues there had logged upward of twenty thousand hours, most of those flying laps around Kauai. It's a tribute to them. But it's also a comment on how beautiful the island is, and how fortunate we felt to be soaring above it, and getting paid to do so. It truly was a dream job, and a perfect way to cap an aviation career. *"The heart of a man can want no more than this."*

I always thought I'd decide when to quit flying, when to hang up my headset, fold my tent and wander away from the flight line. Would it be my decision? Of course it would. As a pilot, I was used to making decisions, being in charge. It never occurred to me that some outside entity would decide for me.

One thing every pilot dreads is the yearly visit to the flight physician. When flying commercially, the required annual medical check makes any pilot anxious. Your flight doc holds your aviation career in his or her hands. With the sweep of a ballpoint pen a physician can end that career, forever. I've seen pilots become physically ill prior to a yearly checkup. Some have no issue, no problem with high blood pressure, until the white-frocked one with the clipboard enters the exam room. Then...BP goes through the roof. There's even a name for the event: White Coat Syndrome. But no flight doctor grounded me.

I took off that December day feeling fine, looking forward to another great tour. At 12:45 I lifted off for a harbor departure, cleared LiHu□ airspace and cruised past MaunaWaiPuna falls. Then I flew on to Waimea Canyon.

A passenger asked about the barren tree limbs scattered over the island, like volunteer weeds in new corn. I told him it was remnants of Hurricane Iniki in 1992. With winds of 170 miles per hour the storm had stripped those trees bare. "Remind you of Vietnam?" he asked.

I hadn't expected anyone to make the connection, but the damaged trees did take me back to the war. He was right; the landscape looked like parts of Southeast Asia. "Yeah, I guess it does kinda remind me of that," I said.

"Thanks for your service over there," he said, and other passengers chimed in with their gratitude as well.

The mention of Vietnam was unusual. The reminder wasn't. With the terrain, the tropical weather, and the amount of flying, cruising around Kauai did remind me of my assignment as a younger pilot. It took me back for other reasons as well. Local people were equally powerless, in Vietnam and on Kauai. Many islanders hate the helicopter services because of the noise, and the disregard for their care of the land. If I strayed over one of several no-fly zones on the island someone living there would make an immediate phone call to the boss and when I landed he'd be at the helipad to let me know about it. The tension between locals and the haoles focused on helicopter operators to a large extent. We were a highly-visible target of native Hawaiians' disgust over rich Mainlanders forcing their way into Hawaii to enrich themselves. In Vietnam, the local people were dismissed by a government that ignored their needs and wants. In Vietnam, local people's attitude toward GIs was a barely concealed contempt. In their view, we'd forced our way into their culture to take over and enrich ourselves. There were many similarities, so the fellow's question about them hit home.

Because of my longevity in the cockpit, I suppose, I'd taken to reminiscing, going back over old ground. The more I flew the more I noted the recurrence of familiar things, like I was revisiting old haunts, a kind of summation of my career. I'd scan the jungle on Kauai and imagine flying over Vietnam. Once again, it seemed, like traveling to Vietnam all those years before, coming to Kauai I'd packed my bags, traveled across the Pacific to fly over a rich, exotic landscape.

Some of it took me back to St. Louis. It wasn't long before I was Chuck's go-to guy. He assigned certain tours to me, because they furthered his business, and he wanted customers pampered. Those customers represented hotels, or cruise ships, or other referral sources for even more customers. One such client who needed pampering, for example, was a principle in one of the largest banks in the U.S. He chartered the helicopter for a personal 90-minute tour. With his family aboard, I flew over the home the fellow was building on the north shore of the island, a property worth in excess of twenty million dollars. The man and his family reminded me of the wealthy patrons I'd flown in Toledo and Evansville years before. Nice, deferential people, kind and considerate of whatever I did in the cockpit. I gave them a wonderful tour, and they were impressed.

Like my hospital flying, taking tourists around the island day after day was a therapeutic exercise for some of them. There was Wendy, the bucket list woman. There was the woman who came to the flight line the evening before her tour. A fellow who claimed he was claustrophobic flew with me, and his symptoms didn't recur. Indeed, several of my passengers on Kauai mentioned a life-long fear of something. I could only conclude that taking a tour was their way of confronting that fear, staring it down, and dismissing it from their lives.

Circling the island, I looked back at a career filled with all good things, and very few bad. Fort Wolters and my first solo; Wayne's curses and broken pencils in the Texas heat; Vietnam and its defining influence in my career; Alaska and Panama and Guyana with the military. The Ohio Guard, the Medicopter and the closure that mission gave me. Fly By Helicopter in Toledo, and getting fired. Evansville with its coal, racism and the humiliation of scrubbing hubcaps on Betty's Lincoln. Iowa City and my Air Medical career, twenty years of helping people when they most needed help. *"The heart of a man..."*

I'd flown 12,500 hours, carried 100,000 people, 3,200 medical patients, 15,000 tourists. I'd traveled over a million miles in a helicopter, an exciting, exhilarating life in the cockpit. I'd put a lot of sky behind me.

I turned the corner at Ke'e Beach, and headed toward Mount Namolokama. Namo's waterfall gushed down the mountainside that day. Silvery spray foamed from green crevices. Sheets of white water splashed into bubbly pools. I pulled up to Namo's falls, slowed the aircraft almost to a hover, and turned with the pedals so passengers on both sides of the cabin could see and photograph the glorious water show.

Cameras clicked, people chattered. With some reluctance, I turned away, toward the ridge that led into Hanalei Valley, leaving Namolokama behind. Forever, as it turned out.

As I neared the ridge a tingle started behind my eyes. It grew more intense, a buzzing, humming kind of alarm. Then the sparkles started—pinpoints of light, like I'd stood too quickly. My vision narrowed. Blackness seeped in at the corners of my peripheral vision, closing, closing more, leaving a keyhole of light. I swallowed hard, shook my head, and took deep breaths. It wasn't working. A terrifying thought flashed in my brain: I'm going to pass out. I fought against it with every instinct I had, while trying not to be obvious. My passengers were in the dark, and it seemed I was quickly going there myself.

My heart slammed like a hammer. Sweat ran off my forehead and stung my eyes. My chest ached in fear. The sparkles began to dissipate, and slowly my vision cleared. The spell lasted ten seconds. It felt like an hour.

I tried not to think about what might have happened. Had I

gone unconscious for even a few seconds the aircraft would have crashed, and people would have died. I saw the headlines. Saw the arc of my career, from perfect safety for forty years to agonizing, inexplicable crash in forty seconds. As sobering as it was, I knew that gruesome outcome could have happened. There was no denying the gravity of it; I had to find out what happened to me, no matter the consequences.

As I crossed the ridge and dropped into the Hanalei Valley, winging toward the volcano crater, I looked for ways to expedite the tour and keep my passengers happy. I'd show them the heart-shaped waterfall in the valley, then cruise to the crater for a quick turn, then head for home, hoping the spell didn't return. If it started again I'd find a place to land, regardless. Whatever it was, the spell came out of nowhere, a sudden, ominous event that I knew in my bones meant trouble.

I raced toward the crater and hurried inside. Music matched the interior of the nave and waterfalls slicked the sides of the blackened flue. I hovered in the mist, while my passengers clicked, ooohed and ahhhed. All the time I kept my eyes on Jack's spot in case I felt the need to land. But at that point I felt fine, with no indication that anything untoward had happened.

I left the crater, and aimed the aircraft for home, still feeling fine. I queued up Louis Armstrong, and soon *Wonderful World* echoed through the cabin. *"I see skies of blue... clouds of white...bright blessed days....dark sacred nights...And I think to myself.....what a wonderful world..."*

I entered the traffic pattern and turned final. *"...The colors of the rainbow so pretty in the sky...are also on the faces of people going by...I see friends shaking hands saying how do you do...they're really saying I...love...you..."*

I stopped at the arrival pad, hovered in... *"I hear babies cry, I watch them grow...*

They'll learn much more than I'll never know...and I think

to myself...what a wonderful world...
    Yes I think to myself...what a wonderful world..."
    The landing gear touched the pad... *"...Oh, yeah..!*

28

Learning to Fly

My wife and I visited nearly every doctor, every clinic in Hawaii. I had every test, every alphabet procedure the medical experts thought appropriate: MRI, CT, EEG, BP, lab tests, X-rays, eye tests, treadmill. I lay on a table while a doctor filled my ears with ice water, and then spun the table around to make me dizzy. I didn't get dizzy; I felt fine. I stared into a cone filled with sparks of light, pressing buttons when I saw a flash. I passed with flying colors. I was poked and prodded, tested and tried more than some of the patients I'd flown in Iowa. No physical, or medical, or psychological symptom or deficit ever showed itself, no simple, straightforward explanation why I'd nearly passed out in the cockpit. No matter what medical test or protocol or procedure I had, the symptoms couldn't be duplicated. (And they've never returned.)

When I told the flight doc what had happened he grounded me, as I expected he would. I assumed it was just long enough for the aforementioned tests. I was hoping, of course, that as dire as the diagnosis might be, that test, whatever it was, would show something wrong, some medical anomaly that could be addressed and fixed. When nothing showed up it was disheartening. I was left trying to prove a negative. Will I get dizzy again? Might I have those symptoms again? Lacking a diagnosis I can't prove that I will not.

My flying career ended that day. The job I was born to do was over. It took a lot of time to sink in that I was done flying, because at first I simply couldn't accept it. I was fifty-five years old, otherwise in terrific shape, happy, extremely competent, with the best flying job I'd ever had. I'd planned to fly until at least sixty and beyond. It simply could not, *could not* be over.

Could I have ignored the spell, returned to the cockpit like nothing happened? Certainly. It would have been easy enough to do that, to assume that the near syncope, its medical term, was a passing thing, a case of dehydration, something I ate, too much caffeine, too little protein, something. Yes, I could have kept quiet about it, climbed back aboard, taken the chance that I'd never experience another spell.

At the time, I'd flown for almost forty years, more than 12,000 accident, incident-free hours. After all those years and hours in the air, thousands of miles, thousands of passengers, in all kinds of weather, in a war with live ammo, days and days after nights and nights, I had not one negative event in my record. Could I take a chance and put all that in jeopardy? I could not.

Losing my career put that spotless record in high relief. I'd attained a place of honor, a reputation any pilot should strive for. I couldn't jeopardize it.

Once, at the hospital, I overheard a flight nurse ask the dispatcher which pilot was on duty with him that night. When he asked the question I was in the next room, behind a partition. The dispatcher said that I was the pilot that night. The nurse responded, "Good, we all relax when Byron's on duty." Another similar circumstance happened at the Guard hangar. I overheard the enlisted crews bantering about different pilots, so I decided to eavesdrop, in case my name came up. And then it did. "I'd fly with Edgington to hell and back," the fellow said. There's no better feeling than that. It had been my goal from early in my career to have people relax and know they were safe with me at the controls. The knowledge that they were was worth more than platinum.

As difficult as it was, and it was heartbreaking for me, overnight I became a former pilot. I had to learn to fly all over again.

Like a lot of people who've had marvelous lives my first instinct was to deny that all of that joy, success and affirmation were gone. I'd been so good at what I did, for so long, with so much recognition and compensation for it that my mind rebelled at its ending. I simply couldn't convince myself that I'd never fly again. Flying had been such an integral part of my life, such a part of who I was that I felt invisible. I crashed, hard.

Everything I touched turned out wrong, or awkward, or badly. I was anxious getting out of bed in the morning, unsure what the day would bring, absolutely sure that I'd fall short in some way. It seemed I couldn't do anything right. I craved some kind of success, something I could do that didn't end badly. I was experiencing the classic symptoms of depression, I just didn't acknowledge it. My wife recognized what was happening to me, but she didn't know how to help. All she could do was watch and wait for me to pull out of my nosedive, and find something else.

But what? I felt I had no purpose, no reason to keep trying anything when it might be wrong. The last thing I needed right then was another failure. I'd forgotten who I was. Like I was radiating some kind of aura into the universe, the offers, scams and get-rich propositions arrived in my mailbox. Perhaps I'd always been getting that junk in the mail and tossed it aside. But I started reading those hyped mass-mailings like a desperate drunk, clinging to shreds of hope that those snake-oil schemes, those never-before-tried money tricks were the ticket. Looking back, I have to laugh at the inane appeals to the desperate, the conniving part of human nature. Those copywriters knew exactly how I felt. They wrote that hype just for me, the poor, desperate schmuck who'd see the dangled bait, and lunge at it for all he's worth. The offers always demanded action right now, today, don't wait, because it expires at midnight and we're giving very few people the opportunity! Those writers knew exactly what makes us tick, and it has a lot to do with cash.

But it wasn't the loss of income that bothered me so much. The last year I flew I earned more money than I ever dreamed of. But losing that, while inconvenient, wasn't the source of my anguish. I'd lost my identity. My connection with people who are good at what they do, and are recognized for it.

Something else I never understood until I was grounded was this: I had indeed been privileged to fly, and I would not have thrived on the ground. Like Wayne Alexander, I didn't so much board the helicopter as put it on, become a part of it. Not to go into the airey-fairey, but flying is a unique interaction between human, machine and the elements. I kept that balance, and did it very well for forty years. With every machine I took into the sky I learned its quirks, its characteristics, its limits. I discovered each one's mechanical strengths, and performance parameters too, but that's not it. Every aircraft has a personality, a particular feel and response that a pilot is aware of, or not. I always tried to learn those traits about every helicopter.

Every AStar I flew took off with a strange kind of wobble. Each one yawed at times for no apparent reason, and landed differently, every time. Snowflake landings, the nurses called them. No two alike.

Every Huey I flew welcomed me aboard, like slipping into an old loafer. And the UH-1 gave plenty of warning when a system was about to spit up, which seldom happened. Hueys felt, every one of them, like coming home to the sky. I'd fly a Huey today if they'd let me.

Every JetRanger had a different shimmy, different blade

bounce, different skitter on the pad when lifting the collective. I never flew a Bell JetRanger or LongRanger while sensing danger, or a threat. Like their big brother the Huey, the 206 series Bells are like happy pups out for a walk, and eager to please.

Then there's the Chinook. The Boeing Vertol CH-47, the Army's tandem-rotor cargo helicopter is a beast. Its temperament is like a fragile, moody, overweight tyrant whose subjects learn to tiptoe around lest it lash out at any moment. Like a Jabba the Hut of rotary wing flight. Every Chinook I flew reacted differently to thrust movements, control inputs, pedal travel. Every one had quirks and hidden mysteries, airframe or systems idiosyncrasies that no amount of maintenance attention could ever find. Vibrations, blade bounce, AFCS (automatic flight control system) excursions for no apparent reason, electrical jerks and snaps, gauge flip-flops, odd smells, seeps and hydraulic leaks throughout the airframe. Every Chinook was different. Unlike the Huey, which was the most forgiving helicopter I ever flew, the CH-47 had a hundred different ways it could kill me, if I let it. I loved flying the 'Hook.' The '47 is a great helicopter, with amazing capability, tremendous lifting power and ungodly speed for a helicopter. I logged several hundred hours in a Chinook cockpit, flying missions that could only be done with that beast of an aircraft. But I never trusted it. Maybe that's why I flew it so well?

Despite my obvious adoration of helicopters in general, arms-length treatment was the way I conducted business in the cockpit for almost forty years. I never felt apprehensive about any aircraft. But I always had a great deal of respect for each one, its immense power, its ability to do what it did and do it well, provided I did my part equally well. I knew from day one that if the interface between myself and the aircraft wasn't a smooth, graceful match of man and machine the result could be ugly.

Not all my flights were spiritually energizing, soul-gratifying endeavors. Some of them, even a few tours of Kauai were tedious, grinding efforts to get things over and done. Some flights in Iowa on chill winter nights, when a victim was trapped in the wreckage, air filled with the smell of gore, alcohol and two-cycle stench of the Jaws of Life,™ those flights were hard, demanding work. As much as I miss the gratification and challenge of air medical flying, I don't miss those two a.m. frostbite affairs along Iowa's roadways. I couldn't believe they paid me to fly. But sometimes I couldn't believe how *little* they paid me to fly. Those times were far between, but they existed nonetheless.

In every flight I made, every takeoff, every time I lifted the collective and took a machine into the sky there was an element of grace. Any memoir needs a summary, whether to cap things off, or to announce the end. I'll try to finish with grace, because much of my flying had a touch of it, and I must recognize that. And now, it seems, I must widen my perspective to include the grace found in life all around me.

29

Takeoff

I slip the car into gear and ease it forward. This moving around on the ground will take some getting used to, but I'm sure I can handle it. The flight doc may issue me an up slip, he may not. If not, I've got my sweet wife, I have my health, mostly, and I have a few years left to make a difference to some people, which is kinda what I've always wanted to do anyway, airborne or on the ground, to make a difference to other people. It was a great life cruising around through the atmosphere, one adventure after another. Maybe it's time to get to know people who spend all their time on earth.

I stop at the light by the airport exit, and flick my blinker on. There's a lot of those folks right here, people who come and go all day, never leaving the ground. They pass the airport without so much as a glance. They seem to do fine, seem to enjoy their lives, have their own adventures. Maybe it won't be so bad.

The light changes. I turn left, head down the hill when another of my former colleagues rumbles overhead, starting his tour of the island. I watch him go. The guy behind me honks, so I look ahead and step on the gas. Just as well. I have a doctor's appointment, and some serious planning to do. It's called the rest of my life.

At that moment, my colleague's helicopter getting smaller and smaller, I see the tiny machine in which I learned to fly, Wayne beside me yelling and his number two pencil slapping the side of my helmet. "Damn it, Edgington, get it right!" Seems like yesterday. I got it right for a long time, I think. The time quite literally flew by. I went back to where it all started.

Summer 1969. Wayne Alexander was a tough guy with a tough job. He had to teach me to fly a helicopter, so I could get on to Vietnam where pilots were getting scarcer by the day. Wayne had no time for friendship, or sentiment. He taught me basic flying skills that would determine my chances of survival a year later when a stable hover, level flight, jerky collective inputs and a good crosscheck were the least of my worries.

Mister touchy-feely he was not. When a maneuver didn't go well, and he had to intervene to save two lives, his own and mine, Wayne screamed at me in the tiny cockpit, "Goddamit, Edgington! I've got a lot more fuckin' to do and you're tryin' to kill me!" He grabbed the controls, set the ship aright and demanded that I do the maneuver again, correctly this time. "You're a day late and a dollar short! Do it right or you'll be humpin' a ruck in Vietnam next month!" With my every miscue Wayne pummeled my helmet with a pencil, often snapping them in half. I began to wonder if the flight helmet was for crash protection, or against Wayne's pencil assaults. His tolerance for error was indeed pencil thin: altitudes had to be dead on, airspeed exact, vertical speed perfect, alignment with landing markers absolute. My autorotations had to be to a full stop, with no power recoveries, so every aspect of those power-off maneuvers demanded utmost precision.

Like all the instructors at Wolters Wayne had served a tour in Vietnam. Getting me through flight school meant one more pilot name on the roster ahead of his second tour overseas, one more pilot slot filled that he didn't have to worry about. But a poor pilot, or a dead pilot, was a black mark on any instructor's reputation, so *his* investment in teaching me was rather high as well. I absorbed

Wayne's verbal abuse, his screamed instructions, profanity-laced efforts to make me a pilot. Wayne broke a lot of pencils that summer. Then one day...

One day it all came together. Something rearranged itself in my hands, or my brain, likely both, and I flew. I just flat took off, and flew. I started the engine, checked the gauges, called the tower and scanned outside. Then I eased the collective up, added just enough pedal and lifted, smooth as smoke, to a clean, stable hover. It seemed so easy I couldn't imagine *not* doing it. Wayne sat with his arms crossed, pencil safe in his pocket. I took off, cruised, landed. I did it again. And then again. My airspeed was exact. Altitude solid. Engine and rotor rpm like they were painted on the gauge. Wayne didn't say a word. No pencils died that day.

While I happily flew, Wayne scoured the Texas real estate passing below, his head bobbing to some inner music. I took the machine where he told me to. Matched the airspeed he called for. I did a one-eighty turn, and the compass stopped exactly where it ought. I did a max-performance takeoff, a steep approach, a go around. Then a perfect autorotation, sliding only one aircraft length, kissing it on like butter. Wayne was pleased.

Friday, June 27th 1969. Again, I flew all the maneuvers Wayne ordered—takeoff, straight-in landing, steep approach, a passable, (survivable) autorotation and nominal slide-on landing. Halfway through the session Wayne pointed to the base of the control tower. "Land over there," he said. "...and go back to idle."

I aimed the helicopter where he pointed, stopped near the tower and landed. Then, not sure what he was up to, I cut the engine back, and waited. Wayne unbuckled his seat belt and stepped out of the cockpit onto the tarmac. His helmet was still plugged in. "Okay, Edgington," he said. "Give me three laps around the traffic pattern, then land back here." He unplugged his helmet. Then he thought of a last bit of advice, and plugged in again. "Remember," he said. "It's gonna fly different without my fat ass in it." He unplugged again and walked away.

I stared at the empty seat beside me, and a shiver chilled my arms. The word *solo* floated through my brain. From your Funk & Wagnalls: Solo, meaning alone. I'd never felt so alone in my life. I'd had a great training session, did everything well. I felt like I was in control of the helicopter. I could make it do as I wished. Wayne seemed content. He hadn't raised his voice, or cursed, or broken one pencil. When he pointed at the tower and told me to land close to it, I simply did what he told me to do, that's how dumb *I* was. I angled for the tower, landed there and waited. Until that moment it didn't occur to me what Wayne had in mind, what I was about to do. I watched him walk away. "Solo," I whispered. A smile curled my stupid face. "Holy crap."

I brought the rpm up, gulped really hard, called the tower for a takeoff clearance. "5-6-8-3, solo on lane one."

"5-6-8-3 is cleared for solo takeoff, lane one." The call echoed in my headset and my arms chilled again. "Holy crap." I took a deep breath and lifted the collective. The little ship skittered on its landing gear. It rose on the left side first, just as Wayne said it would *without his fat ass in it.* With a touch more power, and a hint of collective, I hovered. Clean. Solid. I moved to the departure pad, and took off. I flew. And I didn't stop for forty years.

30

Goodbye to the Sky

I admit to being a bit of a romantic. Perhaps that explains why I was attracted to aviation in the first place. My aspiration to fly started as a dream of a religious life. I wanted to soar above mundane, earthly concerns. Perhaps because I was second of ten kids, I thrived in crowds. But I didn't wish to disappear into one. I wanted to be separate from people, with a higher calling, not immersed in the daily exertions and hardships my parents endured.

Aviation writers of the past, Ernest K. Gann, Richard Bach, Barry Schiff, all wrote beautiful, one might say soaring prose. Then there was St. Ex, who tied aviation and life together in a way I can only admire from a distance. Charles Lindbergh may have thrilled the world with his 1927 solo Atlantic crossing. But his writer wife, Anne Morrow Lindbergh, thrilled us with her lofty, intelligent prose, inspiration found in *North to the Orient*, and *Gift from the Sea*.

Between flying and life, metaphors abound: Leaving the earth under our own power, soaring through clear air and cloud and rain and wind, and then landing successfully, if always too soon. It's as close to the birth and death story as we can hope to come. So I use that metaphor for my own purposes. I learned a lot in the sky. It taught me much. In a kind of upside down way, I learned that the sky suits my temperament better than earth does. In the ethereal, insubstantial air I was at home, at ease, filled not with fear or apprehension, but with a sense of satisfaction and even comfort. On the ground, early in life, I learned the harsh truths of hypocrisy and venality, the various evils that human beings are too quick to adopt. My preference was the sky.

Because of my early disappointment, and the dismissal of my first dream, I let go of my religious background and found spiritual sustenance in the sky. As Richard Bach writes, *"The pilot's religion is flight...his way of finding out about the sky. And he has to obey those laws."* Bach mentions the laws of aerodynamics, and how indifferent they are to man's pleading, or supplication. *"...it's following those laws that matters, not whether you believe in them or not."*

The sky held the truth I'd lost, and there was much comfort in that discovery. Flying felt safe to me, simpler, less threatening. In the sky no hypocrisy, no venality can survive. In the ethereal air there is hard truth. Another aviation maxim states that gravity isn't just a good idea; it's the law. Amen to that.

I was never fearful in the cockpit. It confused me when people asked if I was afraid. I never was. Instead, I wondered the opposite. How do others go through life plodding, trudging, always a mere six feet above one's final destiny? I chose a bit of distance from the earth and its depressions, held it at bay as long as possible. I found balance in the sky, and living there fed my soul.

My only fear had nothing to do with an aviation mishap. The thought of an engine failure, a blade strike, a system malfunction, none of those things frightened me. I understood the systems and I knew what to do for any malfunction. The most frightening thing in life for me has always been the prospect of living someone else's. There are those who spend a lifetime pleasing others, acting as they think someone else wants them to, keeping their true selves hidden. "Every time you take off," Wayne said. "...you gotta decide if you're a pilot or a passenger. You can't be both." I was a pilot. In the cockpit, I called the shots. I moved the sticks around, made the aircraft go where I wanted. I was never a passenger.

I don't believe anyone should be. Life's too short to be a passenger. Helicopters were exactly right for me. If you've learned to hover and do it well, you'll have a happy life. I grip the collective with my left hand, fingers wrapped around its barrel and I pull up. My right hand holds the cyclic like an old friend. As power rises, engine noise deepens, wind blasts outward, dust and leaves and debris gush up. Needles rise in gauges, power surges and the skid gear skitters on the sticky ground. The aircraft reaches the balance point between gravity and lift, and lift wins. Smooth as smoke, up, up, up I rise, hovering like a hummingbird, in perfect balance. Once, during a tour, a fellow said to his wife, "...can't even see his hands move, amazing!" I smiled, and nodded. Good pilots make it look easy. Holding the cyclic, feeling its contours and heft, the various buttons and devices on it I smile. It feels good. It always has.

I have a souvenir in my office of a cyclic grip. It was taken from the AStar I flew at the hospital in Iowa. Once in a while I'll take that cyclic grip down from the shelf and hold it again, feel its contours, the rough texture on its sides, the heft of it. I may have held a cyclic in my hand for forty years, but in reality I know it was actually the other way around.

Aviation and life really are about balance. Aircraft aren't designed to fly backward, and neither are we. Living, like flying, means moving forward, always forward, always looking for balance. Even through cloud and rain and fog we must force our way ahead, often blind, hoping the way is clear. Often it means making mistakes. Minimizing those errors may be more critical in the air, but perhaps not. If we make a mistake, up or down, we should correct it as soon as possible to balance things out. If we hurt someone else we must make it better for them. That makes it better for us, too, so we can fly on. The heart of a man can want no more than this.

On most aircraft I flew the rpm gauge was marked not in numerals, but in percent. As might be imagined, the optimum rpm figure was 100%. Just so, life is meant to be lived at 100%. When life's rpm sags we descend to a level in our personal, or work, or social lives that's disappointing and unworthy of our best. Keeping the rpm at 100% may not guarantee success, happiness or reward. But it allows us to climb as high as possible, and to make the most of whatever life presents.

To fly means to be aware of wind at all times. Wayne's words: "Know where the wind is, Edgington...and you're halfway home." If we know which way the wind of human emotion and fear is blowing we're halfway to understanding. People send gusts of emotional signals to us every day. They're the winds that warm us, chill us at times, tell us who and what and where people are coming from, where they've been, what they're afraid of and what they need from us. Wetting a finger to sense that wind isn't always enough. Those who know by looking, listening, truly hearing others feel the wind first and best, and are able to turn into it.

To fly means always having a place to go in an emergency. In aviation it's called a forced landing area. If the engine quits, or a system spits up, or a fire breaks out, a good pilot always has a place in mind on the ground to land. Backup plans are a good thing, even when life seems most chaotic, especially then.

Experience shows us the gauge readings, and the gauges never lie, in the cockpit or in life. The night in Toledo with the boss's family aboard, weather was awful, fuel was low and time was short. I looked at the gauges and I trusted them. They took me home. Some pilots become disoriented in poor weather. The aircraft yaws and turns and dives, and the gauges tell them exactly how to make it right. But their body and mind tell them something else, and they follow their senses to a crash. In life, signals and senses sometimes conflict as well. Experience is there for the using. Trusting it is the hard part.

In aviation there are many aphorisms: always fly with your head, not your hands; speed is life, altitude is life insurance; trust the captain, but keep your seatbelt fastened; the only time you have too much fuel is when you're on fire; takeoffs are optional, landings are mandatory. The list goes on.

One of my favorites is this: there are three things you can't use in aviation, runway behind you, fuel back in the truck, and three minutes ago. I always tried to stay ahead of the aircraft, because it's never good to look back; I never assumed a fuel gauge was accurate, that my watch was better; I tried to anticipate as much as I could, to complete a flight without incident. As I sat in my car at the airport that day, watching my colleague take off, I couldn't help looking backward.

Every soldier I carried in the war, every patient to a hospital, every tourist I flew around Kauai taught me something. I've had an examined life, and it's been well worth the living. I'll never regret spending so much of my time in the air. I'd do it again in a heartbeat.

Like the meanings we assigned to cloud shapes as kids when billowing towers of white passed overhead, we can infer almost anything based on our perceptions. But what we must perceive in the end is that we're all just flying through, ephemeral beings in the beauty that is the world we share.

Life is better than good. I have my health, the love of a wonderful woman, three beautiful daughters and a delightful grandson. In September 2009 I returned to college to finish up the degree that eluded me in 1969. In June 2012, forty years after leaving Ohio State, I received my Bachelors in English from that wonderful institution. Now I spend my days writing, inflicting my work on the public and hoping for acceptance. I work for progressive causes such as gay rights and marriage equality, because it's the right thing to do, to procure what my spouse and I have for others who yearn for it. The heart of a man… Guess I'll always be a missionary of sorts.

I never thought I'd say this, much less put the thought in writing, but I'd rather write than fly, even though writing is harder. I don't miss flying any more. It was a wonderful, fulfilling, gratifying way to make a living. A thrill every day. I was one of those fortunate people who loved what I did, and never worked a day in my life. I flew all over the world, carried hundreds of passengers, had an equal number of takeoffs and landings and put a lot of the sky behind me. Thanks for reading my story.

Epilogue:

Extended Downwind
CRM/AMRM & A New Career

Crew Resource Management is a systemic approach to aviation safety. Since its early years, aviation has been plagued by accidents, incidents and mismanagement, neglect that has killed many thousands of people and cost millions of dollars. Studies show that between 60% and 80% of all aviation accidents contain a human error component. Like it or not, people cause most accidents. That's the bad news. But that's the good news, too, since it offers a ready solution to most accidents. The statistic has certainly been true in the arena of Air Medical accidents and incidents. Thus, CRM has a unique application in Air Med, the career choice I selected for much of my flying history, and a job that I truly loved. It even has its own acronym, AMRM, Air Medical Resource Management.

This chapter will detail CRM/AMRM from the standpoint of my completed career, using a kind of show and tell model. Yes, I intend to share with readers, especially those still involved in aviation, a few of my own less than stellar decisions in various cockpits, incidents and potential accidents I managed (somehow) to avoid. I do this partly to advance aviation safety by sharing my own experience, and partly to underline how fortunate I was to have escaped all those times with my clean safety record intact. Looking back at some of those events, it's obvious that a crude form of CRM was at work, even without my awareness of it. Certain crewmembers must have looked out for my well being, and allowed me to steer along a better path. Others intervened in subtle and not so subtle ways to change our direction. I'll use real life examples, situations that actually happened to me during my long career to illustrate what happened, what didn't and how using a little active CRM would have broken an error chain, as they say, and kept me and my crew away even from potential danger.

In the process of this discussion, I'll outline my new career. I've extended my downwind by becoming an instructor and facilitator in Crew Resource Management. As with many things in life, this new endeavor has a rather serendipitous onset. A while ago I got an E-mail from a fellow named Randy Mains. Mr. Mains is a former HEMS pilot like myself, and a career helicopter pilot, CRM instructor/trainer and a man who has worn many aviation hats. Randy is the very first winner, in 1983, of the 'Golden Hour Award,' offered by Airbus Helicopters, and also the 2013 winner of the Jim Charlson award for safety. Randy contacted me after reading a piece I'd written for an on-line publication Ezinearticles.com. My piece titled 'How to Fix The Helicopter EMS Accident Rate' appeared April 27th 2009. (http://tinyurl.com/l4rsg2c) Randy read the piece, agreed with it, and asked if he might use it for an upcoming presentation. Of course I agreed, and that was that. Weeks later I got a phone call from an administrative fellow with Transport Canada. Fred had also read the piece. He asked if I might be interested in traveling to Vancouver BC to be the featured speaker at the upcoming Transport Canada convention.

There are times in life when desire overcomes reality. We've all had the urge to throw caution to the winds and agree to things we know we have no business agreeing to. At the time, I had very little experience in front of a large audience, and no earthly idea what a speech to that august group of Canadian aviators would entail. I was seconds away from declining Fred's gracious invitation and then hanging up, when I thought of an alternative. I told Fred to contact Randy Mains. Randy lived close by, he had the necessary creds, and I knew he'd be able to give Transport Canada a rousing speech. Fred contacted Randy, who subsequently appeared at the convention as their speaker.

The interaction gave Randy a fair amount of exposure and a ticket punch for his resume,' which led to other engagements etc. I suppose that was my first active use of Crew Resource Management. I delegated a task that I knew someone else could do better, and it turned out to be so. It gets better still. Not long ago Randy contacted me again. He'd taken a position with Oregon Aero (http://www.oregonaero.com/) to promote and teach their CRM/AMRM offerings. He asked if I'd be interested in taking the course, learning the syllabus and joining him on the CRM/AMRM teaching road show? I told him I'd enjoy that very much.

So I'm extending my downwind a bit, launching my latest career in aviation. I'll be teaching and promoting Crew Resource Management far and wide, doing my part to help address and hopefully to reduce the accident rate. And confession being good for the soul, herein I add a few of my own flying faux pas, situations in which I could have used CRM, had I known about it and used it. These events will be reflections, some taken from this book, some not, on how I got into a particular pickle and what I could have done to avoid the peril. I'll utilize the error chain approach, giving details of actions along the chain that, if broken, would have saved me some embarrassment—or worse.

First, here's an itemized list of the error chain on which I base these critiques, interventions I refer to along the way. Post-accident investigations reveal a minimum of four warning signs in every aviation accident sequence that, if broken, could have prevented the accident being studied. The average number of links is seven. Eleven items have been identified. Here's the list:

1— Ambiguity
2— Fixation or Preoccupation
3— Confusion or an 'Empty feeling'
4— No one flying the aircraft
5— No one looking out the window
6— Use of an undocumented procedure
7— Violating limitations or minimum operating standards
8— Unresolved discrepancies
9— Failure to meet targets
10— Departure from SOPs
11— Incomplete communications

The first example I'll discuss concerns what I believe was the closest I ever came to killing myself and my crew and destroying a perfectly good UH-1 helicopter. It happened in Vietnam, and almost caused me to rethink my career choice.

I'd been requested to sling load a piece of armament, a quad-fifty that had broken down. I would hook it onto my sling, fly it to Phu Bai and drop it off. It appeared to be a simple, straightforward mission, one I thought I could perform blindfolded. Well, I did in fact put the blinders on, and doing so almost made me a casualty. The complicating factor was that the heavy equipment in question was on a barge several hundred yards offshore in a small bay.

I approached the barge, and hovered close to the deck while the crew beneath attached the sling to my hook on the belly of the Huey. One important factor is this: hovering over water is one of the most difficult maneuvers there is. As the rotors whip up the surface, a pilot loses all reference to movement, direction, altitude, everything. There's no way to orient in relation to anything, and hovering becomes an exercise in frustration.

While hovering my Huey above the barge I had no trouble. I could see the corner of the boat, a small section of its rail in my chin bubble that gave me a reference point. But once the load was hooked, and I rose straight up, the reference point disappeared under me. My crewchief informed me that I was forward of the load, with the sling at a high angle instead of straight up and down. He told me to back up. I tried, I really did, but I didn't know what *back up* meant. With water whipping up, and no point of reference, I was unable to detect movement in the aircraft—back, forward, sideways, up or down.

Added to the quickly forming error chain was the fact that the load was much too heavy. I glanced at the torque meter: forty-eight pounds, and the load hadn't budged. I shouldn't say that; it had skidded across the deck perhaps two feet. My crewchief again yelled for me to back up; I tried, but couldn't find reverse, the churning water by then giving me vertigo. One more look at torque, and I made a decision that likely saved my life. The gauge read 50 pounds, the maximum power available in the Huey. The load had not moved. I told my copilot to punch the sling off. He did that, and it dropped onto the deck. We flew back around and landed on the barge, where I explained what had happened. The barge crew thanked me anyway, and I went on my way.

Going over the scenario in my head, I began to understand the peril I'd faced, the various links in the error chain that would have been written in the accident report. As per number one, ambiguity, and number eleven, incomplete communication, my crew and I failed to talk through the difficulties. Per number 10, I failed to conduct a briefing as SOP required. Number seven refers to limitations. I discovered later that the equipment I tried to lift weighed in excess of 3,000 pounds. The cargo hook on my Huey had a maximum limit of 2,500.

Much later, I realized my near fatal error. Had that three thousand pound chunk of metal slid off the barge and into the water it would have taken me with it. There would have been no time to pickle the load. The accident sequence would have happened much too fast. I consoled myself by thinking that the guy in the right seat would surely have hit the pickle switch and saved the day. Wrong answer. I looked overhead at the cluster of switches and breakers and realized that I'd not armed the cargo hook! My right seat pilot could have punched that electrical pickle switch all day long and nothing would have happened. Number four link in the error chain came into play as well. No one was flying the aircraft as it should have been flown. My copilot kicked the manual release to set the load free. So the links that could have broken the error chain that day are number 1, 4, 7, 10 and 11. The old aviation maxim is true: The rules are written in blood.

Next on the list is a near accident I mentioned in the book. It covers a night takeoff for a heart attack victim where I entered fog at four hundred feet, and then pushed forward for twenty miles to get home. Again, looking back on the mission, I can see the accident report bearing my name.

The flight happened in 1985, when Air Medical aviation was in its infancy. In those days accidents happened with alarming regularity. And most of them were related to weather, namely poor visibility. The short version of the event is as follows: When I launched on the mission at eleven PM the sky was clear, temp/dewpoint separated by six degrees. A slight breeze kicked the windsock around, and stars littered the night sky. The patient lived twenty miles away in farm country. After a fifteen-minute flight I landed near his home, shut down the aircraft and the crew went inside. We expected to be on the ground twenty minutes, tops, so I walked around the aircraft, waiting. Twenty minutes passed. The breeze stopped. Temperature sagged. A fine mist formed on the helicopter's windscreen. Twenty more minutes passed. Stars winked out overhead. A faint haze settled over nearby fields. Twenty more minutes, then ten more and still no sign of my medical crew.

Cut to the chase, after an hour on the ground my crew arrived with our patient. I climbed into the cockpit, fired up the Lycoming and took a deep breath. I'd have been better served to shut off the engine and camp out for the night, but I didn't. I took off, climbed to two hundred, three hundred, four hundred feet…and ran into a wall of fog. I angled back to where I'd just taken off. No use; I couldn't see the ground. So I elected to continue, plowing ahead through a cloaking fog, with a half-mile visibility at most, sometimes near zero. With the crew's exertions doing CPR etc. the cabin steamed up, and the windscreen fogged over. I grabbed the defroster knob and turned…and nothing happened. The knob was jammed. It wouldn't budge. I opened the vent in my side window and flew along, almost at a hover, three hundred feet off the ground, looking, desperately hoping for the lights of Iowa City, and home plate. It was perhaps the longest thirty minutes of my life.

So here is the error chain. First, there was no briefing, no discussion with the crew what time pressure awaited us. I didn't discuss with them what weather conditions might be, and in truth turned out to be, asking them to expedite interactions with the patient. The second flaw was my decision to take off with the patient at all. I acceded to the oldest pressure a pilot puts on himself, get-home-itis. Third was my continued attempt to fly out of a dangerous situation. The four Cs are there for a reason: Control, Climb, Confess, Comply—Conserve being a fifth C, if fuel is low. The local ATC agency was shuttered for the night. But altitude would have been my friend, allowing me to steer clear and to talk with a Center controller, perhaps the sixth C. Instead, I chose to hug the ground, and nearly got hugged back as a result. One last digression from CRM was that there was no post-flight debrief, either. As I said, the mission happened in 1985, when Air Medical flying was new and CRM itself was never mentioned. At that time no one even know how to spell CRM.

So the links that could have broken that error chain are numbers 1, 3, 6, 7, 9, 10 and 11. Perhaps the most important lost potential in that flight was the debriefing, and the transparency that might have resulted but did not. The upshot is that to this day I have no idea how the medical crew felt about what happened in the fog that night. I'm not even sure they knew how close they were to yet another Air Medical helicopter accident. If they did, they never mentioned it. This illustrates a prominent break in the error chain, and a common challenge to safety among Air Med crews, particularly in single pilot aircraft configurations, which arrangement describes the overwhelming number of those crews, at least in the United States. The problem lies not in the single pilot factor itself, but in the dismissal of CRM as a useful tool because of it.

In 1985, when my flight in the fog happened, the Air Medical helicopter business seemed to be suffering from a kind of (no pun intended), collective denial of the opaque situation surrounding us. Pilots demanded sovereignty in their cockpits under FAR pilot in command authority; customers honored that, for the most part. Meanwhile accidents continued to plague the young, accident-prone business. And when close calls, and unsafe events happened, the event may have been discussed and bemoaned for a time, but it was quickly forgotten in a rush to get back in the air. The bottom line was that we had no sense of crew monitoring, no perceived duty to watch each other. Individual roles were considered sacred. On a big airplane, a part 121 carrier, when we strap in and prepare to travel we hear flight attendants launch into their mandatory safety spiel. They gather the seat belt sample, the oxygen mask and the over water flotation gear, and the lead attendant rattles on about loss of cabin pressure, seat belt use, the prohibition against smoking in lavatories etc. When they're done, the attendant says "doors secured and cross-check," what they mean is, let's all monitor each other and make sure nothing is missed.

No one was watching me that night in the fog. I was on my own, partly because the medical crew was busy saving a life, partly because mentioning our dilemma would have been blurring the lines between my authority and theirs. I made no effort to help with CPR; they didn't tell me how to fly—or how not to. There was no crosschecking to be had. Years after the flight in the fog I began hearing stories about similar situations involving other pilots and crews, other near misses and close encounters of the perilous kind. If not hearing about danger until many years afterward isn't a good case for CRM/AMRM I don't what is. An important element of CRM/AMRM is the team concept. Members are trained to act as a team, not as individual, albeit highly technical actors. As a final note in this particular story, the patient was pronounced dead within minutes of my landing on our helipad that night. I offer no editorial comment here, but it disturbed me then. I endangered myself and my crew for a dead man. Triage as a CRM/AMRM tool? Perhaps.

Good applications of CRM apply to every member of the crew, not just the flying staff. It's called *Crew* Resource Management for a reason, and virtually every aviation accident can be tied in some way to the same error chain. The missed maintenance detail, forgotten logbook signature or glossed over inspection item can lead to an accident almost as readily and quickly as any pilot error can.

One of the stylistic differences between my wife and me is this: I'm always shutting cabinet doors, putting items away, securing things, often before she's done with them. It happens a lot in the kitchen, often enough that I've become keenly aware of the tension caused when I slip the butter back in the fridge before she's finished frying the mushrooms. "I wasn't done with that." My sweet spouse once again gives me 'the look.' Sheepish and apologetic, I put the butter back on the counter, another marital crisis averted.

She asked me once, "why do you do that?" I explained to her that the predilection to put things back, to secure loose items around me, derives from one of two sources: either I aspired to aviation because I understand the value of securing things before walking away from them; or I was successful and safe in aviation for so long because I learned that practice early and well as a new pilot. An old aviation aphorism states that if you want your kid to grow up to be a pilot, teach them to put things back where they found them.

This is where good CRM comes in. And this near-accident scenario is an excellent example of why putting things back and not walking away until they're secured can make all the difference.

For a fellow with little experience Jim Bradshaw was a reasonably good pilot. Jim and I flew together years ago for a company called Air Kauai. He and I shared the duty often, launching thirty minutes apart from our helipad at Lihue airport on Hawaii's 'Garden Island' to fly tours. The boss, a fellow named Chuck, scolded Jim on a regular basis for being inattentive while the line crew fueled his aircraft after each tour. Instead of staying close by the ship, as Chuck demanded he do, Bradshaw would often wander off to smoke a cigarette and to chat with his girlfriend on the phone.

One afternoon I landed after a tour, and Chuck met me at the helipad. He was clearly at a seven-foot unstable hover. "Take these to Bradshaw," he said. Fuming, he handed me a set of keys. Bradshaw had, once again, neglected his duty to supervise the refueling. The fueler hadn't done his job, either, and Jim took off with twenty-percent showing on the gas gauge. Ten minutes into his one-hour tour, the low fuel light illuminated and Jim had to land at the Air Force base on the west side of the island to gas up. When he tried to open the fuel port he had the wrong key, which is why I had to veer away from my tour to fly the appropriate key to him.

After Jim finished his interrupted tour, Chuck fired him. The error chain could have been broken a number of times, and a number of ways: Jim could have done what the boss demanded and monitored his refueling; the fueler could have done his job; Jim might have done a bit better crosscheck of the gauges prior to liftoff. It's not a stretch to mention several other crews in close proximity, other refueling crews who might have sensed what had happened—or had not.

The best outcome Jim Bradshaw realized from the incident was getting fired. Others might not have been so attractive: Lacking sufficient fuel to complete his flight, he'd taken off in violation of regulations; he'd endangered his passengers and himself, plus the reputation of the company—indeed the tour industry on Kauai, already perceived as a risky endeavor—and he'd lost his job. But had the low fuel light in his caution panel been inoperative, the bulb burned out, or the system non-functional for some reason, it's not likely he would have noticed anything amiss until the engine quit. He would have flamed out along the northern coast of Kauai, a rugged section of the island lacking acceptable forced landing areas. Bradshaw would have crashed into the cliffs or the ocean, and people would have died. So numbers 1, 4, 6, 7, 9 and 10 would have broken the chain leading to an accident that, lucky for Jim Bradshaw, never happened.

On a tragic followup note, Jim died in the crash of an Air Medical helicopter in November 2009, in Lassen County California. Weather may have been a causal factor. There was no post-crash fire.

Another episode where good CRM comes to mind is this one from my days as a lead pilot in Iowa City. It's safe to say my program and I dodged a bullet that day, and looking back, I'm ashamed of myself for my lack of due diligence.

Bob Goss was a good, conscientious pilot. He flew for the AirCare program in Iowa City for about three years. I was Bob's lead pilot during that time, and he and I shared the duty in the early, crazy-busy two-pilot crew days. So I got to know Bob pretty well, and thought highly of him. Then he nearly crashed, and if he had, I would have been implicated in the incident.

Bob was in the middle of a nasty divorce, his second, and his personal challenge affected his aviation skills, not in an overt, but a subtle way, which was much more perilous. Seeing him struggle with the divorce, watching him interact with his soon to be ex, dealing with property issues, relocation, dividing financial assets, the emotional toll involved and the whole tedious regimen that divorce demands, Bob neglected his flying duties. His head wasn't in the game. After the mechanic had performed minor maintenance on the AStar, Goss received an Air Med dispatch call, and he left the rooftop pad without doing the necessary walk around inspection. The oversight nearly cost him his life, and the medical crew's along with him.

A few miles from the hospital, outbound for the patient, Bob leveled off at two thousand feet and increased airspeed. It was a beautiful, cloudless VMC day, late September with temps in the delightful seventies. A gorgeous day to fly. As soon as Bob leveled the aircraft, the crew heard a terrible bang, then continuous slapping, popping and grinding noise from the rotor system, and a steady shudder in the airframe.

Goss dropped the collective, and headed for the ground. He landed in a farm field, killed the engine and stopped the blades. When he stepped from the cockpit, he saw the source of the slamming, banging sound. Left unlatched, the transmission cowl had flown up into the rotor system, where the pitch change rods chewed it to pieces. Bob removed the entire damaged cowl, stowed it on board and flew the aircraft to our hangar. Fortunately, no one was injured, and the only casualty ended up being the cowl.

Bob called me right away and told me what had happened. I told him to take a few days off, get his head straight and report back to work. The incident happened in 1984, long before I'd been exposed to CRM and its systematic methodology. When I think about how close we came to another Air Med accident with fatalities, like the battered cowl that day, I shudder, too. Why those push-pull tubes didn't break off as they slammed against the cowl is a mystery.

The bigger mystery is this: Why did I not ground Bob Goss indefinitely, or at least long enough for him to put his personal challenge behind him? Why did I not bring the company into the problem? Why did the customer not step in? Why did Bob take off again to fly to the hangar before the mechanic could look over the aircraft? Why did any of us assume that a new cowl was all that was needed? Why, why, why?

I can answer two of those questions. It may sound as if I'm ducking my own responsibility in that near accident, and perhaps I am, but in those days operators had little sensitivity to staffing issues. Indeed, in 1984 the crew rest and pilot staffing challenge was issue number one, the biggest bone of contention in Air Medical aviation. I could have called the company to request a relief pilot, until Bob returned to full duty. But I knew it would never happen. He and I flew for Omniflight Helicopters at the time. Omni was a good company, but, like every other operator, their pilot staffing stretched only as thin as the payroll and contractual obligations allowed, and no further. The FAA would not be helpful. That august agency struggled at the time with interpretation of crew rest regs just like we did. The customer wouldn't have helped either, seeing the problem as an aviation challenge.

I should have grounded Bob while he faced his personal issues. He should have grounded himself. He should have done his walk around inspection. The entire crew should have done a walk around inspection. The mechanic should never have left the aircraft unbuttoned. The hospital administration should have sensed that additional pilot staffing was needed. (At the time, as members of the two-pilot crew in Iowa City, Goss and I spent exactly half the week—84 hours apiece, at work). The company should have… The could'a, would'a, should'a drill is pretty obvious, and 'could' go on ad nauseam.

The bottom line is that, had proper CRM been in place and actively used, that particular error chain would have been broken pretty early. The only reason no accident occurred is because we got lucky, nothing else.

Sadly, Bob Goss was killed with two medical crewmembers in an Air Med crash near Corpus Christi Texas in February 2008.

Yet another incident that lends itself to good CRM dissection happened to me in the mid eighties, this one with several points of entry. I was flying an old 'D' model AStar at the time equipped with the much-maligned Lycoming LTS-101 engine. The small Lycoming was a good powerplant, but it was not very dependable long-term. In Iowa City, a busy program, we'd swap out engines every two or three hundred hours, which for us meant an engine change every three months or so. When the engine began coking up, demanding a change, it started using quantities of oil. One quart per hour was not unusual. So checking oil level prior to flight was crucial.

Another feature of the 'D' model AStar was its white plastic oil reservoir that had no sight gauge. The reservoir was an opaque cylinder, eight inches across or so which held eight quarts of turbine oil. To check it, I lifted the cowl, peered at the plastic reservoir and noted the dark line around it near the top indicating oil—I thought.

I'd reported in to work, and within minutes the pager squawked for a patient flight. So I went to the pad, walked around, and lifted the cowl to check the oil. Spying the dark line, I assumed the level was good, so I dropped the cowl and secured it. Then I hopped aboard, fired up the Lycoming and lifted into the Iowa sky. Five minutes outbound, the torque gauge did a little whifferdill, the needle jerking and dancing with no power change from me. The needle jumped, jerked again, fell to zero and then leapt up, skipping all over the gauge. The torque measuring system in that aircraft was a wet gauge arrangement, so I sensed that the problem might be oil related. I told the nurse I was aborting, called dispatch and returned to the helipad.

When I shut the engine down and checked the reservoir, it held perhaps three tablespoons of turbine oil on the bottom of the can. The dark line I'd seen was a stain that had grown there from repeated filling to that level.

The error chain was this: Number two, for sure, as I was fixated on the dark line instead of actual oil; number five, because I wasn't flying the aircraft, I was flying the mission; number eight and unresolved discrepancy, because I failed to do an adequate check; and number eleven, incomplete communication because both my mechanic and I should have seen the potential danger in the stain on that plastic reservoir. Sometimes good CRM involves projecting ahead to what can happen if left untended. Pilots hear a lot of wise and worthwhile adages. One is this: if it's bad on the ground, it can only get worse in the air. Another addendum to this incident. The manufacturer should have seen the potential involved here as well. Good CRM only happens when every entity involved performs at full potential. Shortly after that incident the manufacturer installed a metal oil reservoir complete with a sight gauge in those aircraft.

The last example I'll mention involves the new fascination and utilization of metadata. Many employers are beginning to use applications and algorithms that screen for personality in their hiring and placement, looking at applicants' so called 'behavioral DNA.' Such tests as the Hogan Personality Indicator,[1] Cattell's 16 Personality Indicators[2] and Caliper Profile[3] help employers make these determinations. When I began flying Air Med in 1983, the administrator at the time greeted me with his assessment of working with flight nurses. "It's like herding cats," he said.

I soon discovered he was right. Flight nurses tend to be aggressive, goal-oriented, hyper-competent egomaniacs with a tendency to overachieve. And that's the modest ones. Here's an example of how this lends itself to good CRM.

Larry and Bill (I've changed the names to protect the guilty) were flight nurses I flew with routinely. They were both terrifically competent in a clinical sense, with a dedication to the job and the program that was exemplary. On one particular flight, they showed me an ugly side of their ego-driven natures, an astonishing breakdown of the CRM atmosphere.

I'd flown to a small Illinois hospital for a trauma patient. The man had sustained numerous ortho injuries, but was otherwise stable. We loaded him on the helicopter, and fully conscious and alert, he settled in for the half hour flight back to Iowa City. Larry and Bill boarded, and I spun up the blades.

The two nurses had been bickering all evening about something, a topic I paid no attention to. On the flight to Illinois they argued, their body language revealing a rather heated dustup of some kind. I dismissed it, and flew on.

After we loaded our patient, the confrontation between Larry and Bill reached a climax for some reason, and the next thing I knew, as I prepared to lift off, they got into a shoving match in the cabin. Arms flew, curses yelled and the temperature spiked.

The patient observed all this and his jaw sagged. Were his two flight nurses really fighting in the aircraft? Were they neglecting his care while they sparred with each other?

Yes, they were. Astonished, I held the collective down and turned to stare at them. "Gentlemen, shall we go home?" I said, stopping the argument. They fell back to neutral corners and Larry apologized to his patient. I took off and flew home.

That flight showed a need for the personality profiles that have come in vogue, and it poses a question to all Air Med and other flight crew employers: have you screened your people to see who might optimize the strengths and deflect the weaknesses of the other team members? Should you use the information gathered in the screening to schedule certain staff members together, or to keep them apart? Using the CRM model, have you used the data to optimize safe practices?

The questions go way beyond intervening in fisticuffs in the aircraft. The mission to Illinois is an extreme example, but personalities play their part in every endeavor, and everybody has one. One application I imagine for the use of such data, besides scheduling of crews, is in the hiring process itself. Flight crews do tend to be highly motivated, goal oriented people. We have a reputation for seeing risk as a necessary part of life, not something to be shunned. We're not daredevils by any means, but in an ironic way, those who gravitate to Air Medical aviation may be the wrong people to undertake that particular profession. Instead of probing for risks, examining every aspect of a flight to discern its dangers, we assume the risk and go on. Despite our exposure to the terrible tragedies and grisly vicissitudes of trauma and medical emergency, the reality of death and morbidity we observe every time we take off, we're damn good at denial. Often we stare a grave risk dead ahead, and ignore its presence, to accomplish the mission at hand.

Maybe the personality screening should be done to discover those tendencies. At least the knowledge we gain from knowing our own predilections may assist us in our CRM usage. And it may allow a scheduler to pair us up with a crewmember who compliments our skills, and shores up a weakness. Or at least keeps us out of a fist fight.

Another note on this incendiary incident involves me as the pilot. After we landed in Iowa City that night and the patient left us, I forgot about the argument. Should I have taken the information to the chief flight nurse? Probably. Should I have confronted Larry and Bill? Absolutely. I did neither. I allowed the incident to go unremarked. The opportunity to discuss the misplaced focus in the cabin that night passed us by, and we failed to take advantage of it. If an Air Med crew or any other consists of people who don't fit, that arrangement needs to be addressed. A non-communicating crew is not a safe crew.

Finally, the fistfight incident suggests another CRM driven safety initiative: mandatory disclosure. Like many laws in society that require us to report certain things, safety of flight items lend themselves to transparency. At the program or admin level, supervisors should make the reporting of incidents mandatory. This way, staff members are essentially removed from the loop of repercussions from other staff. When an incident occurs, if crews know they're required to report them, this mandate gives them protection from backlash. Making reporting incidents a condition of employment should serve to enhance transparency, and used correctly opens up communications for everyone. Like the NASA reporting system, comments may be anonymous, and should be targeted not at individuals but at situations. The hallmark of good CRM/AMRM used correctly and well is the elimination of oversights and lingering safety concerns.

1— http://www.hoganassessments.com/content/hogan-personality-inventory-hpi

2— http://personality-testing.info/tests/16PF.php

3— https://www.calipercorp.com/products-and-solutions/pre-employment-assessments-3/caliper-profile/

Final Approach

Put to good use, with its ability to open up communications and shine bright lights on deficiencies and oversights, Crew Resource Management will work to reduce or eliminate human error accidents. As an instructor in this life-saving application, and as a twenty-year veteran Air Medical pilot I feel an extra responsibility to disseminate this program. If you're aware of an incident, or a potential accident waiting to happen and can't get anyone's attention, feel free to contact me. Any such information can, of course, be entirely confidential. Look for further literature and additional books from The SkyWriter Press about aviation topics in general, and CRM oriented topics in particular.

For those who enjoy aviation fiction, my novel *'Final Sky'* will be available soon from The SkyWriter Press. *Final Sky* is an Air Medical love story filled with a fascinating inside look at Air Medical aviation, the people who labor in that field, their exciting true-to-life adventures and the perils they encounter not just in the air, but in their personal lives as well. If you've ever been a member of an Air Med team you'll recognize every one of the people in *Final Sky*.

Want to read a ripping aviation war novel? You'll love, *Waiting for Willie Pete, a Helicopter Novel of Vietnam*. *Waiting For Willie Pete: Moby Dick* meets *Chickenhawk*. Look for *Willie Pete* soon from The SkyWriter Press. Thanks for reading TSBM and fly safe!

BE Columbus Ohio
www.byronedgington.com
www.theskywriterpress.com
@byronedgington

Available at Amazon.com, and at Smashwords.com for E-readers. For more titles from The SkyWriter Press, visit the website: www.byronedgington.com

For forty years I thought I held a cyclic stick in my hand, when in actuality it was the other way around.

I had a marvelous life in the sky, and I'd do it again in a heartbeat.

Made in the USA
Monee, IL
07 July 2026

56552283R00184